TOLSTOY ON WAR

D1525321

TOLSTOY ON WAR

Narrative Art and Historical
Truth in "War and Peace"

Edited by
Rick McPeak and
Donna Tussing Orwin

Cornell University Press   *Ithaca & London*

First published 2012 by Cornell University Press
First printing, Cornell Paperbacks 2012

Printed in the United States of America

Library of Congress Cataloging-in-Publication Data
Tolstoy on war : narrative art and historical truth in War and peace / edited by Rick McPeak and Donna Tussing Orwin.
    p. cm.
  Includes bibliographical references and index.
  ISBN 978-0-8014-4898-0 (cloth : alk. paper)
  ISBN 978-0-8014-7817-8 (pbk. : alk. paper)
  1. Tolstoy, Leo, graf, 1828–1910. Voina i mir.   2. War in literature.
3. History in literature.   I. McPeak, Rickie Allen.   II. Orwin, Donna Tussing, 1947–
    PG3365.V65T65 2012
    891.73'3—dc23   2012015299

Cornell University Press strives to use environmentally responsible suppliers and materials to the fullest extent possible in the publishing of its books. Such materials include vegetable-based, low-VOC inks and acid-free papers that are recycled, totally chlorine-free, or partly composed of nonwood fibers. For further information, visit our website at www.cornellpress.cornell.edu.

Cloth printing   10 9 8 7 6 5 4 3 2 1
Paperback printing   10 9 8 7 6 5 4 3 2 1

Contents

Acknowledgments

The Social Sciences and Humanities Research Council of Canada (SSHRC) contributed funds to realize this project. We thank Anton Nonin for his help gathering permissions, Dr. Edith Klein for editing the final manuscript for submission to Cornell University Press, and Arkadi Klioutchanki for his preparation of the index. Many thanks to John Ackerman, Susan Specter, and Jamie Fuller of Cornell University Press for their help. We thank Victoria McPeak and Clifford Orwin for their patience and understanding during the process of assembling this volume.

Note to the Reader

Unless otherwise stated, throughout the volume we use the English translation of *War and Peace* by Richard Pevear and Larissa Volokhonsky in the Alfred A. Knopf edition (New York, 2008). We also use their translation of Tolstoy's "A Few Words Apropos of *War and Peace*," available in the same Knopf edition of the novel. References in Russian and all writings by Tolstoy are, unless otherwise stated, to the so-called Jubilee edition, L. N. Tolstoi, *Polnoe sobranie sochinenii* [PSS], 90 vols. (Moscow: Gosudarstvennoe izdatel'stvo Khudozhestvennaia literatura, 1928–58). Most references to the novel in the text and notes are by volume, part, and chapter; references to the epilogue, however, are by part and chapter. Where necessary, page numbers to the Pevear/Volokhonsky edition of the novel and volume and page numbers to PSS are included as well. References to the Pevear/Volokhonsky translation of "A Few Words Apropos of *War and Peace*" are in the text, by page number only.

Throughout the book, except in quotations and titles, we have used conventional English spellings of well-known Russian names. Where the name is not familiar, and in Russian quotations, we have followed a modified version of Library of Congress transliteration to render Cyrillic into the Latin alphabet.

All ellipses in quotations from the novel, unless enclosed in brackets, are in the original.

Introduction

———

DONNA TUSSING ORWIN

The year 2012 is the two hundredth anniversary of Napoleon's fateful invasion of Russia and the Battle of Borodino. This book marks the occasion with essays on Leo Tolstoy's epic novel *War and Peace* (1865–1869), which is set in the period from 1805 to 1820 and describes the struggle between Russia and France through 1812. As a founding epic for modern Russia and a meditation on war and history, *War and Peace* is one of the most read and most important novels ever written. Ernest Hemingway, Vasily Grossman, and Vikram Seth are just three of the many prose writers from different cultures who have acknowledged their indebtedness to it. In it the lives of five fictional families intertwine with real historical events and actors to an extent never before achieved in fiction. Neither strand of the novel is subordinated to the other: the fictional characters are not merely historical types, and history is not merely setting. The personal, which can be imagined only through a fictional narrative, enters history, while the gap between the personal and large trends of history visible only in hindsight narrows, though it does not entirely disappear.

The novel's profundity grows out of contradictions that it is too true to life to resolve: this is why it eludes labeling. Its fictional narrative demonstrates both the necessity of human freedom and, paradoxically, the extent to which history and its actors must be determined; its digressions argue for each of these fundamental imperatives in different places without explaining how the two can coexist. The tension between the two is maximally on display in times of war, and it is no accident that interest in *War and Peace* intensifies then. This happened during World War II, and it is happening now during what has been provisionally named the Long War against Terrorism.[1]

Tolstoy On War: Narrative Art and Historical Truth in "War and Peace" is also a product of this situation. In April 2010, a group of scholars gathered at West Point to discuss Tolstoy's great novel. They presented and debated before an audience of mostly cadets and their teachers, some military and some not. Tolstoy's representation of war took on real urgency as the cadets, who had all studied the novel, wrestled with his take on their deadly, idealistic profession. It was a lesson for professors used to working in an environment in which war themes are often treated ironically or as metaphors for something else closer to their own experience and that of their students. My coeditor, Colonel Rick McPeak, reports on the reactions of the cadets in this book's concluding chapter.

The premise underlying *Tolstoy On War* is that the issues in Tolstoy's novel are too complex to be comprehended satisfactorily within a single academic discipline. No one discipline owns war. Literary criticism, history, social science, and philosophy—all represented in this volume—do not necessarily agree about what is important or even true; therefore, by its nature the volume cannot have the unity of a monograph or a collection within one discipline. Its great strength lies in its diversity of approach. It is not intended to provide a single unified reading of *War and Peace,* nor are the different authors necessarily supposed to engage one another where they disagree. Instead, the debate is supposed to take place in the mind of the reader or among its readers, as it did at West Point. As I argue below, Tolstoy intended *War and Peace* to transcend conventional forms of writing; therefore, we can and should measure it by criteria from different disciplines. It will be flawed where it oversteps itself, but it still gets a lot right. We hope that this volume will facilitate the use of *War and Peace* in multidisciplinary classrooms and discussion groups.

War and Peace as Literature

War and Peace is "not a novel, still less a long poem [*poema*], and even less a historical chronicle." So says its author in "A Few Words about the Book *War and Peace*" (1868).[2] Tolstoy as realist may want to deny as much as possible that his work has a literary shape, but it does, and he knows it. In fact, his disclaimer notwithstanding, its formal uniqueness and use of various genres make *War and Peace* both the quintessential Russian novel and perhaps its greatest example. This Russian type of novel grew out of the Hegelian culture of the nineteenth century. Struggling to establish themselves as a world historical people in the Hegelian sense, Russian thinkers claimed that they stood at the apex of history as Hegel defined it. In this self-conception, their distinctive contribution to world culture was to understand and synthesize all that had come before them. Tolstoy's great novel achieves this ambition to an astonishing extent and in so doing can claim both Russian and universal status.

Novel, long poem (epic), and historical chronicle: the three genres that Tolstoy says his work is *not* are the ones that it both incorporates and supersedes. They are the genres most important in the work but they do not determine its final shape. The book is woven from these different strands along with other generic threads intermingled but less important.

In "A Few Words" Tolstoy attributes to the "author" the determining role in *War and Peace*. He tells contemporary readers puzzled by his unique masterpiece that it can be understood only as "that which the author wanted to and could express in the form in which it is expressed." Certainly an authoritative narrator speaks loudly and clearly in it. *War and Peace* is composed of a fictional narrative and a commentary on it that stretches from embedded maxims to historical digressions and long philosophical essays. Tolstoy himself was uncertain that these last belonged in the book. This may be why he does not mention the essays in his summary of the important genres present in it and why he relegated some of them to appendices in its 1873 edition. Still, he subsequently restored them to the main text, and they remain there today in the authoritative version of the book. Tolstoy's uneasiness about these digressions tells us that he regarded himself—the author—as more artist than essayist and his text as more literary than expository. Knowing that it was important for a writer of fiction not to break the spell that bound his reader to the world he was creating, he worried that too much open philosophizing would do that. The author had something to say, he informs us, but it seems that he had to work within artistic rules that in certain ways constrained him. The critic Boris Eikhenbaum has interpreted him as a kind of historical chronicler. Medieval chronicles have narrators who openly comment on the events they compile, and Eikhenbaum has made a powerful argument for the presence in the narrative commentary of *War and Peace* of style and themes borrowed from Russian chronicles.[3] If Tolstoy's authorial narrator indeed owes something to medieval chronicles, one must keep in mind that chroniclers represent a general universalizing perspective rather than the opinions of an individual. At his most grandiose, the narrator of *War and Peace* is a kind of Hegelian transcendentalist who attributes the Napoleonic wars to "Providence"; this is a modern version of the medieval chronicler who saw world history in Christian terms. Yet one cannot simply equate the narrator of *War and Peace* with its author: even his portentous tones do not tidily sum up the work. As a result, the relation among the different strands in the novel has been a subject of critical speculation since it was first published. This volume's contributors from different disciplines demonstrate how one can engage the book in quite different ways depending on one's own concerns.

War and Peace as History

The first four chapters of *Tolstoy On War* explores history in the novel. In chapter 1 ("Tolstoy on War, Russia, and Empire") Dominic Lieven concedes the enormous influence of *War and Peace,* which he attributes to its intrinsic virtues—especially its psychological portrait of Russian soldiers—as well as to its myth-making power. As national myth, the novel told Russian readers what they were already primed to hear and still hear until the present day. Thus in Lieven's reading, *War and Peace* is bad history that makes subsequent history by contributing immensely to the self-understanding of subsequent generations of Russians.

   Tolstoy did a huge amount of historical research in writing the novel. This does not in itself nullify Lieven's claim that he distorted the historical record, but it allows us to look at his practice of history from another, more positive perspective. When criticized for his portrayal of historical actors by veterans of 1812 and military historians, he declared defiantly in "A Few Words about the Book *War and Peace*" that it was true to the data he uncovered (PSS 16:13). Dan Ungurianu's investigations in chapter 2 ("The Use of Historical Sources in *War and Peace*") substantiate that claim. According to him, Tolstoy rarely changes historical fact in the book, and where he does, it is insignificant or unintentional. While romantic authors like Nikolai Gogol in *Taras Bulba* play fast and loose with facts, Tolstoy, as a realist, strives to be true to the historical record available to him. He does not put history first, however. Instead he "tackles historical sources, numerous as they were, on his own terms." Elsewhere Ungurianu writes that "Tolstoy approaches the historical material as a scholar but one whose critical arsenal is enriched with artistic tools." Ungurianu's (and Tolstoy's) equation of historian and scholar is significant. In the 1860s historian Leopold von Ranke (1795–1886) had already set the standards for a scientifically valid discipline of history. Though his own historical sources for the war were not all empirical, Tolstoy may have had primarily this scientific, scholarly version of history in mind when he distinguished so sharply in "A Few Words" between the tasks of history and literature. Empiricist history as practiced by von Ranke and his followers left methodologically generated gaps about the human dimension of epochs and events that only fiction, with its privileging of the imagination, can fill. Eikhenbaum concludes that Tolstoy believed that history could be profitably taught only through art, and he quotes to this effect from Tolstoy's notebook in 1870: "History-art, like every art, is not broad, but deep, and its subject can be a description of the life of all of Europe and a description of a month in the life of a single moujik in the sixteenth century."[4] In *War and Peace* Tolstoy is not striving for a full account of the 1812 war, and we must be careful not to equate the fictional world of the novel with a record of events based on historical documents that he believed the historian should provide. Readers of *Tolstoy On War* might want to ponder where Tolstoy's artistic approach to history is preferable or inferior to the Rankean one.

Tolstoy shapes the world of *War and Peace* subjectively and on his own terms by excluding points of view with which he is not sympathetic. Alexander Martin in chapter 3 ("Moscow in 1812: Myths and Realities") notes an important respect in which the fictional world of *War and Peace* does not correspond to the historical realities of the 1812 campaign. Tolstoy portrays the occupation and burning of Moscow from the point of view of the gentry, not the townspeople. These last, an incipient middle class left behind when all who could do so had fled, recalled these events very differently from the way Tolstoy describes them. The raw energy that Tolstoy celebrates in his book threatened the law and order essential to their security. They blamed the aristocrats for deserting them and the peasants for sacking the city rather than, as *War and Peace* would have it, rebuilding it. They left behind vivid descriptions of disorder, filth, and violence that Tolstoy would have had to take into account to do full justice to the situation.

In chapter 4 ("The French at War: Representations of the Enemy in *War and Peace*") Alan Forrest reports on another point of view that Tolstoy did not conscientiously research, namely that of the French invaders. Not surprisingly, and in accordance with Tolstoy's representation of them, the French considered Russians exotic, although one might retort that Frenchmen and Germans are in turn simplified into types in the novel. Forrest discusses the nature of his sources and their reliability. Mostly memoirs, they have the advantage of being eyewitness accounts. They are all written after the fact, some many years later. The experiences of their authors have crystallized into narratives with plotlines that require that some things be emphasized and others left out. In this respect as in others, memoirs are closer to fiction than to "scientific" history.

Like memoirists and the nationalist historians whom he criticized, Tolstoy had his own axes to grind. As a veteran of the Crimean War, he wanted to connect his own time with the earlier period when the French under another Napoleon invaded Russia. Lieven analyzes his prejudices against the non-Russian officers in Russian service, and he notes that Tolstoy and other Russian commentators are silent about Russian achievements in 1813–14, even though in military terms they exceeded those of 1812. This otherwise inexplicable modesty among Russians about their own military triumphs is due, Lieven concludes, to the rise of nationalism and its imperatives. Later Russians, including historians, military men, and Tolstoy himself, were not sympathetic to the prenationalist goals of Alexander I in 1813–14, when he set out to save Europe. They preferred to focus on the nation-building moment of the 1812 expulsion of the French from the homeland. In the same vein, Lieven disparages Tolstoy's representation of partisan warfare as an expression of national spirit. On the contrary, Lieven asserts, those whom Tolstoy calls partisans in the Russian army were irregular units and light cavalry (especially Cossacks) led by regular army officers. Furthermore, the greatest feats of these groups were not on Russian soil but later on in Prussia, after Napoleon had been chased from Russia.

Tolstoy's Worldview

If Tolstoy's great work did help form modern Russia, that in itself makes it imperative for all students of Russia, whatever their discipline, to understand its author's worldview. Like certain other great nineteenth-century Russian writers (Pushkin and Dostoevsky, for example), though in his own inimitable way, Tolstoy is both an Enlightenment figure and a romantic. He very much admired unbiased reason, but he did not believe that people are able to transcend their own will and their desire to impose it. He was, therefore, very suspicious of supposedly rational action and speech and privileged the irrational and spontaneous in war and politics (as in all spheres of human life) above the rational and planned. The former can often be more reasonable than the latter because it may transcend the calculations of narrow egotism. In chapter 5 ("Symposium of Quotations: Wit and Other Short Genres in *War and Peace*"), Gary Saul Morson examines the literary expressions of the kind of intelligence valued in *War and Peace* and the kind scorned there. These different exercises of the mind are encapsulated in various small genres represented liberally in the book. The bon mot even as practiced by the truly witty diplomat Bilibin is always ignoble, because in Tolstoy's view, it always serves self-congratulatory pride and competition. Similarly, heroic pronouncements by both Napoleon and Alexander in the novel come across in Morson's reading as deliberately theatrical and self-serving. Sayings and aphorisms, on the other hand, appear as distillations of folk wisdom when anonymous or spoken by the humble peasant soldier Platon Karataev and as reflections by wise men on the complexities of life when their authors are the likes of Pascal.

Rationalists (like Mikhail Speransky or old Prince Bolkonsky) are not reasonable in *War and Peace,* and political and military leaders almost never act from reasonable motives. The exploits of Napoleon are denigrated, while Karataev stands at the top of the novel's pyramid of values. Jeff Love in chapter 6 ("The Great Man in *War and Peace*") explores the philosophical implications of this hierarchy. Love associates Napoleon with the modern philosophical project of the conquest of nature through science. According to him, Napoleon practices military theory based on scientific principles and, more important, on "modern mathematical physics" "that should allow us to impose our will on nature in a way that the ancients might have imagined but never dared to realize." Napoleon epitomizes "the modern will to mastery over all impediments to human power, the impetus of the finite being to overcome finitude, to wrestle with fate and win." Prince Andrei, an admirer of Napoleon, starts his quest for military glory with just such ambitions. Taking a different approach to war, Kutuzov mostly eschews aggressive decision making on the battlefield. He "simply dismisses out of hand the elaborate science of war the Austrians employ against Napoleon." He "suppresses will" so as to gain an "unclouded apprehension of events that cannot be reduced to strategy, formula, or method." Love calls this "cognitive humility" and associates it with classical Greek thought. The wisest man in the novel in this respect is not Kutuzov, however, but Karataev. No military man can completely embrace Karataevian wisdom: "Karataev misses nothing, needs nothing, wants nothing: he is as he is. There is no striving, no problem of will, no need for reasons to be. Karataev is disinterest incarnate, to engage a paradoxical expression." Love wonders whether at its deepest philosophical level the novel is not a patriotic epic but an exploration of wisdom that undercuts all ways of life except that of the sage. Since, however, no one else in the book seems capable of the purely disinterested stance of Karataev, all the other characters, even Pierre Bezukhov, fall back into fantasies generated by the will. Platon figures as an unrealistic ideal, and in Love's reading, the narrative illustrates the failure of human beings to achieve what Tolstoy regards as philosophical perfection.

Tolstoy's military readers were deeply suspicious of this strand of *War and Peace.* In chapter 7 ("*War and Peace* from the Military Point of View") I evaluate their reactions to the novel. While praising Tolstoy's unrivaled understanding of the psychology of the Russian army and his portrait of its everyday life, they attacked his theory of history and especially his military theory. General Mikhail Dragomirov, the author of the most extensive review of *War and Peace,* castigated Tolstoy's poor grasp of strategy, tactics, and logistics. In different ways Tolstoy's military readers all objected to his historical determinism and especially to his denial of the possibility of control of the battlefield. They had personal reasons to take offense. "If officers do not think or rationally maneuver on the battlefield, if wars make no rational sense from the human perspective—if they just happen by themselves and armies coalesce, fight, and die without any guidance from leaders—then Dragomirov and the others were simply wasting their time." The last part of my essay explores an important limitation in the perspective of the military readers and defends an aspect of Tolstoy's psychology that they rejected as harmful to their task as soldiers.

Theories of War and History in the Novel

It is not easy to separate fiction and essay in *War and Peace*. Tolstoy's theories derive much of their power from their illustration in the fictional narrative. In chapter 8 ("The Duel as a Microcosm of War") Rick McPeak forcefully demonstrates how parallels between Clausewitz's and Tolstoy's military theory play out in the fictional narrative of the book. Both writers compare war to a duel. The principles of war as enunciated by Prince Andrei and Tolstoy's narrator govern Pierre's duel with Dolokhov, which takes on a dynamic of its own that Pierre cannot resist even as he repudiates it. In chapter 9 ("The Awful Poetry of War: Tolstoy's Borodino"), I first show how Tolstoyan war psychology blends with his theories of war in ways that make it difficult to separate them. I then demonstrate how Tolstoy mythologizes the physical setting of battle and its terrible dynamics.

Although Jeff Love and I discuss different ways in which Tolstoy's theories about war and history are hostile to practical life, they also contain much useful commentary on it. Andreas Herberg-Rothe in chapter 10 ("Tolstoy and Clausewitz: The Dialectics of War") compares Tolstoy's ideas with those of Clausewitz, who, although a Prussian, participated as a Russian staff officer in the 1812 campaign. An episode just before the Battle of Borodino in which Clausewitz makes a cameo appearance wrongly locates the theorist in the Prussian school of military strategy. According to Herberg-Rothe, Tolstoy, though he may not have known it, agreed with Clausewitz's own early "existential" view. Ironically, Clausewitz's experience of the Russian campaign changed this view to an "instrumental" one, and it is this later iteration of Clausewitz's ideas that Tolstoy is criticizing in the scene in which he appears. Herberg-Rothe distinguishes Clausewitz's later instrumental from his earlier existential views as follows. "In the first, war is primarily a means of policy to pursue goals, whether political ones or some other kind. According to the second, the warring parties are fighting for their very existence, either as a political body or for their physical existence or their identity. When Prince Andrei says before Borodino that one should fight only for a cause for which one is willing to die, he is expressing the existential concept of war." As Herberg-Rothe explains, Clausewitz first thought that Napoleon's aggressiveness was the proper way to conduct all war. After the Russian campaign he came to see that Napoleon's "boundless violence" had been the only right response to the emergency in which he and France continually found themselves up to this point. Clausewitz believed that in 1812 Napoleon did everything the same as before, but this time his aggressive strategy led inevitably to defeat by so exhausting the French forces that they could not exploit their own successes. In other words, he had not altered his strategy as the particular circumstances required. Clausewitzian instrumentalism, which Tolstoy (like John Keegan today) considered immoral, was influential in the Russia of Tolstoy's time, but, Herberg-Rothe argues, it too was not Clausewitz's ultimate position. While Tolstoy became a radical pacifist in his later years, Clausewitz, who would have considered such a stance naive, eventually tried to combine the various aspects of war in order to do full justice to its complexity.

In embracing existential war, Tolstoy was thinking of his own experience in the Crimean War, while the early Clausewitz had in mind the battles of the Prussians against Napoleon. Though he was no democrat, Clausewitz, according to Herberg-Rothe, saw the universal mobilization required in existential war as an important step toward creating a German nation. Here too there is an ironic parallel to the role of *War and Peace* as a founding epic of modern Russia.

Reconfigured in certain ways, Tolstoy's theories can be remarkably relevant today. Tolstoy's contemporary readers were themselves transcendentalists of some kind, and therefore his claim that Providence in some way was directing the war of 1812 did not in itself seem outlandish to them. Most modern readers find it bizarre and unacceptable. Ignoring Tolstoy's transcendentalism, Elizabeth Samet focuses in chapter 11 ("The Disobediences of *War and Peace*") on his rejection of history as neatly shaped by a few dominant minds. She argues that the "disobedient" "hybrid" form of Tolstoy's book parallels this rejection. Samet reminds readers that "[i]n being what it is, the novel resists not only 'conventional forms of artistic prose' but also—notwithstanding that it is drawn from actual events—historical narratives of cause and effect. 'A historian has to do with the results of an event,' he explains [in "A Few Words"], 'the artist with the fact of the event.'" Tolstoy emphasizes not links forged through cause and effect but what happens in the moment and how it unfolds. On the surface this emphasis on the moment seems contrary to the circular yet relentlessly unfolding pattern of epic, but it is not necessarily so. Samet cites what David Quint has called the losers' epic, "which embraces contingency and resists the linear march of victory," as a version of epic with features that fit Tolstoy's vision. One of these is to not only start in medias res, but end there too. This highlights the moment rather than its antecedents or consequences. The focus on the moment jibes with that of individual experience: no matter how commonplace the decisive life events of each of us may seem to others, we each experience them as fresh and uniquely powerful. Tolstoy's fiction captures this central dynamic of individual existence. As Samet shows, this emphasis on the individual links him to nineteenth-century American military thought.

In the last part of her essay, Samet suggests that today's warfare may resemble the paradigms suggested by Tolstoy and that his mathematical modeling of war may prefigure present-day theories that use computers to predict patterns in asymmetric warfare. Updating Tolstoy's argument and thereby rendering it relevant to political science, David Welch in chapter 12 ("Tolstoy the International Relations Theorist") substitutes what he calls the structural arguments of International Relations theorists for Tolstoy's metaphysical determinism. Like Samet, he thereby makes use of Tolstoy's argument against the influence of great men in history while disregarding its most radical conclusions. By "structure" Welch means the larger forces generated by political institutions and constraints within a country as well as by constraints internationally. This structure limits the individual agency of even the most powerful political actors. In International Relations, Welch explains, most people would say that the reasons for events rest somewhere on a sliding scale between the two kinds of causes. In other words, the actions of individuals matter while always being influenced and limited by structural considerations.

Tolstoy does not answer the question "What force moves people?" but he poses it better than anyone Welch knows. Early on, Welch quotes Tolstoy on the difficulty of explaining how ideas actually influence culture, but then in the final section of his essay he points out correctly that it is precisely *ideas* to which Tolstoy is most sympathetic. Welch points out that the will of the people is itself an idea or influenced by ideas. Substituting ideas for God as the formative element of culture, Welch avoids debate over whether those ideas and hence the will of the people might be divinely inspired. Welch's approach exposes an underlying irony in Tolstoy's position. As an artist Tolstoy affects culture no less than does the philosopher or the soldier-statesman, and perhaps he does so more directly than the others. He himself is a great man, in this case in competition with Napoleon. Tolstoy, however, makes no claim to control the future (as opposed to influencing it) and to this extent is true to his own thought.

What makes *War and Peace* uniquely valuable across the disciplines is its broad combination of modes of discourse. Readers who compare the fictional narrative and the essay part of the book reap the greatest benefits from it.

No one would deny that human subjectivity needs the steady hand of reason to control and guide it. Readers therefore ignore narrative digressions and commentary in the book at their peril. Those who don't ignore them have every right to subject both them and Tolstoy's fictional narrative to the scrutiny of reason. On the other hand, Welch points out that International Relations theorists and social scientists routinely exclude what Tolstoy calls "real life"—by which he means life generated by the inner needs of individuals—and yet without it we cannot understand what moves anyone. Herein resides the importance of narrative fiction for the social sciences (and, as seen above, for historians). Only it can describe real life because only art privileges subjectivity as the main truth. The deductive reasoning that anchors social science always reduces subjectivity to something else, something determined and therefore unacceptable to human consciousness when one applies such reasoning not to others but to oneself.

War and Peace derives much of its power from the way its author imagines the lives of its principal characters not only within a historical framework but as actors who themselves in different ways and with different degrees of self-consciousness participate in history, present and past. The results, while usually not what the individual actors intended and therefore not reducible to any one individual will, are produced by them and their deeply personal motivations. Art exceeds its mandate when it reduces everything to the personal and subjective. On the other hand, history and social science need art in order to convincingly re-create, understand, and generalize the past and the present.

1

Tolstoy on War, Russia, and Empire

—◂

DOMINIC LIEVEN

Tolstoy made it clear that for him *War and Peace* was much more than a mere novel. In part through the mouth of Prince Andrei Bolkonsky and in part through his own direct voice as author, Tolstoy used *War and Peace* to express his views on war, history, and Russia. Not surprisingly, military thinkers and historians turned their critical attention to the book, given its enormous popularity and the message it was attempting to convey about their profession. Of these military critics the most senior and also one of the most insightful was General Mikhail Dragomirov. In Dragomirov's case—as indeed was true of other military critics—what was interesting were not only the criticisms that were made but those that were not. The silent assumptions of both Tolstoy and his critics tell one as much about Russian myths and memories of the Napoleonic wars as do the views they actually expressed. Viewing these myths and memories in comparative perspective this not only illustrates the uniqueness of some aspects of how Russia remembered the Napoleonic era but also more generally sheds light on Russian views on war, nation, and empire.

In common with all Tolstoy's military critics, Dragomirov decried the novelist's weak grasp of historical causation, his failure to understand the importance of military professionalism, and his willful ignorance about why leadership remained crucial in war. Key examples of these faults included Tolstoy's almost juvenile account of the causes of Napoleon's invasion of 1812, his foolish comments about the unimportance of choice of terrain and skillful deployment in battle, and the manner in which Tolstoy's stress on the fog of war had led him to deny the possibility of purposeful leadership rather than emphasize its crucial albeit exceptionally challenging nature.[1]

In common with most military critics, Dragomirov paid tribute to the great descriptive power of Tolstoy the novelist,[2] as well as his intimate knowledge of the everyday life of the army, the values and mentalities of its officers and men, and the realities of battle as seen by the officer and soldier in the ranks. Dragomirov went much further, however, than most fellow officers in praising Tolstoy and suggesting that *War and Peace* had much to offer with respect to the education of future officers in war's realities. He argued that Tolstoy, unlike almost all current military historians, discussed and understood "the whole inner aspect of war, which is unknown to most military theorists and peacetime officers." In other words, he revealed the all-important issue of the psychology of the soldier on campaign and in battle, which was of crucial significance to anyone seeking to understand and prepare himself for war's realities. For that reason Dragomirov argued that *War and Peace* would be an excellent addition to any course designed to train officers.[3]

To understand Dragomirov's standpoint it is essential to know his position as a key protagonist in the debates about military doctrine that occurred during the last decades of the nineteenth century. A leading Western historian of the Russian army describes the two sides in this debate as "technologists" and "magicians." The former stressed the impact on war of new elements such as railways, machine guns, and indeed the whole technology of the industrial era, with its inevitable effect on the organization of armies, the planning of wars, and the mentality of soldiers. On the other side, the magicians, led by Mikhail Dragomirov, stressed the eternal truth that morale, motivation, and will were the keys to victory in war. Magicians in general and Dragomirov above all emphasized the uniquely strong sources of morale and motivation for Russian soldiers. Dragomirov was famous for his belief in an indigenous and superior Russian school of war, which he traced back to Aleksandr Suvorov in the eighteenth century. He believed that this powerful indigenous tradition had too often been sidelined in the Russian army because of reliance on alien and usually German teachings about material aspects of war. For Dragomirov there was a direct line between pedantic German military thinkers of the Napoleonic era with their abstract formulas and the technologists of his own times.[4]

It is therefore not surprising that Dragomirov sympathized with key elements of Tolstoy's interpretation of the Napoleonic wars and saw him as a potential ally. After all, among the strongest threads in *War and Peace* is Tolstoy's stress on Russian ethnic patriotism and on the overriding importance of the moral factor in war. His contempt for staffs and staff officers owed something to the fact that more than half of the tsarist general staff officers in 1812 did not even have Slavic, let alone Russian, names. Very many of them were Germans. In the midst of Prince Andrei's outburst on the eve of Borodino about the meaning of a national war for Russians, Tolstoy depicts Clausewitz and Wolzogen riding by within earshot and discussing the conflict in terms of strategic abstractions. As is often the case, Tolstoy's judgments—in this case about German theorists—are partly true and partly false. In the person of General Karl Pfühl, who devised the fortified camp at Drissa and the strategy that revolved around it, "German staff-officer theory" was indeed worthy of mockery. But this was hardly true of Clausewitz, who understood at least as well as Tolstoy the anarchic power of war but had a far more realistic and terrifying sense of how this power might be harnessed and what the implications of modern, national war might be.[5]

Tolstoy argues that the retreat of the Russian army from the empire's frontier to Moscow was the unplanned result of wholly unpredictable circumstance and chance (III, 2, i, 682–86). Again his judgment is partly correct. With Russia having chosen to wage a defensive war and surrender the initiative to Napoleon, the French emperor had to decide whether to march toward Moscow, Petersburg, or Kiev, or indeed—most dangerously—to end the 1812 campaign at Smolensk and organize Lithuania and Belorussia as a base for further military operations in 1813. It is also true that by driving between Barclay and Bagration's armies and thereby keeping them disunited, Napoleon inadvertently made it easier for Barclay to justify and execute the strategy of deep retreat that ultimately led to Napoleon's downfall.[6]

Nevertheless, the argument that the Russian strategic withdrawal was pure chance flies in the face of overwhelming evidence from Russian intelligence documents and from the correspondence of Alexander I and of Barclay de Tolly. It was above all Barclay who was responsible for conceiving and executing this strategy. But Tolstoy was disinclined to acknowledge such merit in a man whom he described as "an honest and very precise German," a "stranger" to Russia who was unfit to command "precisely because he thinks everything over very thoroughly and precisely, as every German ought to do" (III, 2, xxv, 772). Unlike some of Tolstoy's military critics, Dragomirov held an ideological position that made it unlikely that he would come to Barclay's defense. His praise for Russian generalship at Borodino and during the campaign is confined to ethnic Russians such as Kutuzov, Ermolov, Dokhturov, and Raevsky, and to Petr Bagration, whose Orthodox religion and assimilation into the Russian aristocracy allowed him to be seen as "one of us."[7]

A key motif in *War and Peace* is that Napoleon was irresistible until stopped in his tracks by Russia and above all by the patriotism of the Russian people. Once again, there is a good deal of truth in this claim, but Tolstoy exaggerates it because of his Russian patriotic and populist bias. It is true that Napoleon's empire was greatly weakened by 1812 and that without the successful Russian resistance to his invasion the subsequent European coalition of 1813–14 that destroyed Napoleon could never have occurred. In 1812 the Russian army showed extraordinary courage and resilience in surviving the long retreat and the devastating losses at Borodino without losing its cohesion and morale. Probably no other army in Europe could have done this. Nevertheless, the 1812 campaign did not destroy Napoleon or make the collapse of his empire inevitable. He very nearly won the spring 1813 campaign and recouped most of what he had lost in 1812. Moreover, in claiming that "Borodino was the first [battle] that Napoleon did not win" (III, 2, xxviii, 785; IV, 3, i, 1031–32) Tolstoy is betraying the element of national smugness and the ignorance of the broader European context that runs through *War and Peace*. Three years before Borodino the Austrians had defeated Napoleon at Aspern, displaying both then and at the subsequent battle of Wagram great courage and steadiness in the face of heavy casualties.[8]

Tolstoy's silence about Aspern reflected not just the fact that, as one critic wrote subsequently, he was interested only in Russia and not at all in Europe or in international relations.[9] The essence of Tolstoy's "military doctrine" is that battles are won by morale and morale itself is rooted in national spirit and consciousness. How could the armies of the polyglot Habsburg Empire be so motivated? As to the Russian army, in a key passage in *War and Peace* Tolstoy argues that it lost the battle of Austerlitz because this was not a truly Russian cause and the soldiers therefore had nothing to fight for. As Prince Andrei insisted on the eve of Borodino, the national war of 1812 in defense of family, home, and country was a very different matter (III, 2, xxv, 773–74).

There is actually strong evidence to suggest that the Russian army fought with particular stubbornness and ferocity in 1812. The troops had watched as Smolensk was burned to the ground by foreign invaders, including—very much to the point—the ancestral Polish enemy. Unlike not just the French but even the British army of that era, every Russian regiment had chaplains, and Orthodoxy was an integral part of army daily life and ritual. There is no reason to doubt that the clergy's calls to defend the Orthodox fatherland and its protector, the tsar, struck home. It is impossible to prove this by reference to soldiers' own comments since almost all the rank and file were illiterate, and very few records remain in which they speak on their own behalf. But their officers were certainly motivated by strong feelings of patriotism and believed that this was also true of their men. One senior officer wrote in his memoirs that so long as the commanders and officers were motivated and effective, the men would follow. That this was an elitist and patronizing view does not necessarily make it incorrect, especially where premodern and colonial armies are concerned.[10]

Still, there are problems with the assumption that what most strongly motivated Russian rank-and-file soldiers at this time was patriotism, however that is defined. Almost all military specialists stress that the key motivator for soldiers in battle tends to be small-unit loyalty—in other words, loyalty to comrades and regiment. Even Dragomirov left some hints that he found Tolstoy's explanation of soldiers' motivation inadequate. He wrote of one officer described by Tolstoy that "the regiment was his fatherland." The single issue to which Dragomirov took most violent objection in Tolstoy was the latter's description of regimental flags as "pieces of cloth on sticks" (III, 2, xxxix, 819). In Dragomirov's opinion Tolstoy's words were so foolish and unworthy that he was convinced that the novelist would remove them in subsequent editions of War and Peace, which of course did not happen. Dragomirov insisted that for humans material objects could take on near-sacred connotations as living symbols of "the inner spiritual unity of the people who make up any unit." As John Keegan reminds us, regimental identities and loyalties symbolized in flags and other material objects were the key building blocks in the British army that defeated Napoleon at Waterloo. For illiterate Russian soldiers removed forever from any contact with their families and committed to a lifetime's service in their regiments, such loyalties were likely to be particularly strong. A German prince with decades of experience of both the Russian and other armies wrote plausibly in his memoirs that the uniquely strong loyalty of Russian soldiers for their regimental home was the single greatest key to the army's strength and resilience.[11]

There is in any case a fundamental problem in taking Tolstoy's interpretation as the final word on what motivated Russian soldiers. If it is indeed true that Russian troops failed to win at Austerlitz or Friedland because of lack of motivation, how does one explain the fact that in 1813–14 they scored a series of victories on foreign soil alongside the very same allies whom Tolstoy dismisses with such contempt in 1805–7? It will not do to suggest that Napoleon's armies were too weakened by 1812 to put up a stout resistance in subsequent years. On the contrary, he put more than half a million troops on the German battlefields in 1813, outnumbering the allies by two to one at decisive moments of the spring 1813 campaign. Nor is it true that in 1813–14 Russia was playing a secondary role, with the main effort in the allied coalition falling to the Prussians and Austrians. In fact Russia deployed more than five hundred thousand troops beyond the empire's borders in 1813–14 and played the leading military role in the coalition.

Perhaps it should not be too surprising that in professional military terms the Russian army fought better in 1813–14 than in 1812. Peacetime training is no substitute for the experience of campaign and combat where performance is concerned. On the battlefields of 1813–14 staff work was more efficient, reserves were better employed, and light infantry skirmishers were more proficient than in 1812, to take but three examples. Since Tolstoy was not really interested in professional military training or qualities, he might have shrugged off this evidence. Harder to dismiss as irrelevant is the evidence of the enormous courage and steadiness of Russian troops on a number of German and French battlefields in the face of casualties as high as and sometimes higher than those suffered by most First Army units at Borodino. Something beyond Tolstoy is needed to explain the exceptional staying power and commitment of these Russian soldiers, which make a mockery of some Soviet-era historians' efforts to claim lack of motivation as the cause of setbacks in spring 1813.[12] Small-unit loyalty to comrades and regiments is the best explanation, along with the fact that their Orthodox and monarchist loyalties had an impact even when the troops were operating outside Russia. For all its heroism, the main Russian army scored few clear-cut victories in 1812. By contrast, in 1813–14 the army scored a string of victories in which it was generally the main and sometimes the only element engaged on the allied side.[13]

Tolstoy's novel essentially ends with the Russian army in Vilno in December 1812. He therefore did not need to contemplate ways in which the victories of the following two years might have called into question some of the assumptions and assertions that went into *War and Peace*. What interested Tolstoy was not the army's triumphs abroad and the establishment of a stable and peaceful international order but rather the war's impact on Russian society and mentalities. Initially he had intended to write a book that would devote much attention to the Decembrist movement, and it is this movement rather than the fall of Paris in 1814 that shadows the later chapters of the book.

Even more interesting than Tolstoy's lack of concern for 1813–14 is the fact that this attitude was shared by his critics, none of whom seemed to much care that Tolstoy's novel ended with the story of Napoleon's defeat still only half-finished. Among the many often quite sharp criticisms of *War and Peace* by military commentators this is remarkable, for the campaigns of 1813–14 were the most glorious in tsarist military history and the capture of Paris in 1814 the army's most spectacular achievement. Moreover, without some grasp of the 1813–14 campaigns it was hard to make sense of Russian grand strategy in 1812 since Alexander and Barclay had always seen the defensive campaign of that year as the first stage in a longer war that would drain Napoleon's resources and open the way for Russia to counterattack across its western border and raise a pan-European coalition against Napoleon's empire.

Aleksandr Mikhailovskii-Danilevskii was really the first Russian official historian of the campaigns of 1812–14. Tolstoy drew much information and maybe some inspiration from his work. Mikhailovskii's diary for summer 1815 offers some hints as to why Tolstoy's concentration on 1812 to the exclusion of 1813–14 seemed natural to many Russians. Mikhailovskii-Danilevskii at this time was serving in Alexander's entourage and in close proximity to the monarch. He recorded that the emperor was very un-Russian in sympathy, that his diplomatic advisers were almost never Russian, and that he sometimes behaved in ways that humiliated Russians before foreigners. Characteristically, Alexander did not like to be reminded about Borodino, where, in Mikhailovskii-Danilevskii's opinion, Russian courage and Kutuzov's wisdom had saved the country. Instead the emperor took more pride in subsequent campaigns and victories. For Mikhailovskii-Danilevskii this made no sense. "What are other battles in comparison to Borodino?" he asked, adding that "at Borodino there was a battle of the nations, Russia against Europe." In his opinion, Leipzig by comparison was a paltry affair, with Napoleon half-beaten before the battle even began.[14]

From Mikhailovskii-Danilevskii one gets the sense that whereas 1812 was a national war, the subsequent campaigns were almost Alexander's private affair, an imperial and dynastic war remote from the interests of the Russian nation. Tolstoy himself contributed enormously to this idea, and it became firmly fixed in Russian memory and perception. In the process the reality of Russia's war effort became distorted.

One example of this is the historiography of the Russian partisans and their place in Russian folk memory. Tolstoy was very interested in partisan warfare, which he described as "always successful, as history demonstrates." To some extent this reflected his belief that partisan warfare was rooted in popular support and that the masses were not just more virtuous but also more powerful than their leaders. He was indeed an early exponent of "history from below," even arguing that "power is the sum total of the wills of the masses, transferred by express or tacit agreement to rulers chosen by the masses." Though this might seem a strange comment on the tsarist system of government, Tolstoy's populist sympathies inevitably won him much sympathy in the Soviet era. In addition, even without strong official pressures to equate the partisans of 1941–45 with the earlier opposition to Napoleon, these comparisons would have come naturally to Soviet citizens who had witnessed the carnage but also the heroism of popular resistance to Hitler in the Soviet territories he conquered.

The Tolstoyan and Soviet mythology about partisan war has a foundation in fact. Napoleon was seriously impeded by the popular resistance to his foraging parties as they sought food and fodder for his army in Moscow. Partisan units farther afield threatened his communications, carried off his stores, and forced his commanders to disperse their troops to keep these partisans at bay. But one should not exaggerate the significance of partisans in 1812. It was

Spring 1813: the Cossacks in Hamburg.

not they who defeated Napoleon but Kutuzov's army. Moreover the term "partisan" in its modern rendering conceals the reality of partisan operations in 1812. Partisans were not the people in arms but rather units of regular light cavalry and Cossacks operating behind enemy lines under the command of regular officers.[15]

Perhaps most shocking of all to Russian popular memory is the fact that the most successful Russian partisan operations occurred not in 1812 but in early 1813, and not in Russia but on Prussian soil. Partisans in 1812 were a major nuisance to Napoleon but no more. They were of tactical rather than strategic importance. The partisan raid deep into the enemy rear in January–March 1813, on the other hand, had major strategic results. It precipitated the retreat of the French from the line of the River Warthe on the Prusso-Polish frontier right back to the Elbe, in the process liberating Berlin and the Prussian heartland and hastening Prussia's entry into the war. Had the spring 1813 campaign begun on the Warthe with most of Prussia still under Napoleon's control and restless Poland within range of his advance, then Alexander's campaign to liberate Europe would probably have been wrecked before it had truly begun. If the liberation of Berlin is not a usual part of partisan mythology, neither are the men who led this raid. Aleksandr Chernyshev was a brilliant spymaster and leader of cavalry raiding parties behind enemy lines. He was also a consummate Petersburg courtier, as unscrupulous and opportunistic as Tolstoy's Prince Vasily Kuragin but a great deal more formidable. A pillar of Nicholas I's regime and a man who played a key role in the suppression of the Decembrist movement, for both Tolstoy and popular Russian memory he is an almost perfect antihero. Yet even Chernyshev pales in popular mythology before the memory of his second in command, Alexander Benckendorff, a nicer man than his chief in the 1813 raid but as a Baltic German noble and the chief of Nicholas I's security police a figure who is the exact antithesis of the accepted Russian picture of the partisan. In fact, to describe Chernyshev and Benckendorff as Russia's most successful partisan leaders in the struggle against Napoleon is more or less to stand Russian popular memory and mythology on its head.[16]

Of course, Russians were by no means unique in distorting the true story of wars to suit subsequent political and cultural assumptions and priorities. War is the best breeding ground for the myths and memories around which societies and polities cohere. It provides unparalleled examples of heroism and sacrifice for the community, as well as striking examples of united action against a common external threat. The Napoleonic wars provide a powerful illustration of this trend, not just because they lasted so long and had so deep an impact but also because they occurred at a time when the key ideas underlying modern nationalism were beginning to emerge and when the modern, urban, and literate mass societies that are the best environment for nationalism were just over the horizon.[17]

Spain is the most striking example from the Napoleonic era with respect to the role of partisan warfare in the creation of national myths. A leading Anglophone historian of Spain writes that "Spanish historians are agreed that the myth of Spain as a nation was born around 1808 or 1812."[18] Much of this myth revolved around the role of the partisans. By contrast with Russia, the Spanish monarchy and state had more or less collapsed, and the poor performance of the regular army did not make it a good source of heroic myths. As in Russia, regular military forces had played a crucial role in defeating the foreign enemy, but since in the Spanish case this meant Wellington's British army, there was no mileage to be made from this fact by nationalists. In addition, unlike regular forces, the partisans could easily be equated with "the people." Subsequently, different political tendencies in Spain could interpret the partisan movement to suit their own ideologies and interests. For the right, the partisans had fought for traditional Catholic and royal Spain against the godless French. For the left, they were a shining example of the people taking up arms to defend their rights against alien and authoritarian rule. But on both sides of the debate it was more or less agreed that the partisans were true patriots who had played the crucial role in liberating their country from foreign rule.[19]

Recent historiography has called all these judgments into question. Though not to the same extent as in Russia, many partisans in Spain were in fact also regular soldiers on detached duty and operating behind enemy lines. The more genuinely popular elements in the resistance were very often hardly distinguishable from bandits and were regarded as such by much of the population. Though the guerrillas undoubtedly did make a big contribution to Napoleon's troubles in Spain, they were not the main cause of his defeat there. Nor in the European context were they either unique or invincible. On the contrary, revolutionary and Napoleonic France had faced and defeated many similar movements beginning in the Vendée in 1793–95 and subsequently covering parts of Belgium, Italy, and the Tyrol. In their opposition to the ideas of the Enlightenment and, above all, to newly intrusive and oppressive government, all these movements had much in common, not least the extent to which resistance could often overlap with mere banditry. With the exception of Spain, the Napoleonic regime and its allies did in fact suppress all these revolts and pacified these territories by a combination of fierce repression, exploitation of divisions within local communities, and playing on elite and public exhaustion and desire for order. First British intervention and then Napoleon's debacle in Russia were the main reasons this did not happen in Spain.[20]

The British myth of the Napoleonic wars was inevitably very different from the Spanish one. Britain had never been invaded, so there was no partisan movement to celebrate. On the other hand, the British state had displayed formidable naval and financial power in the wars against Napoleon and had been revolutionary and Napoleonic France's most consistent enemy. The final destruction of Napoleon at Waterloo was a powerful memory that helped to legitimize the British aristocratic elite and polity. It helped that the allied army was commanded by that archetypal English aristocrat the Duke of Wellington and that Napoleon's final assault was repulsed by the British Guards, who acquired their now-familiar bearskins in memory of their triumph over Napoleon's Immortals. Even more than is usually the case with Napoleonic-era mythology, there was a solid basis in fact to British memory. The British state and armed forces had indeed proved formidably effective in the wars of the late eighteenth and early nineteenth centuries. Nevertheless, public memory far from coincided with historical reality. At Waterloo barely a quarter of the combined allied armies were British, and even a good many of them were Gaels from the Scottish highlands and Ireland. Moreover, the idea that Britain had fought for freedom against despotism was also largely a myth. Britain did fight against empire in Europe and for a European balance of power because this served its interests. One key advantage of a European balance was that it allowed Britain a free hand to secure a massive overseas empire. During the revolutionary and Napoleonic wars the expansion and consolidation of this empire advanced at great speed.[21]

The Prusso-German myth of the Napoleonic era shares common elements with European mythmaking but has its own specific traits, above all linked to the desire of the Prussian state to legitimize its subsequent unification and domination of Germany. Once again the "Borussian myth" had a solid foundation in fact. The Prussian achievement in 1812–15 in mobilizing a large, well-led, and well-motivated army from a war-ravaged land with fewer than six million people was indeed astonishing. Nevertheless, the official Prussian myth that Frederick William III had led a united Prussian people in a crusade to liberate Germany was rather far from the mark. It concealed Prussia's purely self-interested role before 1806 as a species of Napoleonic jackal. Even in 1813 the Prussian king had no interest in a German national crusade. His goals were far narrower and more self-interested. As to his peoples, they differed greatly in their commitment to the war, with some regions and social groups much more enthusiastic than others. Moreover, whereas in East Prussia enthusiasm for the war ran deep in almost all parts of society, that had less to do with Prussian—let alone German—nationalism than with visceral hatred of the French occupiers who had stripped the province bare in 1811–12. The Prussian myth was also careful to sideline the Austrian contribution in 1813–14 and to play down the fact that Prussia's restoration owed a huge amount to Russia, which was always the most powerful member of the allied coalition.[22]

European comparisons put the Russian case into perspective without, however, solving all the puzzles aroused by the study of Russian memory of the Napoleonic era. Whatever their differences, the Spanish, British, and Prussians did after all agree on exaggerating and glorifying their own achievements, usually at the expense of their allies. The strangest aspect of Russian memory of the Napoleonic wars is the extent to which it underestimates the Russian achievement.

For this Tolstoy is partly to blame. His version of "history from below" ruled out any awareness of the actually rather formidable achievement of Russia's government in planning and executing an effective strategy to defeat Napoleon. His belief that morale counted for far more than military professionalism or leadership equally ruled out a fair evaluation of the Russian army's often outstanding performance in these years. By ending the war part of *War and Peace* in December 1812, he automatically diverted attention from the two subsequent years when the Russian army reached the peak of its performance and Russia led a coalition to defeat Napoleon and restore a stable international order in Europe.

For all his greatness as a novelist, however, Tolstoy could never have done all this unless the soil had been well prepared in Russia for his message. One key to this was that it was precisely in the first quarter of the nineteenth century that there began the parting of the ways between the tsarist state and elements of Russian educated society.[23] In the eighteenth century the monarchy was almost always seen as the key force for modernization in Russia. Enlightened despotism also enjoyed legitimacy in much of Europe. The French Revolution helped to change this. The Decembrist movement emerged from this parting of the ways and played a huge role in entrenching the divide.

But there was also a structural element to this division between Russian state and society. The eighteenth-century Russian polity had been dominated largely by the aristocracy. In the nineteenth century power increasingly shifted to the growing bureaucracy. Tolstoy's rather disdainful portrait of Speransky in *War and Peace* illustrates his own resentment and that of his aristocratic peers at this phenomenon. In *War and Peace*, however, Tolstoy's aristocratic disdain for the bureaucratic state is a minor theme. By contrast, in *Anna Karenina* it looms far larger. The competition for Anna's love between the desiccated, conformist bureaucrat Karenin and Count Vronsky, the vibrantly human aristocratic Guards Cavalry officer, accurately reflects attitudes widely held but seldom so artistically expressed by the Russian social elites.

To some extent Tolstoy's quarrel with the tsarist state is familiar to historians not just of Russia but of Europe. It is the age-old struggle between court and country, with the aristocracy claiming its "natural" right to speak for society in opposition to the demands of a state power often seen as not just arbitrary, artificial, and amoral but also cosmopolitan and alien to the land over which it rules. Oliver Cromwell would easily have empathized with many of Tolstoy's instincts. In nineteenth-century Russia there were, however, specific reasons why the tension between court and country was particularly great. The tsarist bureaucracy and its Petersburg headquarters were very obviously in key respects a foreign import. Moreover, the social elites, unlike those almost everywhere else in Europe, did not possess representative institutions through which they could exercise some surveillance over state power or indeed the guaranteed civil rights that would ensure their freedom from bureaucratic and police interference in their lives. It was by no means purely personal accident that the Russian aristocracy and gentry produced two of the nineteenth century's most famous anarchists, Petr Kropotkin and Mikhail Bakunin. On the whole, as one might expect, most Russian aristocrats and members of the gentry were never fully alienated from the regime. As Russia modernized in the second half of the nineteenth century, however, the traditional elites lost their monopoly on the right to speak in society's name. The new plebeian elements who filled the ranks of the intelligentsia were much less inhibited in their outright rejection of the imperial state.

To understand the full implications of this alienation, especially in the context of this chapter, requires one to tease out the meanings of the words "empire" and "imperial." One key aspect of empire is power, especially "hard" military and diplomatic power exercised in the sphere of international relations. Russian society's alienation from the state entailed also a distancing from the latter's military and diplomatic aims and achievements, including Russia's key role in European politics in 1813–15. Tolstoy both reflected and encouraged this distancing.

The other key aspect of empire is multiethnicity, and here too, though less obviously, a gap widened between Russian society and the state. Leo Tolstoy was much more of a Russian ethnonationalist than Nicholas I or Alexander II, the cosmopolitan imperial dynasts under whose rule he passed his youth and middle age. His heroes, the Decembrists, were motivated not just by the desire to impose society's control over the absolutist state but also by deep resentment at what they perceived as tsarism's favoritism toward non-Russians and its disdain for the empire's core people and elite. The most striking Decembrist leader and thinker, Pavel Pestel', was a far more thoroughgoing centralizer and Russifier than even Alexander III. To put things in twentieth-century comparative imperial context, he was in fact a precursor of the Young Turks, who wished to assert Turkish ethnonational preeminence in what had traditionally been an Ottoman empire legitimized in religious and dynastic terms. In the twentieth century, a narrow and assertive ethnic nationalism of the core-majority people put at risk interethnic harmony and the survival of the multiethnic imperial polity.[24]

The biggest single reason that Russian memory underestimates the Russian achievement in 1812–14 in fact derives from the dilemmas of empire and nation in the Romanovs' polity. Britain, France, Spain, and Germany were or aspired to become nations. Their mobilization of ethnonational myths served this purpose. But the Russia that defeated Napoleon was a multinational, dynastic, and aristocratic empire. It derived part of its strength in 1812–14 from this fact. Given its multiethnic complexity and the principles on which it had been founded, it could never hope to become a nation. Inevitably the Russian ethnonational myths and memories that derived from the Napoleonic wars not only distorted but also diminished the Russian achievement in these years. Tolstoy played his part in this, but the complications and dilemmas arising from Russia's history as empire, nation, territory, and people went far deeper than the impact of his great novel and affected issues far more important than the distortion of Russian memory of the Napoleonic wars. From the 1930s the Soviet regime increasingly incorporated a semi-Tolstoyan interpretation of 1812–14 into its canon of Soviet patriotism. At one level this is ironic since in many key respects the Soviet regime was even more imperial and even more divorced from Russian ethnonational identity than was tsarism. But in principle if not always in practice Soviet imperialism was a rival and not a continuation of tsarist empire. Indeed in theory it defined its identity against imperialism in general and tsarist empire in particular. In the Soviet canon Alexander's vision of European security in 1812–15 and the policies he pursued to sustain this vision were driven by the reactionary ideology of the Holy Alliance and the vested interests this ideology served. This added a further element to Russian public misunderstanding and amnesia about key aspects of Russia's achievement in 1812–14.[25]

2

The Use of Historical Sources in *War and Peace*

———

DAN UNGURIANU

As with any work involving documentary material, the problem of historical sources in *War and Peace* can ultimately be reduced to two basic questions. First, how solid is the novel's documentary base, or in other words, how knowledgeable is the author? Second, how responsible is the author in his use of the material—that is to say, is he guided by the primary sources, or, on the contrary, does he manipulate them in order to validate his own opinions? Acknowledging the inevitable naïveté of such formulations, let us take them as a point of departure, which is all the more appropriate because Tolstoy himself chose to comment on both of these questions: *"Wherever in my novel historical figures speak and act, I have not invented, but have made use of the materials, of which, during my work, I have formed a whole library, the titles of which I find it unnecessary to set down here, but for which I can always give the reference"* (Pevear/ Volokhonsky, 1222; PSS 16:13). This passage appears in "A Few Words Apropos of the Book *War and Peace*," an essay published in March 1868, when Tolstoy's novel—or rather his "book," as he called it— was still coming out. There is little ground to doubt his sincerity, especially given his worship of truth as a supreme ethical and aesthetical category. One need only recall the powerful final words from "Sevastopol in May": "[T]he hero of my story, whom I love with all my heart and soul, whom I have attempted to portray in all his beauty and who has always been, is now and will always be supremely magnificent, is truth."[1] We will not find in Tolstoy literary games and provocations surrounding the truthfulness of one's own narrative that were so common among romantic authors and, during the subsequent periods, among modernists and postmodernists. However, his statement in "A Few Words" contributed, perhaps unwittingly, to heated debates in critical literature, as Tolstoy teases the reader with a promise of a bibliographical list that he ultimately chooses to withhold. To complicate the matter further, both in the text of *War and Peace* and in "A Few Words" Tolstoy explicitly mentions only a small number of very basic and obvious sources, as if undermining his own claims of thorough historical preparation.

The ensuing debate has been dominated by strongly polarized opinion, as most of the critics who address the problem of historical sources in *War and Peace* neatly fall into two opposing camps: the skeptics who question almost every historical aspect of *War and Peace,* exposing what they see as Tolstoy's meager preparation and considerable license in his handling of sources,[2] and those who, taking Tolstoy's assurances at face value, speak of the novel's colossal factual foundation owing to which the "words and deeds of historical characters are rendered in complete accordance with the truth of history."[3] There are surprisingly few commentators who occupy a middle-ground position and conclude that Tolstoy's rich documentary base was combined with a sui generis approach to sources.[4] The trajectory of this debate in itself constitutes a fascinating chapter in the reception of *War and Peace*. Initially vigorous, the voices of Tolstoy's critics gradually gave way to laudatory assessments of the novel's historical underpinnings, as the "Sage from Iasnaia Poliana" became canonized in Russian and Soviet culture. Any potentially subversive discussion of historical license in the novel all but vanished in the 1930s and resurfaced only in the mid to late 1980s, when cultural iconoclasm started to come back into vogue.

The most drastic instance of the discord surrounding the treatment of historical sources in *War and Peace* is found in two monographs that appeared in 1928 amid the heightened attention to Tolstoy during the centennial of his birth. The first was *Lev Tolstoy over the Pages of History* by Nikolai Apostolov (Ardens), a prominent Tolstoy scholar who had first approached the topic in the 1910s, and in the 1920s collaborated with the Jubilee Commission. The second was *Material and Style in Lev Tolstoy's Novel "War and Peace"* by Victor Shklovsky, one of the founders of Russian formalism in whose work Tolstoy also occupies a special place. (In 1917, developing his concept of art as device—which became a staple of the nascent formalist theory—Shklovsky coined the term *ostranenie* ["defamiliarization"] to describe the hallmark Tolstoyan technique and then kept returning to Tolstoy's work throughout his life.) Apostolov considers Tolstoy's preparation massive and the historical aspect of the novel impeccable. Shklovsky, drawing on the same evidence, speaks of a sketchy preparation and a rather peculiar selection of sources and concludes that in Tolstoy's novel the style—the author's poetics combined with his polemical ideological intent—overpowers and supplants the material—reality as reflected in historical sources. Looking back at his polemics with Shklovsky more than three decades later, Apostolov reiterates his highly positive opinion of the novel's historical aspect: "[U]nder all layers of artistic invention in *War and Peace* there is a solid foundation of precise historical knowledge. [...] In essence, for every 'fictional' episode or even detail of the novel one can find historical parallels and social traits reflected in documents or memoirs. [...] The use of 'historical sources' by Tolstoy was very responsible. There is no ground whatsoever to claim that there exists a break between the material and stylistic features of Tolstoy's novel. Isolated instances when Tolstoy erred as a historian do not undermine our general conclusion."[5] Far from being a matter of the past, arguments about Tolstoy's use of historical material in *War and Peace* continue today.

Taking into account this rich and controversial tradition, I revisit the question of the novel's historical base. I outline the scope of Tolstoy's sources, his treatment of historical material, and its implications for the overall artistic system of *War and Peace*. Finally, I examine the arguments of skeptics who question Tolstoy's historical accuracy.

The Scope of Tolstoy's Sources

Tolstoy names some of his sources in the text of the novel, its drafts, and his correspondence. Many of these are preserved in the Iasnaia Poliana library and bear marks of his work. Yet other sources can be reconstructed through textual parallels, although here one should be mindful of possible cross-contaminations. The first comprehensive list of materials used by Tolstoy was compiled almost a century ago, in 1912, and has been expanded several times.[6] New discoveries are still being made, so the list is not yet finalized, but it is safe to say that we know the greater part of Tolstoy's sources. They include the following:

1. Works of historiography dealing with the Napoleonic era and some of its major figures. Here Tolstoy explicitly mentions the multivolume histories by Aleksandr Mikhailovskii-Danilevskii (published in the mid-1830s–1840s) and Adolphe Thiers (the mid-1840s). Several critics—beginning with the military historian Aleksandr Vitmer in 1869—have rebuked Tolstoy for exaggerating the importance of these works, something that, in their opinion, serves as a proof of how limited the novel's historical arsenal is. Additionally, many commentators point out that Mikhailovskii-Danilevskii and Thiers were chosen as easy polemical targets and convenient irritants. One can also surmise that Tolstoy singles them out because they happen to be the most comprehensive and detailed narratives relatively close to the events in question in terms of chronology. He perceives them as primary sources of sorts—Mikhailovskii-Danilevskii

was actually a veteran of the 1812 war—and largely dismisses the more recent history of Napoleon's invasion by Mikhail Bogdanovich (1859–60) as
secondary and derivative.

2. Reference materials, including a dictionary of historical biography and an
   illustrated history of Russian military uniforms.

3. Numerous memoirs of civilians and combatants of various ranks from subal-
   tern officers to Napoleon himself.

4. Numerous official publications (proclamations and manifestos, military reg-
   ulations, et al.).

5. Periodicals, including Russian journals and newspapers of the epoch.

6. Religious, moral, and mystical literature, especially that related to Free-
   masonry.

7. Literary works of the period and about the period, including some Russian
   historical novels set in the Napoleonic era and published in the 1830s. Their
   authors happen to be veterans of the war of 1812 who fought on both
   the Russian side (Mikhail Zagoskin and Rafail Zotov) and the French side
   (Faddei Bulgarin). These novels provided Tolstoy with some stock-in-trade
   adventure situations that are quite prominent in *War and Peace* and coexist
   with its serious philosophical dimension.[7]

8. Pictorial materials of the era (including reproductions from the Military
   Gallery of 1812 in the Winter Palace that supplied details for many of
   Tolstoy's portraits).

9. A variety of unpublished archival documents and private letters.

10. Something that nowadays would be termed oral history: interviews with
    surviving eyewitnesses and also family lore, as many of Tolstoy's relatives
    were closely involved in the events described in *War and Peace* and served
    as prototypes for the heroes of the novel. Family connections also helped
    Tolstoy to procure some valuable documents—for example, the letters of
    Mariia Volkova to Varvara Lanskaia, which served as the main source for the
    correspondence between Princess Marya and Julie Karagina in the novel.
    Tolstoy's request concerning these letters addressed to his "aunt" Tatiana
    Ergol'skaia (who happens to be a partial prototype for the novel's Sonia)
    vividly illustrates the sense of family involvement and homeyness inherent
    in Tolstoy's work on *War and Peace:* "Do me a favor, auntie, in the book-
    case in my study, on the third shelf from the top, you'll find bundles of let-
    ters from Mar['ia] Apol[lonovna] Volkova. Pack them in oilcloth and send
    to me by mail" (PSS 61:130).

In addition to consulting the materials he had at Iasnaia Poliana, Tolstoy
worked at the Rumiantsev Library (during the Soviet period transformed
into the Lenin Library, now the Russian State Library), the Chertkov Library
(later known as the State Historical Library), and the Archives of the Palace

Title page illustration from Faddei Bulgarin's *Petr Ivanovich Vyzhigin*, vol. 1 (1831), engraving by S. Galaktionov. Russian novels of the 1830s provided Tolstoy with some stock-in-trade adventure situations pertaining to the war of 1812. Thus Pierre Bezukhov's exploits in occupied Moscow find parallels in Faddei Bulgarin's *Vyzhigin*, whose protagonist, also disguised as a commoner, stays behind after the retreat of Russian troops.

Ministry. He utilized the help of several consultants, including a prominent historian of the older generation, Mikhail Pogodin, and Petr Bartenev, editor of the recently founded *Russkii Arkhive* (*Russian Archive*), a historical journal that published a number of materials related to the period in question. Additionally, Tolstoy made a field trip to Borodino in order to familiarize himself with the site of the battle.

Well aware of all this, Shklovsky nonetheless downplays the seriousness of Tolstoy's historical preparation and speaks of merely two bookshelves of material browsed by Tolstoy. Apostolov, on the contrary, measures the sources read by Tolstoy in "tens of thousands of pages."[8] Shklovsky manipulates the facts to make his point: he takes the nominal list of the established sources of the novel (some fifty items as of the late 1920s), many of them multivolume works, and, ignoring the periodicals and archival materials, counts each entry as a "book": hence the two shelves. Apostolov, who reveres Tolstoy, is

A. Volkov. Caricature from the satirical magazine *Iskra* (1868, no. 16) depicting Tolstoy at work on *War and Peace*. The cartoonist emphasizes the eclectic nature of Tolstoy's sources, which include ready-made figurines of historical characters (among them is Napoleon III posing as Napoleon), two novels about the war of 1812 dating back to the 1830s (Zagoskin's *Roslavlev* and Zotov's *Leonid*), and even *Adventures of the English Lord George*, a lowbrow novel from the late eighteenth century, which was not among the sources of *War and Peace* and was included for comic effect.

perhaps too generous with his estimate. While I would refrain from quantitative assessments, one thing is clear. The preparation that went into *War and Peace* is extraordinary by any standard. It is true that in his selection of historical material Tolstoy was omnivorous and, as a result, his sources were quite eclectic, something that was gleefully emphasized by a contemporary cartoonist. One might argue, however, that this eclecticism was natural and inevitable, given the immense scope of *War and Peace*. Overall, in all of Russian literature there is perhaps only one work that involves a greater amount of historical material. I refer to Alexander Solzhenitsyn's colossal *Red Wheel*, which took decades to create but whose impact on Russian, let alone world, culture has been extremely limited.

Transformation of Historical Sources in *War and Peace*

Tolstoy's approach to using the historical material has also been studied by generations of scholars. There are many detailed textological comparisons of the novel and its sources that usually entail two types of questions. What is Tolstoy's attitude to a given source, and does he more or less accept or argue against it? How does he handle the material in technical terms? Here one can discern the following scenarios.

1. Frequent open quotations from historical documents. Needless to say, each quotation interacts with the broader novelistic context, but in some instances this does not subvert documents as such, while in others it exposes their absurdity and constitutes a polemical device. The most conspicuous example of this kind involves the beginning of the Austerlitz dispositions by General Weyrother quoted in the German original. This failed battle plan with its proverbial prescriptions—"Die erste Kolonne marschiert...Die zweite Kolonne marschiert..." (I, 3, xii, 261)—epitomizes for Tolstoy the futility of attempts to control the flow of raw life. Similar to this are the letter of Barclay de Tolly that assures the governor of Smolensk that the city is in no danger (Alpatych reads these words during the fierce French bombardment) and Napoleon's dispositions for the Battle of Borodino. In this second case, Tolstoy points out that not a single goal outlined by Napoleon was or could have been attained.

   Sometimes, in a variation, the historical source is itself fictionalized. This can amount to a satirical commentary, as in the episode of Napoleon's conversation with a "Child of the Don" documented by Thiers. In the novel, the supposedly naive Cossack turns out to be Lavrushka, the roguish orderly of Nikolai Rostov who fools the emperor of the French and his retinue.

   Other contextualizations of extensive quotations are more ambiguous. For example, the novel contains the full text of the Holy Synod's prayer for Russian victory written in Church Slavonic and read in churches at the beginning of Napoleon's invasion. The author interjects with a clearly positive remark concerning the voice of the priest—it is meek and lacks affectation— but also comments on the confused reaction of Natasha, who is preparing for communion. While she tries to follow the prayer with all her heart, Natasha cannot ask for the destruction of the invaders because Christians should forgive and love their enemies. An even more complex clash of perspectives accompanies the reading of Alexander's manifesto that takes place soon thereafter at the Rostovs'. Far from satirizing the document in question, contextual frames in the last two examples underscore the multiplicity of meanings inherent in a historical event.

2. Extensive unmarked borrowings from sources with minor stylistic alterations. They are plentiful and sometimes occur in unexpected episodes. For example, as was discovered in the mid-1990s, Pierre's Masonic dreams can be traced almost word for word to the diary of a Moscow Freemason, Petr Titov, read by Tolstoy at the Rumiantsev Library alongside other Masonic manuscripts.[9] On several occasions, even when Tolstoy uses the raw material provided by a source, he tends to downplay any lofty rhetoric in the original.

3. A significant expansion of an episode or situation found in a source. It may closely follow the original, as in the scene of hussar officers courting Maria Genrikhovna, the pretty wife of the regimental doctor, based on the corresponding passage in the memoirs of Il'ia Radozhitskii,[10] or it may reinterpret it, sometimes in a drastic fashion. For example, Mikhailovskii-Danilevskii recounts how dismounted Pavlograd hussars, under French canister shots, set fire to a bridge across the river Enns. His terse and approving account is turned by Tolstoy into an entire novella that casts the action in a very different light, exposing petty ambitions of commanding officers that lead to unnecessary casualties.

4. Literary "montage" (to quote the formalist term applied to Tolstoy by Boris Eikhenbaum) or "mosaic" (to use an earlier term by Konstantin Pokrovskii). It may be neutral—for instance, information from several sources combined without contradicting them—or it can produce a picture not found in any given source.

In short, while there is a large mass of primary material in the novel used "passively," there are also numerous instances of sources being transformed or, in Shklovsky's terminology, deformed in accordance with Tolstoy's vision of events. This raises the question of historical license in *War and Peace*. In several instances Tolstoy does indeed bend his sources. When General Balashov parts with Napoleon, for instance, Tolstoy's Napoleon, in a gesture almost insulting in its familiarity to the forty-year-old Russian general and the emissary of Emperor Alexander, pinches Balashov's ear. However, according to Bogdanovich's *History,* which served as a basis for this episode, Napoleon in actuality pinched his own general, Caulaincourt. Thus Tolstoy adopts a mannerism typical of Napoleon's behavior in his own court and transfers it to a person who does not belong to this court, emphasizing the emperor's blind self-infatuation.[11]

Another instance involves the famous episode with Alexander I and biscuits. On his visit to Moscow shortly after Napoleon's invasion, the Russian emperor, standing on the balcony of the Kremlin palace, throws a frenzied crowd of enthusiastic Muscovites pieces of a biscuit he is eating. Prince Petr Viazemskii, who knew the late emperor, found this detail highly improbable.

> This account betrays a total lack of knowledge of Alexander I's personality.
>
> He was so measured, so careful in all his actions and slightest moves; he was so apprehensive of anything that could seem ridiculous or awkward; he was so deliberate, so proper, so imposing, so cautious and scrupulous down to the smallest detail that he would have rather jumped into the water than appear before the people *munching a biscuit,* especially on such a solemn and remarkable day. Moreover, he amuses himself by throwing biscuits into the crowd from the balcony of the Kremlin Palace—as if he were some sort of backwoods squire pitching gingerbread in order to provoke a fight among village boys on holiday! This is again a caricature, which by any rate is absolutely out of place and is out of keeping with the truth.[12]

Viazemskii was right to criticize Tolstoy in this instance. The scene in the novel emerged from a conflation of two sources: Sergei Glinka's *Notes* and the *Memoirs* of a certain Riazantsev.[13] Glinka attests to the enthusiasm of huge crowds gathered in the Kremlin, while Riazantsev writes that the emperor benevolently handed out some fruits to the people. Tolstoy combines both accounts and also adds strong disparaging details absent from the sources. Perhaps most fascinating, Tolstoy, faced with Viazemskii's refutations, was certain that his description was fully grounded in primary sources and asked his consultant Bartenev to locate the relevant passage in Glinka (PSS 61:214). Thus we are dealing here with an honest mistake conditioned by certain filters through which Tolstoy perceived his sources and by a not surprising lack of academic discipline on his part. On occasion, Tolstoy ignores, even if he doesn't actually suppress, inconvenient aspects of historical record. For example, in his emphasis on the uniqueness of Russian resistance in 1812, Tolstoy "forgets" about Napoleon's hard-won victories and the setbacks he suffered in previous campaigns.

Commentaries to *War and Peace* point out a number of unquestionable factual mistakes and inexactitudes. For example, Tolstoy confuses Alexander I's name day and birthday. Combining Russian and European sources, he mixes up the Julian and Gregorian calendars. He mentions Russian army divisions in 1805, though this military unit was not introduced until 1806. (This last detail is important because poor coordination above the regimental level was largely responsible for the Russian defeat at Austerlitz.) In a similar mix-up of dates, Nikolai Rostov receives the soldier's cross of St. George in 1805, whereas this decoration was established only in 1807. Finally, there are mistakes pertaining to ranks, titles, designations of military units, descriptions of military uniforms, and other details. (One scrupulous commentator remarks that when Pierre was riding a horse at Borodino, his glasses should not have been sliding down as described in the novel because at this time a different frame was used, with strings tied at the back of the head.)[14]

Such errors are inevitable given the magnitude of *War and Peace,* which has more than five hundred characters, some two hundred of whom are historical, and in which twenty battles are described.[15] There are also, to be sure, numerous cases when Tolstoy, in his revisionist portrayal of events, openly disagrees with historians and questions primary sources. As Iurii Tynianov pointed out, "Documents lie like people," and Tolstoy on such occasions behaves like a historian who critically approaches both his material and its interpretation in historiography. A classical example here is Tolstoy's plan of the Russian positions at Borodino. But I am aware of only one place in the entire novel when Tolstoy knowingly alters indisputable facts.

The episode in question concerns Nikolai Rostov's improvised attack against the French dragoons at Ostrovno. According to the novel, Nikolai serves in the Pavlograd Hussars, an actual regiment of the Russian army that, as Tolstoy certainly knew, was not involved in the battle. Moreover, the regiment was at that time stationed hundreds of miles away, being part of the army covering Kiev. And yet Ostrovno provided an excellent opportunity for developing Nikolai Rostov's plotline. Transferring him to another unit posed unnecessary complications and would also undermine a crucial aspect of the scene: Nikolai must remain in the regiment with which he saw his first action, with old comrades who have become a second family of sorts. Therefore, Tolstoy, deliberately sacrificing factual accuracy in the interest of the novelistic narrative, redeployed the Pavlograd Hussars from the relatively insignificant Tormasov's Third (Reserve/Observation) Army to Barclay's First Army at the center of the unfolding dramatic events.[16]

But this exception only reinforces the rule. In romantic historical novels such alterations of facts and anachronism are numerous and constitute an important element of a larger system. In Tolstoy we have only one isolated instance of this nature. With all his idiosyncrasies and deformation of sources, Tolstoy follows the paradigm of literary realism based on a monistic outlook and devoid of tension between the truth of art and the truth of fact so prevalent during the romantic period. Literary fiction is no longer an antonym to nonfiction; in realism it functions instead as a supporting discipline in the writer's comprehensive analysis of the world. In *War and Peace,* Tolstoy's novelistic narrative merges with his historiographical findings and philosophical musings to form a quasi-scientific analysis of the past. In this respect, despite his somewhat confused thoughts about the difference between the writer and the historian, Tolstoy approaches the historical material as a scholar but one whose critical arsenal is enriched with artistic tools. At the same time, he obviously lacks the discipline of a professional historian. His overpowering personality and propensity for strong opinions and paradoxes also play a role. Consequently, he tackles historical sources, numerous as they are, on his own terms. In the formulation of Liia Myshkovskaia, "Tolstoy treated his sources as *one having authority*—he used them, but did not follow them."[17] Given the manner of Tolstoy's subsequent examination of the Gospels and his role as a moral guru, the allusion to the Sermon on the Mount seems quite appropriate: "For he taught them as one having authority, and not as the scribes" (Matthew 7:29).

Attacks on the Historical Veracity of *War and Peace*

Two well-known participants in events of 1812, Prince Petr Viazemskii and Avraam Norov, sharply criticized *War and Peace*. The brilliant thinker and literary critic Konstantin Leontiev explains outbursts like theirs as reactions to the stylistic inappropriateness of Tolstoy's realistic narrative, with its attention to physiological detail and its tendency to debunk, for conveying the atmosphere of the earlier and glorious time depicted in the novel.[18] For such readers the novel's tone was anachronistic. While some aspects of the critiques by eyewitnesses are justified, we can also observe a fascinating phenomenon of how Tolstoy's text seems to defend itself and—in a boomerang effect of sorts—criticism directed against *War and Peace* tends to backfire. Thus Viazemskii, who countered Tolstoy's version of Borodino with his own memoirs, inadvertently supports the main ideas of his opponent by describing the chaos of combat and providing numerous "lowering" details. The conclusion of Viazemskii's report on Borodino sounds almost like a quotation from Tolstoy.

> And that is my entire *Iliad*! Of course, following the example of others, I could have consulted dispatches and descriptions of the war in order to present a more detailed account of the positions of various units and troop movements on the Borodino field. But I never liked being a charlatan. [...] During the battle I was as if in a dark or, rather, a burning forest. Owing to my shortsightedness I saw poorly what was before my eyes. Owing to my lack of any military abilities or mere experience, I could not understand anything of what was going on. [...] And I might well be inquiring during the battle: "Are we beating them or are they beating us?"[19]

And overall, Viazemskii, himself essentially a civilian who toured the battlefield out of curiosity, is uncannily similar to Tolstoy's Pierre.

Norov, who had lost a leg at Borodino as a young second lieutenant, likewise disliked irreverent details. Tolstoy's Kutuzov reading a sentimental novel by Madame de Genlis especially irritated him: "Before and after Borodino, all of us, from Kutuzov down to the last artillery lieutenant, like myself, burned with the same lofty and sacred fire of patriotism; we regarded our calling as some kind of religious rite; I do not know how comrades-in-arms would have treated someone who had among his belongings a book for light reading, especially a French one, such as a novel by Madame de Genlis."[20] However, shortly after Norov's death in 1869, the novel *Aventures de Roderick Random* (a French translation of Smollett) was found in his library. Norov's own inscription on the book's cover attested that he had read it in Moscow, after being wounded and captured by the French, in September of 1812.

Victor Shklovsky's *Material and Style,* the quintessential scholarly monograph representing the skeptical approach to historical aspects of *War and Peace,* also leaves a very mixed impression in this regard. Its resounding paradigmatic title clearly echoes the tradition of grand Russian binaries—*Fathers and Sons, Crime and Punishment, War and Peace*—and evokes a fascinating theoretical issue. It introduces several useful terms and contains a thorough comparison between Tolstoy's novel and its sources accompanied by some insightful and witty remarks. And finally, the "dissident" thrust of *Material and Style* serves as a much-needed antidote to the syrupy "jubilee" rhetoric that weighs down much subsequent Tolstoy scholarship in the Soviet Union. At the same time, Shklovsky's book combines elements of formal analysis with rather clumsy nods to the sociological approach. (An earlier version that appeared in *LEF* is actually subtitled *A Formal Sociological Study.*) In Shklovsky's reading, Tolstoy emerges as a representative of a retrograde social class driven by revanchist impulses both in domestic policy (irritation against the Great Reforms of Alexander II) and foreign affairs, his fantasies about the war of 1812 being a compensation for Russia's loss in the recent Crimean War, of which he was a veteran. Shklovsky's book also suffers from the tendency to wholesale denigration of Russian history of the imperial period that was quite common in the 1920s.[21] Additionally, there is a visible stylistic contradiction between Shklovsky's sweeping generalizations, categorical statements, and fragmentary and paradoxical narrative and the close reading of the material that three very able assistants—Lidiia Ginzburg, Vladimir Trenin, and Mikhail Nikitin—helped provide.

Shklovsky makes various dubious assertions about the novel. He claims, for instance, that Tolstoy represents Alexander I as an ideal monarch. He says that Tolstoy fails to mention the mismanagement in the Russian military. According to him, Tolstoy downplays the plight of the retreating French army and in so doing follows the official Russian point of view that it was not the winter that defeated Napoleon. Furthermore, Tolstoy allegedly misunderstands and misrepresents the "people's war." He fails to show its cruelty (to back up this claim, Shklovsky quotes a source describing how a crowd of disheveled Russian peasants murdered two tall and handsome French cuirassiers). But even more important, according to Shklovsky, the peasant resistance movement in 1812 was in fact as much antigovernment as it was anti-French, and Tolstoy fails to show this; he therefore ignores its revolutionary potential. He also allegedly ignores the fact that the French guerrilla movement against the invading Russians in 1814 was at least as strong as the Russian guerrilla movement in 1812 and failed only because France did not have the advantage of the Russian space. In this case Shklovsky cites just one absolutely inconclusive passage from the *Notes* of Il'ia Radozhitskii, adding that many more examples could be provided.

Finally, Shklovsky claims that Tolstoy exaggerates the popular support for the Russian war effort in 1812. Among other things, he cites the uneasiness among the peasants conscripted to the militia who were used only as auxiliaries and did not express any enthusiasm for combat. According to Shklovsky, Tolstoy goes against historical evidence when he depicts the alleged patriotism of the militiamen who declare on the eve of Borodino that they want to throw their weight into battle together with the whole people.[22] Here he blatantly misquotes the novel, in which these words are uttered not by militiamen but by a wounded soldier who is amazed that even peasants are rounded up for the upcoming battle: "They even drive peasants to it. [...] They want the whole people to throw their weight into it" (III, 2, xx, 759). While Shklovsky characterizes Tolstoy's preparation for *War and Peace* as sketchy, his own preparation for *Material and Style* seems to have been so meager that he did not even reread the novel carefully. Furthermore, the claim that style overcomes material in *War and Peace* most definitely applies to Shklovsky's own book, where the "style"—that is, the revisionist intent—overcomes and distorts the material, including both the novel itself and its sources.

Since the term "revisionist" has been mentioned several times, a clarification is due. This term in itself by no means represents some kind of negative tag. Tolstoy's own *War and Peace* was a sharply revisionist work, as it assailed the traditional notion of 1812 inspired by the doctrine of official nationality with its three pillars of Orthodoxy, autocracy, and nationality. But Tolstoy, always a nonconformist, remained highly idiosyncratic even in his revisionism. Refuting the official mythology, he also snubbed the prevalent political correctness of the radical and liberal camps in his own time. As a result, he was attacked from all sides. The left could not forgive his unrepentant aristocratism, while the right mistook him for one of the fashionable nihilists. The latter verdict, especially coming from Prince Viazemskii—one of the men of

1812, a fellow aristocrat, and a fellow nonconformist—must have been quite painful for Tolstoy.

Usually, however, revisionist strategies are more predictable than Tolstoy's and debunk an established cultural authority. In the case of *War and Peace,* the target is potentially twofold: Tolstoy as a great writer and the war of 1812 as a defining event of modern Russian history. Although in the 1860s, during the publication of *War and Peace,* Tolstoy's greatness could be questioned, by the twentieth century his status in Russia as one of the geniuses of world literature had become virtually unshakable. (The Futurist appeals to jettison Tolstoy, alongside Pushkin and Dostoevsky, from the steamship of modernity only reinforce his extraordinary standing.) However, the angle taken by later revisionist attacks was even more titillating and sensationalist: "Tolstoy was a great artist indeed, but he completely misrepresented the war of 1812."

Prominent in Shklovsky, this matrix has curiously reproduced itself in more recent revisionist takes on *War and Peace.* Here, for example, is the verdict of the academician Iurii Pivovarov, the director of the once highly respected INION (Institute of Scientific Information in Social Sciences) and a public figure known for his strong and controversial opinions: "Tolstoy's *War and Peace* is a cornerstone myth of Russian culture. However, Tolstoy invented everything about the war of 1812. [. . .] The world he created is more real for the Russian consciousness than the actual world of the early nineteenth century. The real Kutuzov has nothing to do with us, while the fictional one is an incarnation of the deep Russian spirit. But in reality Kutuzov was a sluggard, an intriguer, an erotomaniac who adored young French actresses and read French pornographic novels."[23] Shocking as they may sound, these "revelations" do little to debunk Tolstoy. The reader of *War and Peace* knows that Kutuzov falls asleep during war councils, that he is quite partial to the fair sex, and that he is also fond of French pulp fiction.

What is perhaps most astonishing in the revisionist assessments of *War and Peace* is the ease of claiming true knowledge about the epoch in question. Thus, leaving aside the issue of mythologizing 1812, let us look at some factual arguments that can be verified against historical sources. The most recent scholarly study of the revisionist kind, Ekaterina Tsimbaeva's article entitled "Historical Context in a Literary Work: Gentry Society in *War and Peace,*" radically attacks the novel's historical veracity. According to her, even the opening scene of the novel, the soiree hosted by Anna Pavlovna Scherer, is absolutely improbable from the historical point of view. This is a very serious if not shocking claim, one that deserves a careful analysis.

First, according to Tsimbaeva, Anna Pavlovna, as one of the empress's maids of honor, simply could not have hosted a salon because maids of honor were expected to accompany their patrons at all times, and, as unmarried women, they could not invite men, especially in the evening. This is not quite true. Here one can cite the example of the famous Aleksandra Rosset, whose Wednesday soirees took place right in the Winter Palace. Additionally, Anna Pavlovna, at forty years old, is by no means a young girl who could compromise herself, and her soiree is not a regularly held salon, but rather an ad hoc event. (Otherwise, the invitations mentioned by Tolstoy would not be necessary.) In the drafts of the novel Anna Pavlovna remarks that she is old enough to invite men and also emphasizes that she wants to take advantage of a free evening away from her duties at court.[24] Tolstoy obviously considered all these details unnecessary for the final text.

Tsimbaeva goes on to state that some guests present or mentioned at the soiree, specifically the younger Kuragins, have improbable names.

> Prince Hyppolyte's name is blatantly unprincely. A comprehensive review of the genealogies of the Russian princely families reveals that none of their scions born between the early eighteenth and the late nineteenth centuries were called Hyppolyte. In fact, it is not only not a princely name, it is not even a noble one. [...] The name Hélène—Elena—is odd in a different way. It had fallen out of use among early nineteenth-century Russians (except in the vernacular variant Alena) and had been adopted by Russified Germans. [...] Finally, the name Anatole [...] was a rarity in all strata of Russian society.[25]

All of this is simply false. Anatole/Anatolii was not a particularly rare name among Russian aristocrats. Thus Prince Anatole Kuragin has two potential prototypes among Tolstoy's contemporaries: Prince Anatolii Bariatinskii and Anatolii Shostak, a suitor of Tatiana Bers. There were numerous Elenas among Russian princely families, including Tolstoy's distant cousin Princess Elena Gorchakova (the Gorchakovs served as a prototype for the Kornakovs in Tolstoy's autobiographical trilogy). One also encounters an entire dynasty of Elenas: the famous mystic Helena Blavatsky, who was the daughter of the writer Elena Gan, who was the daughter of Princess Elena Dolgorukaia, a contemporary of Tolstoy's Princess Elena/Hélène Kuragina. It is also easy to find a number of Hyppolytes/Ippolits among the Russian aristocrats of the epoch, both titled and nontitled. Therefore, the name is quite realistic. At the same time it has a relevant literary echo. The *Vestnik Evropy* magazine for 1804—from which Tolstoy borrowed details pertaining to the latest Parisian fashions in order to dress some of his characters, including Prince Hyppolyte—contains the tale "Hyppolyte and Laura" by the aforementioned Madame de Genlis.

And one more claim from Tsimbaeva's article. Supposedly, both the soiree at Anna Pavlovna and the fete at the English ambassador's, for which Prince Vasily leaves accompanied by his daughter Hélène, could not have taken place in reality because of their timing. In the novel they occur in July, whereas the social season at that time ended in June, after which the capital became virtually deserted and the court was transferred to a suburban residence. This was indeed the standard practice, but one should not forget that the time of action is the summer of 1805, when active military operations against Napoleon are about to begin. The drafts of the novel say explicitly that although the court of the dowager empress moved to Pavlovsk, Alexander and his ministers were extremely busy in the capital and all of St. Petersburg's elite, despite the summer season, stayed in the city (PSS 13:183). This is confirmed, for example, by the official Russian newspaper *Sankt-Peterburgskie Vedomosti,* according to which the emperor was definitely present in St. Petersburg on June 29, July 4, July 7, July 13, July 18, July 24, July 27, and July 31.[26] Thus it is not the opening of Tolstoy's novel but rather Tsimbaeva's article that is improbable and even fantastic in its sweeping and unsubstantiated revisionist claims. But investigating such claims in a way represents a useful exercise because it demonstrates, time and time again, that despite all of Tolstoy's idiosyncrasies and possible mistakes, *War and Peace* is indeed a great historical epic that rests on a very solid factual foundation.

3

Moscow in 1812

Myths and Realities

———

ALEXANDER M. MARTIN

When he first read *War and Peace,* Prince Petr Viazemskii, doyen of Russian literary critics, was outraged. Having himself lived in Moscow in 1812 and participated in the war, he was appalled at the version of history he encountered in Tolstoy's novel. In a harsh rebuttal, he accused Tolstoy of contributing to the "moral [and] literary materialism," the "historical free thinking and unbelief," that led current literati to deny historical truths and insult the nation's most cherished memories.[1] In the bitter Russian culture wars of the 1860s, he implied, Tolstoy stood with the nihilists.

Viazemskii was right to call Tolstoy a revisionist for his skeptical treatment of generals and statesmen, but where their image of Moscow was concerned, he and Tolstoy thought alike. Both men belonged to the aristocracy (that is, the wealthy, politically influential elite that formed the upper crust of the nobility), and *War and Peace* conveys their shared belief that Moscow was a city of aristocrats where the other social strata were mere bit players in the drama of history.[2] Far from constituting "literary materialism" or "historical free thinking," this interpretation required Tolstoy as well as Viazemskii to set aside social reality, the emerging consensus among writers and social commentators, and most Muscovites' actual memories of the events of 1812.

When Tolstoy wrote *War and Peace* in the 1860s, describing Moscow as a city defined by aristocrats increasingly ran counter to the mainstream of Russian thought. It had been clear to educated Russians since at least the 1820s that western Europe, especially Great Britain and France, had entered a new era in which the middle and working classes of the major cities played a decisive historical role. Many Russians at that time were shocked by the political turmoil and socioeconomic iniquity of the emerging Western order and preferred to imagine their own cities as places of social peace and harmony. However, Russian literature from the 1830s onward—the works of Gogol, Ostrovsky, Nekrasov, Dostoevsky, and others—suggested that life for most people in Russia's metropolitan centers was not really all that different from Dickens's London or Balzac's Paris, and the Crimean War shattered the illusion that Russia could remain a great power while standing aloof from the forces transforming the societies of Europe. In the 1860s–1870s, the abolition of serfdom, the other Great Reforms, and the onset of large-scale migration from the country to the cities finally sealed the doom of Russia's old order, and urban Russia began its rapid descent into the abyss of pauperism, class conflict, and political violence from which the West was just then beginning to emerge.

This crisis of urban society helped form the context for the upsurge of interest in what had happened in Moscow in 1812. Memoirs about the war, especially those by members of the middle classes, were informed by the same sensibility as were the critical depictions of urban life in the present: they highlighted class conflicts, criticized the aristocracy, placed the middle classes at the center of events, and represented an active, interventionist state as essential to the well-being of the city. Tolstoy's depiction of Moscow should be seen as a rebuttal to these views. He roundly rejected middle-class criticisms of the aristocracy. The middle classes saw their own prosperity and security as dependent on the continued exercise of state power and at risk when war unleashed the elemental passions of the populace. Tolstoy, on the contrary, doubted that government could mold society through rational, purposeful organization, and he admired the nation at war as an unstoppable force of nature. As this chapter shows, Tolstoy's position in the polemics of the 1860s caused his representation of Moscow in *War and Peace* to differ profoundly from the consensus of the eyewitness accounts.

The Middle Estate and the New People

The Moscow of *War and Peace* is a city few of its inhabitants would have recognized. In the novel, there are hardly any merchants, artisans, markets, shops, taverns, slums—indeed, little of what made Moscow one of Europe's major cities. Understanding why Tolstoy chose to portray Moscow as he did requires a brief excursion into the history of Russian thinking about cities.[3]

In the eighteenth century, the tsarist regime's social engineering had a utopian and urban focus, embodied most clearly by the founding of St. Petersburg. Catherine II believed that Europeanizing the towns was essential to bringing enlightenment to Russia as a whole. She ordered the reconstruction of existing towns, including Moscow, and the founding of new ones, and while her reforms left the rural masses largely untouched, she endowed the towns with a new infrastructure of cultural, political, and welfare institutions. At first she shared the Enlightenment dream that a radically reformed school system could give rise to "a new race of people"—her term was *novaia poroda liudei,* a Russian rendering of the *philosophes'* phrase *nouvelle race d'hommes*—to spearhead society's march into the future; later, more realistically, she tried to transform Russia's existing middle social strata into a "middle estate" akin to the burghers of western Europe. Since she considered Moscow—the city that controlled the commerce and administration of the entire Russian interior— particularly filthy, archaic, and prone to social instability, she was anxious to make Moscow "European" through urban renewal and social engineering.

Catherine's ideas and initiatives were carried on by her successors, with no fundamental changes, until the middle of the nineteenth century. The central neighborhoods of Moscow were gradually reconstructed, with paved thoroughfares, street lighting, and neoclassical architecture. The estates (*sosloviia*) of clerics and merchants as well as minor nobles (most of whom were landless petty officials) were given a privileged middle status in society through the grant of important legal rights such as access to specially established schools and exemption from the head tax, flogging, conscription, and of course enserfment. Moscow acquired an increasingly European character in its built environment, its infrastructure of public services and institutions, and the division of its inhabitants into upper, middle, and lower classes.

The notion that Moscow was, or should become, "European" grew increasingly controversial in the nineteenth century. Appalled at the squalor and turbulence of early industrial London and postrevolutionary Paris, some Russians in the 1820s–1840s began praising Moscow for being the opposite of the urban West. Redefining backwardness as a virtue, starting at the end of the 1820s Mikhail Zagoskin and other writers created a gauzy stereotype of Moscow as a serene, harmonious place where life revolved around the aristocracy and everything radiated Russian goodness and Orthodox spirituality.[4] No! came the angry response from social commentators, the feuilletonists of the Natural School, the playwright Ostrovsky, realist painters, and public health researchers. Most Muscovites were poor, they argued, and struggled to survive under the boot of the upper class; Moscow was no Russian idyll but a modern European metropolis, a city that never slept, where people felt lonely in the crowd.[5]

Catherine's "middle estate" and "new race of people" also acquired new connotations. By the mid-nineteenth century, when Tolstoy was writing his novel, a stratum of literate, prosperous nonnobles had in fact come into being, but this did not enhance society's cohesiveness as Catherine had hoped. Minor nobles, clerics, and merchants retained distinct subcultures and heartily disliked each other, but they were united in resenting the privileged elites and demanding a stronger role for themselves. Middle-class professionals, such as lawyers or physicians, claimed that only they had the expert knowledge to guide the country's modernization. The clergy, and particularly their sons who entered secular professions, asserted that their education, spirituality, and rootedness in the folk entitled them alone to lead the nation; similar sentiments existed among Moscow merchants and financiers, many of them Old Believers of strongly nationalist persuasion.[6]

What all could agree on was hostility to aristocrats, who at the time owned most of Russia's wealth and dominated the government. Aristocrats were disliked for their haughtiness, pampered lifestyle, infatuation with Europe, and parasitic exploitation of the people. As in Catherine's time, many Russians looked to "new people" to lead the country into a better future, but the way the term came to be used in the 1860s–1870s (most famously in Nikolai Chernyshevsky's novel *What Is To Be Done? Stories about the New People*), the new people were now assumed to be radical critics of the autocracy and enemies of aristocratic privilege.

Competing Conceptions of History and the City

In these midcentury culture wars, Tolstoy was a staunch defender of the aristocracy and made no bones about his contempt for the middle strata that challenged its preeminence. Yet "the people" as a whole, especially the rural people, filled him with awe, whereas he had no patience for aristocrats who took personal credit for shaping the course of history. This ambivalence toward both the aristocrats and "the people" structures his depiction of Moscow in 1812.[7]

His main characters—the Bezukhovs, Rostovs, Bolkonskys, Kuragins, and so forth—are aristocrats, with hereditary titles (count, prince) and sometimes French names (Pierre, Hélène). Authors like Tolstoy, Viazemskii, and Zagoskin liked to portray Moscow at the time of Napoleon's invasion as an aristocratic city, but in reality, the experience of the aristocracy tells us precious little about the city as a whole. Aristocrats were a minuscule minority, and the vast revenues generated by their serf estates allowed them a lifestyle that was inconceivable to anyone else, including the many poorer nobles whose only income was their government service salary. In 1811, according to police statistics, 6 percent of Moscow's 275,000 inhabitants were nobles,[8] but most of these were landless civil servants; only a small fraction were aristocrats. Just how small is illustrated by an evidently representative sample of

281 noble families that reported how much movable property they had lost in the 1812 Moscow fire, which in most cases consumed their entire households.[9] The median value of their losses was 2,500 rubles. In *War and Peace,* Pierre Bezukhov has an annual income of a half-million rubles (II, 2, x, 378); only one of the 281 families owned possessions worth that much. Nikolai Rostov loses 43,000 rubles in a single card game (II, 1, xiv, 339); only 13 of the 281 families reported losses exceeding that amount, which was also more than the combined annual salaries of fourteen provincial governors or forty-one infantry colonels.[10]

Aristocrats were often *in* Moscow, but they were not really *of* it. Their summers they spent in the country, and when they came to Moscow for the winter season, they replicated the autarkic lifestyle of their country estates and interacted little with urban society. They brought their serf domestics, artisans, and even food from the country. Many worshipped in private chapels. Rather than patronize hotels and restaurants, they lived and dined with other aristocrats. They did not participate in municipal government, and they relied on private tutors or boarding schools rather than entrust their children to public education.

Tolstoy describes nonaristocratic Muscovites as well, of course, but he focuses on lower-class people, most of whom his audience would have recognized as having roots in the countryside. The most developed character of lower-class background whom we meet in Moscow, Platon Karataev, is a soldier of peasant origin; others are factory workers, domestics, and artisans, which were common occupations of rural migrants. In 1811, according to police data, 61 percent of Moscow inhabitants were house serfs, peasant serfs, or state peasants—groups mostly at home in rural villages or noble country manors. Though they formed much of Moscow's laboring population, they typically came to the city only temporarily and without their families, often living and working in teams (*arteli*) from their home region. Most never assimilated into urban society.

Peasants, to upper-class Russians, were not individualized social actors like aristocrats. Instead, they were interchangeable members of an undifferentiated *narod* (people) that embodied Russia's timeless essence. Drawing "his" commoners from this milieu bolstered Tolstoy's thesis that history is driven by the unconscious dynamics of large collectives, that is, by self-organizing systems that generate forces against which the individual is powerless. His favorite metaphors for this were entomological. The ghastly slaughter of 1812 did not result from the will of Napoleon or Alexander I, he argues, or any other causation susceptible to rational analysis: rather, "people were carrying out the same elemental zoological law that bees carry out when they kill each other in the fall" (PSS 16:14). Most of the population of Moscow had left before the French arrived, Tolstoy writes, so the city resembled "a dying-out, queenless beehive" (III, 3, xx, 874). Once the French withdrew from Moscow, Russians acted like "ants" scurrying around "a demolished anthill": they poured into the ruined city, each for his or her own purposes but collectively proving the ant colony's tenacious will to live (IV, 4, xiv, 1108).[11]

An authentically urban society, with its diversity of social types and experiences, its social mobility, self-fashioning, and cultural hybridity, had little place in this scheme. The people who gave Moscow its truly urban character were the middle strata—the 30 to 40 percent of Muscovites who were petty nobles, civil servants, clergy, merchants, professionals, foreigners, shopkeepers, members of the artisan guilds, and the like. Unlike the aristocrats and peasants, they were year-round city residents and fully integrated into urban society. They differed from aristocrats in not having influence at court and generally owning no serfs, and hence exercising little direct power in the state or over other human beings. Also unlike the aristocracy, they worked for a living and lacked the wealth for an ostentatious lifestyle. They differed from the lower classes because they enjoyed a modest degree of material comfort and because the law shielded them from the worst burdens—floggings, conscription, enserfment, the head tax—that the regime imposed on the common people. Last, compared with those either above or below them, members of the middle strata were far more likely either to gain or to lose wealth and status as a result of their own individual work, education, or luck.

By the 1850s–1860s, the middle classes had given rise to an intelligentsia that was hostile to aristocrats, demanded a sweeping overhaul of society, and claimed the exclusive right to speak for the Russian nation. Tolstoy hated the intelligentsia and the middle strata from which they mostly arose. Literary scholars have argued that in *War and Peace* his depiction of Napoleon and Speransky as calculating, selfish social climbers lacking in human warmth or any true understanding of life was a dig at the middle-class upstarts who formed the intelligentsia.[12] In an early draft of *War and Peace,* he justified his novel's focus on aristocrats by insulting the rest of urban society—especially merchants and clergy, whom he pointedly lumps together with the lower classes—in terms that verge on the self-caricature of an aristocratic snob. Why had he not curried favor with a mass readership by writing about people other than "princes, counts, ministers, [and] senators"? Because the lives of other classes—"merchants, coachmen, seminarians, convicts, and peasants"—were "tedious" and "ugly" and animated only by "envy" and "greed." They were as alien to him as animals.

> I could never understand what a watchman thinks when he stands by his guardhouse, what a shopkeeper thinks and feels when he hawks suspenders and

neckties, what a seminarian thinks when he is led to be caned for the hundredth time, and so on. I don't understand these things just as I don't understand what a cow thinks when it is being milked and what a horse thinks when it hauls a barrel. (PSS 13:238–39)

As for himself, he was "proud that I am an aristocrat." As such, "I was raised from childhood [. . .] to love beauty, represented not only by Homer, Bach, and Raphael, but also by a love for clean hands, handsome clothes, and fine dining and transport" (PSS 13:239). As an aristocrat he could not imagine, he wrote, finding moral or intellectual qualities in people who picked their noses.

Reflecting this bias, Tolstoy seems to have done little research on the war experience of the middle strata, even though he read widely about the war. Not one of their eyewitness accounts appears in the list of books he consulted (PSS 16:141-145). In an early draft of the novel, he asserts that "memorials of the history of the time of which I write survive only in the correspondence and memoirs of literate people of the highest class [*krug*]," and that "even when I heard interesting and thoughtful oral tales, I heard them only from people of that class" (PSS 13:238-239). At least where the occupation of Moscow was concerned, this seems unlikely. Aristocrats (and peasants) fled the city before the French arrived, so most of the estimated 6,238 people who remained belonged to the middle strata.[13] Accordingly, it was members of these strata, especially clergymen and minor officials, who wrote most of the several dozen published first-person accounts of the occupation. Some of these accounts were already in print when Tolstoy was writing *War and Peace,* and it is possible that he could have learned about others through his contacts with collectors of unpublished manuscripts such as Petr Bartenev, the editor of the popular historical journal *Russian Archive* (*Russkii Arkhiv*). As for commoners having no interesting stories to tell, that was not the experience of the writer Ekaterina Novosil'tseva (also known by her pseudonym T. Tolycheva), who systematically sought out commoners to interview and published dozens of fascinating survivor narratives; the first of these appeared in print in 1865, when Tolstoy was still working on *War and Peace.*[14]

As Donna Tussing Orwin argues in chapter 7, *War and Peace* antagonized military readers by denying the agency of individuals and the power of disciplined, goal-oriented collective action. In a similar vein, although Viazemskii seems to have been alone in addressing Tolstoy explicitly, middling Muscovites who wrote war memoirs in general implicitly dispute his theories when they depict themselves as purposeful actors who were capable of pursuing their own interests if—but only if—they operated within a rational, orderly urban society. Social chaos held a special existential menace for the middle strata. Peasants and aristocrats could seek shelter in their rural homes: as long as the former had their fields and the latter their serfs, their social status and economic viability were secure, and from the safety of the country they could comfortably discuss whether the anarchy in Moscow served some higher purpose. The middle strata did not have that luxury; when the city broke down, they were mortally threatened.

To understand what 1812 represented for them, it helps to have a sense of how Moscow had evolved. The Moscow of the mid-eighteenth century had not been hospitable to an upwardly mobile middle class. Moving up in society required accumulating wealth and adopting elements of elite culture. Since Moscow was largely a wooden city, it periodically suffered catastrophic fires. Wealthy aristocrats could rebuild quickly, thanks to revenue and serf labor from their estates, but because years of savings were required to outfit a business or a young woman's bridal trousseau, the modest assets of the middle strata were much harder to replace. To participate in elite culture, meanwhile, the middle strata had to be able to go out after their workday and find genteel entertainments that were open to paying customers. This was difficult because the streets were unpaved, unlit, filthy, and barricaded at night by watchmen suspicious of anyone who was out after hours. Moreover, because the aristocracy—the principal source of cultural patronage—disdained entertainments other than those provided privately by aristocrats, the commercial market for theaters, restaurants, and so on was weak. Cultural opportunities were thus limited, and Western visitors found that unless one secured invitations to the homes of the aristocracy, there was little to do in Moscow.[15]

All of this slowly began to change under Catherine the Great. Fire safety and sanitation were improved. The streets were increasingly paved and lit. The police tried to make it safe and convenient to go out at night. Theaters and coffeehouses appeared, albeit in modest numbers. For the middle strata, these improvements opened up unprecedented opportunities to pursue social mobility through an engagement with the Europeanized urban culture that the regime was promoting. This mobility is what was at stake when the social order in Moscow collapsed in 1812.

Tolstoy wrote *War and Peace,* and most eyewitnesses told their stories, near the close of a long period of European revolutions in which the liberal urban middle classes faced enemies on two fronts. In France after 1789, they were squeezed between the sansculottes of Paris and an alliance of émigré royalists and pro-Catholic peasants. Determined not to repeat that nightmare, their heirs in France in 1848 both overthrew the king and crushed the revolt of the Parisian workers, and in 1870–71 they prevented the return of the monarchy and drowned the Paris Commune in blood. Their counterparts in the German states, faced with similar threats in 1848–49, went down in defeat because they were unable to stare down both the princes and the populace. The shared theme in each case was that the liberal middle classes felt they faced two enemies. Inside the city, the threat seemed to emanate from radical ideologues and the class rage of the slums; outside the city, it came from selfish aristocrats and sometimes peasants too retrograde to appreciate modern civilization. A similar thread runs through accounts by Moscow eyewitnesses of 1812, although whether the west European template influenced their thinking is difficult to say because the authors rarely provide insight into their own intellectual development.

Radicals and the Urban Mob

The revolutionary threat from within the city took the form of an attack on authority and a revolt of the masses. Muscovites felt that they witnessed and endured both. More than Tolstoy, they focused on the way Napoleon's men systematically violated symbols of religious and secular authority. They desecrated churches by using them as barracks, stables, and slaughterhouses.[16] Romanov dynastic authority was assaulted when the French tried to blow up the Kremlin. Moscow's brand-new boulevard, intended as a promenade for the upper classes, was used as an execution site,[17] and the French vandalized government and aristocratic property by smashing furniture and destroying documents.

This purposeful assault on authority was accompanied by an anarchic revolt of the despairing populace. The looting by uncouth, unwashed Napoleonic soldiers can be seen in these terms, but so can the behavior of lower-class Muscovites. Tolstoy touches only in passing on the collapse of order among the urban masses, yet this was such a cliché in nineteenth-century Europe that the same images recur in fiction and memoirs from different countries. One example is the frantic drunkenness that accompanied civil disorder. The most influential nineteenth-century novel about revolution was *A Tale of Two Cities* (1859) by Charles Dickens, whom Tolstoy much admired. Early in the novel, Dickens shows that lower-class Parisians are on the verge of a bloody revolt by describing how, when a barrel of wine shatters on the street, the hungry and destitute gather at once to lick up the blood-red liquid from the pavement.[18] In 1872, an elderly former serf told virtually the same story about Moscow: as Napoleon's army approached, "orders were given [by the Russian police] to smash the liquor barrels in the taverns. The common people then fell on them and got utterly drunk. The liquor was flowing in the streets, and some people lay down on the pavement and licked the stones."[19] Though no doubt unaware of each other's existence, Dickens and the Russian serf drew on a shared oral and literary tradition that shaped how Europeans remembered the revolutionary turmoil of earlier decades.

Another sign of the collapse of order was the remorseless popular violence against anyone who looked foreign, which of course included many Russians. Unlike the aristocracy with their servants, the middle strata depended on the authorities for protection. In 1812 their sense of security collapsed. A young nobleman recalled that "at that time, there was more to fear from Russian peasants than from the French." One time he saw "a crowd of peasants coming my way, and as they are walking, each has an iron over his shoulder. [...] One says to the other, 'Hey, look, isn't that a Frenchman?' I come up to a church and start to pray, so the other answers him: 'No, he's from here, one of ours,' and so the prayer saved me." Another time, "a sick Frenchman is walking along, a couple of peasants come toward him, and he goes up to them and says: 'Gentlemen, where is the hospital?' One of the peasants glances at him, mutters, 'How long do we have to put up with this!', hits him over the head with an iron bar, and that was the end of it."[20]

An aristocrat's rank was clear to anyone who saw his horses, carriages, and servants, but the middle strata depended on their clothing to signal their position. In 1812 the rules correlating appearance with status collapsed. Napoleon's soldiers, their own gear in tatters, donned whatever they could find, which shocked Russians accustomed to ancien régime sumptuary rules. Some dressed in priestly vestments or women's clothing, both out of necessity and simply for fun.[21] Russians, too, joined in the reversal of roles: a French officer noted the incongruous sight of prostitutes wearing stolen aristocratic finery as they consorted with soldiers, a spectacle that reduced elderly Russians to tears.[22]

French eyewitnesses—whose memoirs filtered into Russia and were read, for example, by Tolstoy—sometimes employed the language used in France to describe revolutionaries. Like the Russian authors of eyewitness accounts, they equated cities with civilization and were shocked at Moscow's disintegration. They recalled, with bitter hatred, the released convicts who allegedly helped set Moscow ablaze and thereby sealed the French army's destruction. In early modern Europe, the ruling elites had usually assumed that the lower classes were by nature turbulent but could be controlled through the exemplary punishment of isolated ringleaders. This is, for example, how Catherine II had responded to the Moscow plague riot of 1771: by denouncing the people's foolishness and executing a few egregious offenders.[23] Count Rostopchin was operating on the same principle when he arranged the public lynching of the alleged traitor Vereshchagin. Contrast this with the account by General de Ségur, whose memoirs, first published in the 1820s, were read by Tolstoy and many others in Russia (PSS 16:135). Ségur writes

Vasilii Petrovich Vereshchagin, *Execution of Arsonists in the Kremlin* (1897–98). *Otechestvennaia voina i russkoe obshchestvo, 1812–1912: Iubileinoe izdanie,* ed. A. K. Dzhivelegov, S. P. Mel'gunov, and V. I. Picheta (Moscow: Izd. T-va I. D. Sytina, 1912), vol. 4, between pp. 168 and 169.

about the Moscow arsonists in terms characteristic of nineteenth-century antirevolutionary rhetoric—as a dehumanized rabble, out to destroy civilization itself, that needed to be exterminated en masse. The incendiaries "were wild-looking women and men in rags with hideous faces wandering about in the flames, completing an awful image of hell. These wretched creatures, drunk with wine and the success of their crimes, no longer attempted to conceal themselves, but raced in triumph through the blazing streets."[24] When caught, such people were summarily executed. [25]

The collapse of the social order is also indicated by the many references to the disgusting sanitary state of the city. Moscow's public spaces had become gradually cleaner before 1812. This achievement was especially important for the middle strata, for clean clothes, faces, and hands were essential for a respectable appearance, which in turn was a prerequisite for access to genteel public spaces. (As we saw earlier, Tolstoy himself thought that being an aristocrat entailed "a love for clean hands.") Since the middle strata, unlike the aristocracy, had no carriages or capacious mansions to create a protective buffer between themselves and the filth of the city, they depended on the public thoroughfares to be in clean condition.

A separate but related issue was the symbolic dimension of nasty odors. The cultural historian Alain Corbin argues that in nineteenth-century France, the urban middle classes became anxious about putrid smells—urine, feces, decaying flesh—because they were reminders of the threat of social anarchy posed by the unwashed masses.[26] Not until the mid-nineteenth century did large European cities even begin to create effective sewage-disposal systems, so the stench of human waste was always pervasive, but a society's degree of sensitivity to the stench varied according to the middle classes' level of social anxiety. As I have argued elsewhere, Corbin's thesis applies to Moscow, too, since the city's sorry sanitary condition started to be perceived as a public concern only in the middle of the nineteenth century, when many began to perceive a deep crisis in Russia's urban social order.[27]

In *War and Peace,* Tolstoy is sensitive to smells. Nevertheless, while he evokes the horror of war through the stench of field hospitals (II, 2, xvii, 403), he ignores the fact that those same odors—of blood, excrement, and rotting flesh—also pervaded occupied Moscow, for here his focus is on the spiritual dimension of the conflict, not the elemental breakdown of social relations. Because of this breakdown, however, filth and stench are prominent themes in the eyewitness accounts. To Moscow's elites, the French army's filth and boorishness were confirmation of the barbaric essence of the French Revolution and its Napoleonic spawn, but it was nonetheless shocking to see just how low France, that quintessential model of civilization, had fallen. The aristocrat Mariia Volkova, in letters that Tolstoy read for his research, wrote with disgust that even the officers of the French army were not ashamed to relieve themselves in the libraries and ballrooms of aristocratic mansions in Moscow.[28] The director of the Foundling Home, in letters published before Tolstoy wrote *War and Peace,* reported that he had to take in sick Napoleonic soldiers who "fouled everything: where they slept, [that is where] they ate and defecated"; they ruined "the floors, doors, windows, stoves, and walls," and their excrements soaked into the floors and littered the hallways.[29]

The city also reeked of death—another throwback to the past, before Catherine II had ordered cemeteries and slaughterhouses transferred outside the city. When churches were turned into slaughterhouses, they filled with the stink of blood and animal remains. Worse, after the French pulled out, the Russians collected almost twenty-five thousand dead bodies and animal carcasses that had been rotting in the streets in the unseasonably warm weather;[30] the smell was so bad that "15 versts [15.9 kilometers] from Moscow it is already hard to breathe."[31] Disposing of this mountain of putrid flesh was a huge operation that Tolstoy ignores but that made a lasting impression on Muscovites. A priest recalled that "for several weeks, the police were burning them by the banks of the river and sweeping the ashes into the water."[32] A merchant boy who saw this spectacle refused to eat meat for a month, and as late as 1898, the priest's grandson Lebedev recalled that "a horribly suffocating, stinking smoke spread throughout the whole city, and when Grandfather passed by Pskov Hill [near Red Square] and watched as this auto-da-fé was going on below, it nearly choked him. He actually fell and started to cough, and the cough never left him until his very death."[33]

In addition to smelling awful, revolutionary cities were dark. All over Europe from 1789 to at least 1848, revolutionary crowds smashed streetlights, which were symbols of police authority (somewhat like security cameras today).[34] In Moscow, the destruction of thousands of streetlights undermined authority of any sort, making it easier to ambush French soldiers but also contributing to higher crime levels after the war.[35] Revolutionary crowds in France and elsewhere also used streetlights as makeshift gallows: that, too, was a usage that Muscovites discovered in 1812, when Napoleon's soldiers used streetlights to hang suspected arsonists. In some cases, the victims had already been executed by firing squad—another spectacle new to Muscovites. Tolstoy describes such shootings in *War and Peace* but only to explore the inner spiritual state of the Russian victims and their French killers, not to identify the firing squads themselves as a typical accompaniment of urban civil strife, whether in Rome and Madrid under Napoleon or in Paris during the suppression of the Commune.[36]

The order and stability on which the urban middle strata depended thus faced a terrifying threat from within the city. Also frightening, however, were groups based in the countryside—the aristocrats and peasants.

Aristocrats, Peasants, and the City

Beginning with the French Revolution, it became common in revolutionary times to blame the upper classes for the misery of the people. Tolstoy raises these issues when he describes the deceitfulness of Governor-General Rostopchin's propaganda and the crowds' resentment of "the gentry and the merchants" for deserting the city (III, 3, xxiii, 883). In the memoirs by middle-class Muscovites, these themes play a more conspicuous role and come together to form a single antiaristocratic motif. Many blamed Rostopchin's jingoistic propaganda for causing them to tarry in the doomed city.[37] Once the mad rush to evacuate began, the aristocrats, who had horses to move their households and also country estates to go home to, drew

Klavdii Vasil'evich Lebedev, *Flight of the Inhabitants from Moscow* (1912). *Otechestvennaia voina i russkoe obshchestvo, 1812–1912: Iubileinoe izdanie,* ed. A. K. Dzhivelegov, S. P. Mel'gunov, and V. I. Picheta, (Moscow: Izd. T-va I. D. Sytina, 1912), vol. 4, between pp. 56 and 57. The artist highlights themes similar to those in *War and Peace,* with a scene set in the city center near the Kremlin and populated mainly by nobles and soldiers. The poster being read by the man on the far left is recognizable as a propaganda bill authored by Governor-General Rostopchin.

predictable resentment from poorer people whose only options were to stay behind or else leave on foot, with whatever they could carry, and hope for the best. A merchant wrote that while the rich escaped, "the poor"—meaning people like himself—"were forced to stay and breathe the same air with [the French monsters]."[38] According to a priest's son, "The people [...] said that the nobles were saving their own skins while surrendering [the people] and the metropolis itself to Napoleon."[39] A townsman (*meshchanin*) wrote that fleeing noblemen were cowards who evaded combat by dressing up as women, bandaging their sideburns to simulate a toothache.[40] A crippled nun from a merchant family was left behind in Moscow by fellow nuns of aristocratic family whom she bitterly called "our rich miladies."[41]

Feelings toward the peasants were no kinder. As in the Great Fear in France in 1789, rural villagers became suspicious of any and all outsiders, including refugees coming from Moscow. Tolstoy, as we saw, claimed that the urban middle classes' behavior was motivated by greed and envy. This is how some (though not all) Muscovites in turn interpreted the conduct of the peasants. In 1898, the Moscow priest's grandson Lebedev wrote that he had heard that "the peasants came at [grandfather's family] with bear-spears and threatened to slaughter them all for having 'frittered Moscow away' [*Moskvu propili na chaiu*]. They all had to buy their way out with money."[42] Tolstoy likened the peasants who looted Moscow after the French left to ants scurrying about a damaged anthill, their seeming purposelessness masking an unconscious will to rebuild. Lebedev, by contrast, basing his description on stories handed down over the entire nineteenth century, referred to them as locusts—a biblical plague of pure destruction.[43] Others left similar angry accounts. A priest recalled in the 1830s that "[t]hey were merciless in pillaging Moscow and proffered all sorts of insults against the inhabitants of Moscow, calling them runaways and traitors, and declared resolutely that whatever the enemy had left behind in Moscow [now] belonged to them."[44] Another priest, who was a child during the war, heard that his father had returned to find his house still standing, but then "five or so peasants came running to him. 'Where are you going?' they shouted. 'Home,' he answered, 'I am the master of this house.' 'There are no masters here,' one of them screamed."[45]

In *War and Peace,* society acts with spontaneous coordination: when the people flee from Moscow, they create the preconditions for the fire that dooms Napoleon's army, and the peasants who later come to loot thereby help revive the city. By contrast, what stands out in the memoirs is the depth of the social antagonisms, and the civilizational regression when the city folk are betrayed by aristocrats and peasants alike.

For middle-class Muscovites, the fire that engulfed the city in 1812 was a terrifying throwback to the times before Catherine. Decades later, survivors tried to convey the horror through almost magical-realist details: the heat caused water in wells and buckets to boil and flocks of pigeons to fall from the sky, and in a village 30 versts (31.8 kilometers) away, it rained singed paper.[46] A merchant's daughter was haunted for decades by the memory of her merchant landlady. Urged to leave the burning house, the old lady dressed as though for her own funeral, lit the lamps in front of her icons, and announced calmly that "I've lived my life in this house, and I won't leave it alive"; the smoke, she was sure, would suffocate her before the flames could burn her alive.[47]

Darkness and insecurity accompanied the disintegration of urban society. According to a priest, the stillness during the occupation was punctuated only by the cawing of birds and the "unusual barking and howling of the dogs,"[48] and the winter that turned Napoleon's retreat to disaster also struck

Moscow—people huddled around stoves, wrapped in blankets, while the snow blew in through broken doors and windows.[49] Boarded-up windows blocked the light, ruined neighborhoods lay abandoned, streetlights were smashed, and few carriages circulated in the streets. As a result, the long, overcast autumn and winter nights were even gloomier than before: as Dmitrii Zavalishin later recalled, in large areas "there was no glimmer from even the smallest flame," and it was dangerous to go out after dark.[50] The German physician Nordhof blamed the insecurity on the many uprooted peasants from the devastated countryside who survived as squatters in burned-out houses.[51]

People responded in dissimilar ways to the collapse of their civilization. Many found it deeply disturbing: according to the noblewoman Anna Khomutova, "wandering among the snow-covered ruins [during the winter of 1812–13], we did not hear the rumble of carriages, or for that matter, any noise at all: it was the silence of a burial vault. In the evenings, all of a sudden, a pistol shot would ring out; whether it was a chance occurrence or a crime, no one knew."[52] But to others, it was all weirdly liberating: one son of German immigrants recalled,

> As for me personally, I felt very happy. Although [I was] already ten years old, I did not really grasp either the overall situation or my own, and freed from my studies and from supervision, I abandoned myself completely to the joys of freedom, roaming with Pavlushka and the other neighborhood boys in vacant lots, gardens, and kitchen-gardens—at the time, there were almost no fences: the French, when they were looting, had made shortcuts for themselves by knocking them down wherever they stood in the way.[53]

Everyone carried lasting memories of the emptiness and desolation. A physician named Bekker, a son of German immigrants who was eight years old during the war, wrote in 1870 that his dreams still often carried him back to the ruined streets and houses where he and his friends used to play Cossacks and Frenchmen. At the time Bekker was writing, during the Franco-Prussian War, Paris was in the process of being strangled by the German siege, and the misery of the freezing, starving Parisians caused Bekker nothing but glee.[54]

The Moscow of *War and Peace* is not so much a place as an idea. Tolstoy conveys this idea with his entomological metaphors but also by slighting urban sights and sounds and giving center stage to aristocrats whose wealth shielded them from the realities of city life. In one of the rare passages that even mention the dirt and darkness, he turns Moscow's nighttime desolation into an opportunity for aristocratic reverie. On a winter's evening, Pierre, warmly bundled up in his sleigh, sheltered from the danger and discomfort of the streets, returns home from a social visit: "It was cold and clear. Above the dirty, semi-dark streets, above the black roofs, stood the dark, starry sky. Only looking at the sky did Pierre not feel the insulting baseness of everything earthly compared with the height his soul had risen to" (II, 5, xxii, 600).

Tolstoy was, *pace* Prince Viazemskii, no materialist. He did not construct his Moscow from the ground up, one back alley at a time, as writers such as Ivan Kokorev and Aleksandr Levitov did in their gritty Moscow tales of the 1840s–1860s; their sensibility, which is indeed "materialist," is closer than Tolstoy's to that of the eyewitness of 1812.[55] The counts and princes of *War and Peace* had difficulty seeing the world as it appeared to most Muscovites because, as the Russian proverb had it, "a sated man doesn't understand a hungry one."[56] Doomed to a daily struggle for survival and a raw, unmediated physicality in their encounter with the city, common Muscovites could not easily, like Pierre Bezukhov in his bearskin coat and comfortable sleigh, raise their eyes from "the dirty, semi-dark streets" to contemplate with philosophical detachment "the dark, starry sky" above.

4

The French at War

Representations of the Enemy in *War and Peace*

———

ALAN FORREST

Tolstoy makes it clear throughout *War and Peace* that he rejects the great-man theory of warfare and the notion that the war of 1812, or any other, could have been decided by generals, whether by the much-vaunted tactical genius of Napoleon or the dogged and stubborn resilience of Kutuzov. Individual will counted as nothing compared with the spirit of the nation and the desire felt by the army as a whole: hence his concern to discuss the actions of ordinary soldiers and to present the war as a collage of individual initiatives in a host of minor actions.[1] Napoleon's victories could not be explained satisfactorily in terms of his orders alone, as he had no means of ensuring that they were carried out; that depended not on him but on the spirit and motivation of his troops. Nor could he be held uniquely responsible for his defeats, as Prince Andrei explains.

> A battle is won by him who is firmly resolved to win it. Why did we lose the battle at Austerlitz? The French losses were almost equal to ours, but we said to ourselves early on that we had lost the battle—and so we lost it. We said that because there was no need for us to fight: we wanted to leave the battlefield as soon as we could. We've lost—well, let's run for it. And we ran. (III, 2, xxv, 773)

Or consider Tolstoy's verdict on Napoleon's failure to throw the Old Guard into the Battle of Borodino, where he believed that they could have made all the difference in securing victory. It is not "that Napoleon did not send in his guard because he did not want to, but that it could not be done. All the officers and soldiers of the French army knew that it could not be done, because the army's fallen spirits did not allow it" and "because the moral strength of the attacking French army was exhausted." The consequences of this loss of moral force were inestimable.

> The French invasion, like an enraged beast mortally wounded as it charges, sensed its destruction; but it could not stop, just as the twice weaker Russian army could not help moving aside. After the shove it had been given, the French army could still roll on as far as Moscow, but there, with no new efforts on the part of the Russians, it was to perish, bleeding from the mortal wound it had received at Borodino. (III, 2, xxxix, 819–20)

When he discusses the French, Tolstoy is more concerned to understand the thoughts of the rank and file than to discourse on the strategic qualities of Napoleon and his marshals. These for him barely mattered. After all, what Borodino showed was not the efficacy of Napoleon's orders but rather the confusion of the battlefield, the random desperation in the ranks, the chaos and din and carnage that rendered friend and foe indistinguishable. If the French fought bravely, he claims, it was not in response to the orders they received but because "they had nothing left to do but cry '*Vive l'Empereur!*' and go to fight in order to find food and rest as victors in Moscow" (III, 2, xxvii, 785).

And the French did fight bravely—bravely and desperately—in the Russian campaign. It is interesting how little attempt there is in the novel to denigrate or belittle the enemy, even in their hour of defeat, and the degree to which Tolstoy, through his characters, betrays a certain sympathy and fellow feeling for them. They were soldiers, just like the Russians, soldiers hundreds of miles from home, doubting the cause they were fighting for, fearful and desperately weary. Many of them, like their Russian counterparts, were soldiers of necessity, requisitioned or conscripted into a war for which they had little appetite. Some pillaged, got drunk, and mistreated their prisoners, but there is no suggestion that these were peculiarly French traits or that the Russians would have behaved any differently on foreign soil. During his imprisonment after his arrest on suspicion of fire-raising in Moscow, Pierre experienced moments of kindness and shared an unexpected empathy with his captors; when he was befriended by a Frenchman, he clearly felt a shared sense of real humanity (III, 3, xxix, 904–13). They were, in other words, men like any other. And in their final retreat they were soldiers who, through fate rather than any fault of their own, found themselves bereft of hope and forced by circumstance to seek safety in what numbers remained.

> The French, retreating in 1812, though according to tactics they should defend themselves separately, press together in a mass, because the spirit of the army has fallen, and only its mass holds the army together. The Russians, on

the contrary, should, according to tactics, be attacking in mass, but in fact they break up, because the spirit has risen so much that separate persons beat the French without any orders and need not be forced to subject themselves to difficulties and dangers. (IV, 3, iii, 1035)

It is significant that his sympathy is reserved for the men, not for the emperor or the high command, in their moment of epiphany. It is the men who were abandoned to their sufferings in the Russian winter, the ordinary foot soldiers, conscripted across the Napoleonic Empire, whose lives lay ruined on the Russian steppes.

> When the frosts set in, the flight of the French only acquired a more tragic character of men freezing or roasting to death by camp-fires, and of the Emperor, kings and dukes in fur coats continuing to drive on in carriages filled with stolen goods; but in essence the process of the flight and decomposition of the French army had not changed in the least since the departure from Moscow. (IV, 3, xvi, 1066)

Their sufferings stood in stark contrast to the greed and self-interest of their leaders.

It is instructive to compare these views with what the French soldiers themselves wrote of their experience on the campaign and of the Russian troops ranged against them. They and their officers suffered horribly, and they left ample testimony to that suffering in the diaries they kept, the letters they sent home from the front, and especially the memoirs they wrote once they were safely home, often many years after the end of their ordeal. Like Tolstoy they tell stories, except that what they relate they present as personal experience, which appears to give their narratives an added authority. They had been there; they observed and commented on what they had seen, on their spirits and morale, their suffering in the Russian winter, and the horror of death that they witnessed on all sides. Often they felt a compulsion to write about an existence that those who had not shared it could not hope to comprehend. "War is another world," Samuel Hynes reminds us, "where men feel and act differently, and so, when they return to the other world of peace and ordinariness, they feel a need to tell their tales of the somewhere else they have been."[2] Soldiers may not have the novelist's command of literary technique, but at the moment of putting pen to paper they become creative writers in their own right.

The authors of memoirs often have personal agendas, too. This is most evident with memoirs written up for publication many years later, when the soldier, long retired from service, looks back on his campaigns and reflects on what he has achieved; but even the memoirs left in manuscript form, intended to convey the story of one man's war experience to his family or his grandchildren, are not exempt. Even where they are not openly partisan exercises in self-justification, the very fact that they were written after the event allows for benefits of hindsight that the individual would not have had at the time. If memoirs have their genesis in firsthand experience, they should not be confused with experience. Writing memoirs involves drafting a narrative and selecting the events or emotions that will support it. In that sense they, too, must be seen as a form of creative fiction.

Diaries and journals carefully maintained through months of long marches and occasional engagements might seem to provide a less manicured account of events. But because they seldom have any space for reflection, they are often little more than dull litanies of kilometers covered, meals consumed, and villages passed through. Journals can seem lifeless, drained of all color, even rather bleak in their bald listing of facts. They are most lacking, indeed, in precisely the appreciation of sensibility that the novelist is so well fitted to supply. And they generally lack any clear narrative line beyond the basic structure of a day-by-day chronicle. In that respect they may adhere more closely to the reality of military experience, portraying a campaign as they saw it at the time, shapeless and incoherent, a limited vision unadulterated by any sense of the campaign as a whole. They are often grimly realistic, bereft of heroism, with just a suggestion of the futility that we sense in Tolstoy's account of 1812.[3]

Personal correspondence can seem a more promising medium, especially the letters that soldiers wrote to their parents and loved ones back home. They have an undoubted immediacy: letters were scribbled on tables in wayside inns, by candlelight in barracks and billets, or around the campfire on the eve of battle. But the fact of writing to parents imposed its own obligations: expressing their affection, asking about life on the farm, showing concern for the health of aunts and uncles, cousins and grandparents.[4] A letter home could become formulaic, with the family relationship affecting what the soldiers wrote and, just as significantly, what they omitted. So could the established tropes that governed writing: bravery, honor, and military comportment are discussed in a standard way that had been learned from reading manuals and memoirs of past wars as much as from experience of the present.[5] Soldiers were not encouraged to express emotion or to risk being corrupted by pleasure, since these ran counter to prevalent notions of masculinity and the demands of the military code.[6] Would a soldier dare to express fear, for instance, or hint at cowardice or the temptation to desert? Would he risk describing the full horror of the battlefield; the sounds and smells of death; the pleas of the dying; the serried ranks of stripped, pillaged, naked bodies? There is much reassurance in these letters, combined with a hint of bravado: enemies are slaughtered, the French advance, men retain complete confidence in their officers. There is little about sex and virtually no mention of rape, which may at first seem surprising until we remember that these are usually letters written to mothers, a context in which it would not have seemed proper to discuss such subjects.[7] Letters, like other personal accounts, are written for an audience, albeit usually a private one, and for a purpose, most often to reassure. For all their immediacy, they are not value-neutral: they are texts like any other and must be read as such.

But that does not mean that they must be discarded as evidence. For what else do we have that can even attempt to describe individual emotions, explain the decisions taken in the heat of battle, or distinguish the motives and perceptions of individuals from those of leaders and institutions? Here the historian and the novelist may ask similar questions. How did soldiers regard their opponents? How were they affected by pain and suffering, fear and hunger? How damaging was boredom, which was alleviated only by the interspersed moments of military action when the adrenalin flowed, moments for which weary soldiers might actively yearn?[8] These questions were central to Tolstoy: in particular, the interaction of Russians with those who had invaded their country is a key theme in *War and Peace,* just as it was a key interaction during the whole campaign. But did the French depict their adversaries in a similar light? Did they, as an invading army in a very alien landscape, see these Russian opponents differently than they saw the Russians who invaded France after Leipzig less than two years later or those who formed an army of occupation after Waterloo?[9] In war enemies are routinely demonized by governments, and war propaganda is used to motivate both soldiers and civilians; thus Linda Colley claims that it was a shared hatred of the French that helped cement a very fragile British identity during the 1790s.[10] But do such views recur in the opinions expressed by the officers leading the army or in the writings of the soldiers in the ranks? It is fortunate that, in spite of the disruption to supply lines and postal communication, many memoirs, diaries, and letters from the Grande Armée have survived.[11] Rather comfortingly, they do not always substantiate the official line.

The soldiers found themselves far from home, in an alien environment, surrounded by people whose customs they found disturbingly unfamiliar. They could not expect to be warmly received. They were there, after all, as invaders, and it was inevitable that their feel for the land they passed over and their understanding of its inhabitants were very different from those of their Russian counterparts. They came with preconceptions, too, ideas that they had read in books and newspapers, not least from the burgeoning travel literature of the eighteenth century. And, since the Grande Armée contained troops from all over the Empire and not only from France, they brought with them a cocktail of prejudices and presumptions drawn from across the continent. Some came with assumptions of cultural superiority: Germans, in particular, often had firm views about what they saw as a dividing line between civilization and the barbarism that lay to their east.[12] Almost routinely they portrayed Slavs, Poles, and East European Jews as poor, backward, and dirty, the classic depictions of those perceived as belonging to lower forms of civilization.[13] But the assumption that Europe was split into advanced and backward zones, where the north and west were contrasted with the south and east, was not confined to German central Europe. There are traces of it in French accounts of both eastern Europe and Iberia, areas where they encountered guerrilla resistance and civilian atrocities. Besides, more than a third of the Grande Armée was not French. It contained soldiers from all across the empire, regions that France had occupied and colonized. The reactions of the soldiers reflect the collective prejudices of the European continent.

How they talked about the Russians depended on the conditions in which they wrote as much as on their status or level of literacy. During their long march east many soldiers took an interest in the towns they passed through and in the condition of the crops in the fields. Many were country boys at heart, the products of a farming background and accustomed to comparing the condition of the fields, the richness of the soil, or the state of the animals they encountered. At times they commented on the prosperity of the farms and fertility of the landscape, which clearly surprised them. In Lithuania, for instance, René Bourgeois compared the vast cornfields with the Beauce, the breadbasket of France, producing grain of every sort. "There was, in particular, a huge quantity of rye, the plants standing more than six feet high. These great expanses of plain were entirely flat, stretching to the horizon, and all the ears of corn, swaying in the wind, take on the appearance of a gently stirred sea."[14] Behind the farmer's eye there is a hint of the poetic in his description of a scene that he found hauntingly beautiful. The landscape attracted and surprised him, as well, no doubt, as alleviating the tedium of the march. At moments like these the French wrote as simple travelers, military tourists, wide-eyed with innocent curiosity. One young soldier wrote home proudly to say that he was now in Warsaw, adding that it was a fine city and that he had to date passed through three capital cities since leaving home in the Oise.[15] Travel was a source of pleasure, a welcome escape from boredom.

It was also a source of discovery at the end of an eighteenth century characterized by a new appetite for discovery and scientific inquiry from which the army was in no sense immune. On his voyage around the globe in 1767 Bougainville had taken with him two scientists, a botanist and an astronomer. Napoleon's expedition to Egypt was the most famous instance of combining military and scientific motives, the army being accompanied by a rich assortment of botanists and zoologists, archaeologists, and scholars of ancient

Christian von Martens, *The Inhabitants of Dirna* (1812). In Christian von Martens, "Tagebuch meines Feldzuges in Russland 1812," vol. 1, "Vom Ausmarsch bis Moskau, Maez–Sept. 1812," Hauptstaatsarchive, Stuttgart. An officer in the Württemberg army, von Martens went to Russia as part of the Grande Armée. He kept a manuscript diary of his experiences, dated 1812, though it seems likely that the diary and the drawings, given their quality and color, were completed after his return. But they certainly date from the early nineteenth century.

languages. Even in the Italian campaign of 1798 there was a desire to discover and appropriate classical remains and works of art, the iconic representations of a past civilization. The triumphant procession through Paris on Bonaparte's return showcased the great works of art that had been plundered for the nation, but as Eric Leed notes, the procession was spearheaded by "the botanical specimens that Baudin had collected on his first voyage to the West Indies." This demonstrated a desire to counterbalance "a military appropriation of the world through war" with science and culture—"intellectual appropriations through observations."[16] In central and eastern Europe, in contrast, artistic appropriations were restricted largely to theft and looting.

Where an opportunity presented itself, the French also expressed interest in local customs and culture. Désiré Fuzellier, who joined the Grande Armée as a young doctor attached to the medical service, was taken captive in Poland in January 1813 and spent eighteen months as a prisoner in Russia. The captivity diary he wrote while in prison makes interesting reading, the more so since he seemed loath to rail against his misfortune, preferring to comment on what he witnessed around him. There were so many new experiences, unfamiliar rituals, and strange peoples whom he had never encountered in

·civil life in Montreuil-sur-mer. While he suffered individual instances of cruelty from his captors, they were sufficiently rare to merit comment, and for the most part he restricted himself to descriptions of the strange world that had opened before his eyes. He first came across Tatars, for instance, in the city of Kazan. He describes their dress, the colors they wore, their physical appearance. Then, with great perceptiveness, he turns to their character and lifestyle. There was no hostility, no hint of criticism in his account.

> The Tatars scarcely ever get drunk. They are very hard-working; few of them are artists, many are merchants. Those who are rich live a life of ease: they travel only in litters, for they have beds and mattresses. Their houses are kept clean. They are generally very affable, but are tired of living under Russian domination, for the Russians insult them openly and with impunity.[17]

In this passage it is interesting that he should have commented on the cleanliness of the Tatars, since this was a clear sign of respect, an appreciation of their civilization.

A further sign of Fuzellier's respect for Tatar culture can be seen in his description of their capital, Kazan, a city where Tolstoy would spend part of his boyhood. He noted that the city boasted many churches, including two that were very beautiful, as well as a seminary and a number of convents. There was also a Lutheran church, which had been built to accommodate the German residents, for, he observes, this was a cosmopolitan city, with many Germans and Italians living there, as well as a handful of French, mainly in banking. The houses were well built, and there were impressive public buildings and civic amenities, including a range of markets for grain, vegetables, meat, and fish; several bridges across the river; and a fine main square. He goes so far as to identify it as a Western city in many of its aspects: "Certain quarters of Kazan look like a German city," he reports, clearly deeply impressed. In particular, he comments on the theater, which he had not expected to find in a Russian provincial town. "There is a theater where plays are often performed. Curiosity led me to visit it: this is a building perched on top of a mountain. The interior is very simple. The actors, who come from Moscow, cannot be compared to those in Germany, or in France. Only the orchestra attracted our attention."[18] Not everything elicited praise, but the comparisons were with Western cities and culture.

This detailed description underlines the importance of cities and city life as signifiers of culture in foreign parts and of the victory of civilization over barbarism. By that criterion Russia was certainly civilized in French eyes, though the cities were few and scattered, and the troops had to cross many miles of barren waste to reach them. It was one reason why French soldiers found it so shocking when the Russians set fire to their own capital to stop the

French advance. Napoleon himself shared their horror. In a letter to Marie-Louise on October 17, 1812, he wrote, "I had no conception of this city. It had five hundred palaces as beautiful as the Elysée, furnished in French style with incredible luxury, several imperial palaces, barracks, and magnificent hospitals. Everything has disappeared, consumed by fire over the last four days."[19] Napoleon was not alone in his astonishment that the Russians should sacrifice a great city and put two hundred thousand of its citizens onto the streets. Other French observers concurred. It was not the torching of buildings that they found shocking: the French themselves used fire on many occasions to cut off the enemy or to spread terror, burning farmsteads and whole villages in a scorched-earth policy reminiscent of the Vendée. It was the sense that a great city, an integral part of European civilization, was being lost before their eyes. "It's a really ugly thing seeing a great city burn," wrote François-Isidore Parguez, a French officer, to his wife in Paris. His mind drifted to the obvious parallel. "Just think of Paris being burned, all the houses left without roofs, doors or windows, filled with smoking debris, with only a few houses preserved and apparently intact, like the Ile de la Cité or Saint-Louis."[20]

The war itself was a source of untold horror, and soon the French turned their attention to their own fate, as the Russians avoided engagements and pushed them further and further into the open countryside. The sheer savagery they observed, the starvation that led men to slice meat from the corpses of horses that fell by the roadside, the bitter, crippling cold that saw men freeze in their tents all helped make this the cruelest of campaigns. "I had a presentiment of something terrible," wrote Lamy, a supply commissioner in Russia, "and as you know it gave me no pleasure to leave. But one thing which they will scarcely believe back in France is that all those who have fought in Spain look back nostalgically on their time there now that they find themselves here."[21] It is a powerful image and a fitting symptom of the brutality of the fighting on both sides. But even here, as they were being forced back by the Russian winter, officers could behave with honor and dignity to their opponents, and letters bear witness to individual acts of kindness. One officer, his battalion ambushed near Krasnoe (or Krasnoi), was wounded in the neck and forced to hand over his sword; his Russian counterpart helped to staunch the wound before passing him to the care of his general, who had his surgeon tend to the French officer.[22] Russian officers, it is clear, could be expected to understand military concepts of generosity and honor; they had been raised in the same tradition of war and even, in many instances, conversed with their prisoners in French. For their part the French appreciated their courage and occasional displays of chivalry. Russian *molodechestvo* was not so very different from French *élan*.[23]

Christian von Martens, *A Surprise Cossack Attack near Krasnoi* (1812). In Christian von Martens, "Tagebuch meines Feldzuges in Russland 1812," vol. 1, "Vom Ausmarsch bis Moskau, Maerz–Sept. 1812," Hauptstaatsarchive, Stuttgart.

Military culture was a shared European culture: to many it seemed co-terminous with Christendom itself. Beyond the territory defined by that culture, one entered a dangerous and barbarous world with no rules, only ferocity; one crossed, in the words of the nineteenth-century traveler Alexander Kinglake, "the very frontier of all accustomed respectabilities," encountering people "that will be like to put you to death for not being a vagrant, for not being a robber, for not being armed and houseless."[24] The same feeling can be found among the French troops in Russia, for whom the nations of Asia inspired an exaggerated fear. They did not fight with the same rules, the same sense of honor, or the same weapons. When one French officer protested that Bashkir troops had fired arrows at them, he was told by Russians that "in war the essential thing is victory; it matters little what weapons are used."[25] Jakob Meyer, who had volunteered for service in the army of Westphalia, remarked on the unpredictability of the Bashkirs. When one of his fellow captives tried to hide his sword, one of his most precious possessions, he was immediately cut down by a Bashkir soldier. The violence of the response shocked Meyer; it was, he added glumly, "the prelude to the sad days that lay ahead of us."[26]

Of the different groups in the Russian army the Cossacks enjoyed a particular reputation for sadism and cruelty. They were not regarded as being like other Russians—as, indeed, they were not, since, despite considerable loss of autonomy in the eighteenth century, they remained fiercely attached to their traditions and had resisted integration into the Russian imperial order.[27] Their very appearance inspired fear, especially during the French retreat from Moscow, when they were employed to great effect in harrying the army's rear guard and attacking weak links in the main marching column.[28] They moved silently through woods and copses, often by night, falling on their prey like wild beasts. "We were," wrote Bourgeois, "afraid to fall into their hands, for after heaping blows on you they stripped you of all your clothing and abandoned you, stark naked, to the rigors of winter. It would be less barbarous if they killed you."[29] But they were also exceptional soldiers, whose reputation demoralized the French troops in advance of a Cossack attack, and some admitted admiring their wild courage and superb horsemanship. So even, it was reported, did Napoleon, who was impressed by their fearlessness and their warrior qualities. His aide-de-camp, Caulaincourt, reports with apparent approval an exchange between Napoleon and a young Cossack soldier, where the Cossack is quoted as saying the following: "If Alexander's Russian soldiers, especially his generals, were like the Cossacks, you and your Frenchmen would not be in Russia. If Napoleon had had Cossacks in his army, he would have been Emperor of China long ago. It is the Cossacks who do all the fighting, it is always their turn. While the Russians sleep, the Cossacks keep watch."[30] Though this account is heavily partisan, there is perhaps a grain of truth in it, and it is significant that Napoleon did not dismiss it out of hand. The soldiers' view of the enemy was far more nuanced than the unsubtle language of military dispatches. Like Tolstoy's fictional heroes, they did not hesitate to express a degree of admiration for the Russians and their military prowess. Indeed, their observations of the enemy were critical to their appraisal of themselves.

Like any novel, *War and Peace* is the product of the novelist's craft and imagination, but Tolstoy's vision for his work encapsulated a moral and political dimension that aspired to more than creativity or literary excellence. It certainly adopted many of the conventions of the novel, as understood in western Europe, but in Tolstoy's mind it was simply "what the author wished and was able to express in the form in which it is expressed." Elsewhere he stated, even more firmly, that "it is not a novel, even less is it a poem, and still less a historical chronicle."[31] He was writing at a time when the Russian historical novel had lost much of the status it had commanded in an earlier generation, especially during the 1830s, when it had enjoyed a special place in the literary cannon. Dan Ungurianu maintains that it had briefly been "the dominant prose genre," to such a degree, indeed, that "the terms 'novel' and 'historical novel' became synonymous."[32] By the 1840s, however, public taste had changed, and the tendency of historical novelists to paint the country's past in vivid shades and to people it with larger-than-life heroes brought the genre into disrepute. For many critics the historical novel had lost any power of reflection, and it risked being dismissed as fit only for light diversion and as reading matter for children. Only in the 1860s, when writers began to suggest comparisons between the past and the present, did the genre reestablish some of its former authority.[33]

Tolstoy planned *War and Peace* as a form of chronicle that gave due weight to day-to-day events, the everyday and mundane details that collectively constitute human experience, which Liza Knapp calls a "narrative whose flow is determined by experience and time itself."[34] He was fascinated by military life and armed conflict, exploring the mentality of soldiers and especially of army officers, men from his own class and social background facing the challenges and uncertainties of war. As a young man he admired the dash and daring of soldiers in battle, the strength and physical prowess that were the very essence of youth.[35] And there was a strong autobiographical aspect to his observations and in the feelings that he attributed to his characters, feelings he had experienced when fighting in the Crimean War; he understood the values of the officer class, just as he shared the pride and fear that the imminence of battle evoked. And it is this understanding that he brought to his analysis of his military characters. Tolstoy's principal focus is on the experience of war, both military and civilian, and his main concern is to explain the present. At one point he had intended *War and Peace* to be the first part of his projected Decembrist trilogy in which he would "conduct my heroines and heroes through the historical events of 1805, 1807, 1812, 1825 and 1856"[36] and weave these moments of crisis into a single canvas that would illuminate the spirit of the Russian people. He writes about soldiers' views of other soldiers and about their discipline, their sufferings, and their approaches to the art of war. These, he implies, are largely constant over time, from one war to another.[37]

Tolstoy did not, of course, rely wholly on his own experiences of the Crimean War two generations later, however graphically they were inscribed in his memory. For the Napoleonic Wars and the great fires that devoured Moscow were by this time solidly inscribed in Russian collective memory too, in writing and in visual prints, while the Russian resistance to Napoleon, like the risings in Spain and the wars of liberation in Germany, had already passed into legend and been put to a host of overtly political uses.[38] We know how avidly he devoured books on the Napoleonic Wars, and especially memoirs of those who took part in the 1812 campaign, to add precision and vibrancy to his narrative. He studied the strategies of the two armies, the tactical approaches of Napoleon and Alexander, and perhaps the views of Clausewitz on the practice of warfare so that he might claim to foster a greater understanding of the Napoleonic battlefield than those who had fought in 1812 could hope to do. Tolstoy was not a historian, but he sought to use history to deepen his understanding of the wars and enrich his re-creation of the spirit and morale of those who fought them. And he could use all the license available to the novelist by putting into the mouths and minds of his fictional heroes the thoughts of real men in the heat of battle.

Cross-referencing of this kind has inherent dangers, especially because the officer of 1856 was more literate and more affected by nationalist and romantic ideals than was his Napoleonic counterpart. The nature of the Crimean War was different too: it was spread over two fighting seasons, it was not fought at such breakneck speed, and there were long months of relative inactivity during the siege of Sebastopol, when French and Russian soldiers fraternized, shared food and drink, sang songs together, and communicated in sign language.[39] There are few parallel moments in 1812. But the respect shown by French officers for their Russian counterparts and their ability to communicate in a shared language, French, were common to both campaigns. So, no doubt, was the sense of cultural superiority felt by many of the French soldiers, who continued to see themselves as free men, citizen-soldiers in the tradition of the French Revolution, now fighting in a country whose troops were the victims of feudalism and the product of serfdom. But as the Zouave soldier Louis Noir recorded in his memoirs, their pride that they were citizens with rights did not turn them against the Russians; it was just as likely to surface when they compared themselves with their British ally. Disgusted by the ferocity of the beatings administered in the British army, Noir reflected that if the British had had conscription and the sons of the better-off had been obliged to serve, such abuse would surely have been abolished. "The sight of these corporal punishments disgusted us," he remarks, "reminding us that the revolution of 89 abolished flogging in the army when it established universal conscription."[40] Close acquaintance with others, be they Russian or British, served to cement the French soldier's own sense of identity.

If carefully selected, historical parallels can help historians and others to re-create a mentality that they cannot have witnessed and that, by the nature of their sources, can be only very imperfectly accessed. Tolstoy does not hesitate to make use of these parallels, and he claims, in a much-quoted remark at the end of "Sevastopol in May," to be writing something more objective than fiction. "[T]he hero of my story, whom I love with all my heart and soul, whom I have attempted to portray in all his beauty and who has always been, is now and will always be supremely magnificent, is truth." But what, Andrew Wachtel asks, can this mean? His answer is that Tolstoy sought to approach the truth by drawing on the minor details of individual lives—a form of "deep description"—while also "striving for universality" and drawing general lessons from the particular.[41] The interlacing of fictional characters and autobiographical incidents, he believed, entitled him to claim an authority for his work that placed it in a genre apart from mere storytelling.

Tolstoy's view of history, however, is not straightforward, and when analyzing the actions and the values of others he gives vent to his ideas on human psychology and his sense of good and evil. His vision is distinctly Christian, the distance between man and God being taken as a measure of the degree of evil in the human spirit. The idea of freedom lies at the heart of his work: it is "the continuously enticing vitality that is the wellspring of hope."[42] In his analysis of character and his discussion of war these two strands are complementary. *War and Peace* is about Russian spirit and Russian national character, which Tolstoy felt passionately about, but there is also a repugnance at the carnage and wastefulness of war. He refused to share the euphoria of the nineteenth-century nationalists who talked of a war of liberation against Napoleon, the unfettered rising of the Russian people in defense of their country; he preferred to see Napoleon's defeat as the result of his own errors and the implosion of the French army, just as he chose to depict the battlefield less as the site of brilliant tactical maneuvers than as the scene of mindless carnage and confusion. For some Russian officers who were veterans of 1812, Tolstoy went too far in dismantling romantic myths in which they felt they had a personal stake. Like Prince Petr Viazemskii, a survivor of the war who remained influential in Russian cultural circles, they accused him of historical vandalism, of being one of the "killers of history."[43]

Throughout *War and Peace* there is a recurrent reference to the psychology of evil that cannot but affect his view of the military. For soldiers commit acts in war that can easily be equated with evil: they loot and pillage, they rape civilians, they kill and win commendation for that killing. Like the recent work of Joanna Bourke, his depiction of the military places as much emphasis on the act of killing as on the pain of dying.[44] Soldiers, after all, enjoy the right to kill without risking the sanctions that killing entails in civil society, but that right applies only to specific categories: killing committed while in uniform and while subject to military discipline or violence targeted at an identified military opponent. Tolstoy believed, in line with Rousseau and the writers of the French Enlightenment, that men were not naturally driven to evil but rather that they were endowed with the parallel facilities of mind and physical energy—what he termed "force"—which was a natural condition, neither moral nor immoral. In the military force was especially valued, as it played a critical role in saving the soldier's life and protecting those of his comrades. Tolstoy proposed three distinct categories of soldiers: the meek, who make obedient soldiers; those endowed with natural leadership qualities; and the desperate, capable of rash and reckless deeds on the battlefield.[45] He presented war as a part of man's natural condition, which releases force to an unparalleled degree. The more terrible the fighting, he believed, the more the troops displayed fearless energy. It was around such concepts, themselves highly ideological, that he constructed his grand narrative of war.[46]

Like most nineteenth-century Russian intellectuals, Tolstoy saw 1812 as an epic tragedy that engulfed the Russian people. His view would go on to fuel one of the enduring myths of the 1812 campaign, that this defeat could be ascribed to the forces of "geography, the climate and chance" and to the unquenchable spirit of Russian popular resistance. It was a view that reduced the impact of individuals and had the effect of absolving Napoleon from personal responsibility for the terrible hecatomb that ensued. Russian strategy, Tolstoy concluded, was a "combination of improvisation and accident."[47] But that did not devalue his characterizations of army officers or his analysis of their war experiences. What he offered was an acute insight into the sensibility and emotion of the moment, the texture of human experience, which, as both a novelist and an army officer, he was ideally equipped to do.

The pictures of the enemy that he draws in *War and Peace* are largely corroborated by the writings of those who fought in the Moscow campaign. Tolstoy had, of course, read widely in the memoir literature of the war. He knew many of the Russian memoirs at first hand, as well as some of the French, and he valued the opinions of those who had experienced action in the campaign. What is interesting is how international these experiences often were, for, as we have seen, many of the same views and values that Tolstoy ascribes to his Russian heroes were also expressed by their French opponents. Perhaps this should not surprise us, for, though as a novelist he was not constrained by any notion of objectivity and could give free rein to his imagination, he has much to offer the historian of the period too. Of course we would not turn to him for precise details of the campaign or of the orders given to the troops of both sides. But those are not his concern. Tolstoy is at his best in dealing with the human side of war, the pride and honor, the pain and sympathy felt by soldiers in battle. And there he creates a rich and highly credible canvas, a picture that would have found an echo with Russian and Frenchman alike.

5

Symposium of Quotations

Wit and Other Short Genres
in *War and Peace*

———

GARY SAUL MORSON

When we think of literary genres, long forms come first to mind: epics, which demand length to tell the tale of the tribe; novels, which trace the gradual development of character; and perhaps sprawling satires, like the works of Rabelais, Burton's *Anatomy of Melancholy,* or Byron's *Don Juan.* Some long histories, like the narratives of Herodotus or Gibbon, and classic biographies, like Boswell's *Life of Johnson,* also belong to this literary family. We are likely to think next of shorter genres, like sonnets, elegies, and other kinds of lyric; short stories, extending from brief fables to novellas; and various nonfictional forms, like orations and essays.

But we rarely include the shortest literary forms, the ones we might call quotations, since they are brief enough to anthologize in works like Bartlett's or, in an earlier age, Erasmus's *Adages.* Sometimes we call these short works aphorisms, at other times maxims or sayings.[1] We all know many of them, even if we do not remember their author (who said "one swallow does not make a summer"?), and we know that some of them are proverbs, usually authorless.

None of these terms has a clear definition, so if we are to understand these kinds of short works, it would be foolish to try to do so by examining the use of terms. We would do better to identify classes of texts and then, for the sake of convenience, choose a name for them, while recognizing that other names would be equally possible. A witticism by any other name would be as funny.

Although there are many ways to identify classes of literary works, I prefer to do so in terms of worldview. Mikhail Bakhtin offers the clearest account of this approach when he treats each genre as a "form-shaping ideology," by which he means a view of experience, often too complex for ready paraphrase, that seeks appropriate forms of expression.[2] In this classification, forms do not define a genre (as might properly be the case in a different classification) but are the consequence of what does.

This approach readily allows one to see why, on philosophical grounds, a writer might be drawn to one genre rather than another and why, in the course of their history, genres may develop arguments with each other. Utopias and realist novels parody each other, as mock-epic parodies epic. The genres of quotation also dispute each other. Taken together, literary genres may be seen as a great symposium.

Tolstoy loved quotations and anthologies of quotations. Three of the ninety volumes of his Complete Works (PSS 40, 41, and 42) are devoted to them. His *Circle of Reading* (1906) is perhaps the best-known of his collections, but he also produced *Thoughts of Wise People for Every Day* (1903), *For Every Day* (1910), *The Path of Life* (1910), and the *Calendar of Proverbs* (1886). In volume 40 we find his Russian versions of individual authors writing in diverse genres: La Rochefoucauld, La Bruyère, Montesquieu, Lao Tzu, and others. Clearly, the author of *War and Peace* understood the possibilities offered by brevity as well as by length.

Tolstoy recognized that long works often include and develop the wisdom of short genres. Quotations inspire longer works and are often drawn from them. Utopias love and include dicta, short statements of timeless truth professing absolute certainty that error has at last been overcome. We find dicta in thinkers like Spinoza, Leibniz, Bentham, Freud, and Marx. Many appear (and can easily be extracted from) utopias like *What Is to Be Done?* and *Looking Backward*. In *War and Peace,* they belong to generals who believe they have a science of war (General Pfühl) and the "historians" who think they understand the laws of history.

By contrast to utopias and dicta, realist novels are inherently skeptical. They include dicta only as a sign of naïveté. They tend to prefer sardonic maxims like those of La Rochefoucauld. In George Eliot and Anthony Trollope, such maxims occur frequently. These writers treat dicta with considerable irony. So does Tolstoy in *War and Peace*.[3]

Wise Sayings

Tolstoy loved a genre I call wise sayings—the sort of counsel found in the Books of Proverbs and Psalms, in Confucius, and in other wisdom writings. Wise sayings in this sense assert or presume that if one behaves with prudence and righteousness, one will be rewarded, by God, by "Heaven" (in Confucius), or by the very nature of things. The world makes sense. Wise sayings offer a providential view of life, which is governed by rightness and proper reward. The Bible also contains the opposite genre, a type of sardonic maxim that denies purpose and meaning and sets the tone of Ecclesiastes. In Job, these two genres argue.

Several of Tolstoy's late stories take wise sayings as their titles—think of "God Sees the Truth, but Waits to Tell." In *War and Peace,* Bazdeev is drawn to their wisdom, and, of course, Platon Karataev constantly discovers special depth in proverbs—to be sure in a strange and unproverbial way. In his narrative commentaries and inserted essays, Tolstoy himself uses wise sayings. At the end of the book's first long essay, he cites the saying "The hearts of kings are in the hands of God" and adds his own paraphrase: "A king is the slave of history."[4] God and history use us to accomplish their purposes, and wisdom consists in recognizing a meaningful force beyond our ken and will.

Heroic Pronouncements

Tolstoy treats with heavy irony a type of quotation we might call the heroic pronouncement: the grand statement of defiance, purpose, and resolve at a moment of civic crisis, usually in war. In the West, Pericles' funeral oration has served as the traditional model. For Americans, Lincoln's Gettysburg address exemplifies the form. Since World War II, Churchill's "blood, sweat, and tears" and "we will fight them on the beaches" come most readily to mind.

This genre focuses on the citizens, whose sacrifice is demanded, and on the values for which that sacrifice is made. The speaker summons each person to rise above personal needs and think of the people as a whole. He does so himself, and so he must avoid above all any vain display of his own cleverness or rhetorical skill. Lincoln praises "these honored dead," not himself, a modesty all the more evident in the speech's brevity. Legends about Lincoln's speech invariably call attention to his unawareness of its significance and rhetorical power. He believes that the world will little note nor long remember what he says, a belief that itself contributes to the speech's fame.

In *War and Peace,* which satirizes heroic pronouncements, Alexander and Napoleon preen themselves on their own rhetoric. In the received account of Alexander's response to Napoleon that Tolstoy had at his disposal (Mikhailovskii-Danilevskii), the tsar, learning at a ball of Napoleon's invasion, utters heroic words that Russians all remember.

> Then the Emperor sent for Shishkov, the Secretary of State, and said to him: "It is necessary to write an order to the army immediately, and also to send to Count Saltykov in Petersburg, telling him of the enemy's invasion. Say that I will not make peace as long as a single enemy remains on our soil."[5]

Tolstoy mocks these grand words as he mocks conventional heroism in all its forms. He does so by making Alexander so proud of his own words that he repeats and calls attention to them.

To be sure, when Balashov informs Alexander that Napoleon's army has invaded, Alexander spontaneously replies, "To enter Russia without declaring war! I will not make peace so long as a single armed foe remains in my country" (III, 1, iii, 739/611). But having said these bold words, Alexander becomes mightily impressed by them and contrives to show off his great rhetoric on every possible occasion. The passage derived from Milhailovskii-Danilevskii reads,

> On returning home from the ball at two o'clock in the morning, he sent for his secretary Shishkov and told him to write an order to the troops, and a rescript to Field Marshall Saltykov, in which he *insisted on inserting the words* that he would never make peace so long as a single armed Frenchman remained on Russian soil. (III, 1, iii, 739/612; italics added)

It is almost as if the rescript were a pretext for the bombast. The next day, Alexander summons Balashov and entrusts him with a letter to deliver to Napoleon. "As he dismissed Balashov, he repeated to him his declaration that he would never make peace so long as a single armed foe remained on Russian soil, and told him that *he was to repeat those words* to Napoleon without fail" (III, 1, iv, 740/613; italics added). By this time heroic pronouncement has become self-indulgent farce.

Almost every time he appears, Napoleon weaves words into one of his trademark summons to glory. Early in the novel, when Prince Andrei returns to the army from the Austrian court, Napoleon's words ring in his ears.

> [Andrei] remembered these words from Bonaparte's injunction to his army at the beginning of the campaign, and they aroused in him amazement at the genius of his hero, a feeling of wounded pride, and the hope of glory. "And should there be nothing left but to die?" he thought. "Well, if need be, I shall do it no worse than another." (I, 2, xiii, 209/165)

This willingness to die, this treatment of death as a competition in glory rather than a wholly individual experience, is precisely the reaction heroic pronouncements seek to produce.

After Prince Andrei is wounded at Austerlitz and sees the infinite heavens, which reveal the triviality of all earthly glory, he wakes to an exchange between Napoleon and some captured Russians. Their conversation repeats the conventions of heroic pronouncements, which all participants have evidently learned by heart from patriotic histories. Andrei hears it all as unwitting self-parody.

Bonaparte rode up at a gallop and reined in his horse.

"Who is the senior officer here?" he asked, on seeing the prisoners.

They named the colonel, Prince Repnin.

"You are the commander of Emperor Alexander's regiment of Horse Guards?" asked Napoleon.

"I commanded a squadron," replied Repnin.

"Your regiment performed its duty honorably," said Napoleon.

"The praise of a great commander is a soldier's highest reward," replied Repnin.

"I bestow it with pleasure," said Napoleon. "Who is that young man beside you?"

Prince Repnin named Lieutenant Sukhtelen.

Looking at him Napoleon smiled and said: "He is rather young to come and meddle with us."

"Youth is no impediment to courage," murmured the young man, his voice breaking.

"A fine answer," said Napoleon. "Young man, you will go far." (I, 3, xix, 358/292).

At last Napoleon sees Prince Andrei, whom he remembers from the battlefield, and addresses him as "*mon brave*," but Andrei remains silent. The rhetoric, the values it expresses, and the people who honor those values seem so absurd to him that he cannot participate in the scene.

So trivial at that moment seemed to him all the interests that engrossed Napoleon, so petty did his hero himself, with his paltry vanity and joy in victory appear, compared with that lofty, equitable, benevolent sky which he had seen and understood, that he could not answer him. [...] Looking into Napoleon's eyes, Prince Andrei thought of the insignificance of greatness, the unimportance of life, which no one could understand, and the still greater unimportance of death, the meaning of which no living person could understand and express. (I, 3, xix, 358–59/292–93)

Seven years and six hundred pages later, the night before Borodino, Andrei blames chivalry, honor, and the cult of military glory—all valued by heroic pronouncements—for all the slaughter and destruction.

"[Guided by these values, soldiers] meet, as we shall meet tomorrow, to murder one another; they kill and maim tens of thousands of men, and then hold thanksgiving services for having slaughtered so many (they even exaggerate the number). [...] How God can look down and hear them!" cried Prince Andrei in a shrill, piercing voice. (III, 2, xxv, 933/776)

Paradoxically, Andrei's horror at the glorification of killing leads him to want the army to take no prisoners, just kill.

How does horror at bloodshed lead to abandoning all humane rules of war? As Andrei sees the matter, those rules belong to the cult of honor and chivalry, which cause most war. "Eliminate the humbug," he demands. "If there were none of this chivalry in war, we should go to war only when it was worth going to certain death, as now" (III, ii, xxv, 932/775).

Wit

Tolstoy would have agreed with Aristotle's description of wit as well-bred insolence.

War and Peace discredits not only the dictum and the heroic pronouncement but also the witticism. By the witticism I mean the sorts of sharp comments and ripostes that today we associate with Oscar Wilde, Mark Twain, George Bernard Shaw, Winston Churchill, and Dorothy Parker. The form extends back to antiquity. One famous example, retold by Erasmus, concerns the emperor Augustus, who encountered a young man who could have been his twin. Asked by the emperor if his mother had ever been to Rome, the young man replied, "My mother never, my father constantly."[6]

Among the many examples in *War and Peace* we find the famous anecdote of a Russian general, invited by the tsar to name his own reward, who asks to be promoted to a German—an allusion to the number of foreign or ethnically German generals and statesmen governing Russia.

We find as well the anecdote of Balashov's witty reply to Napoleon's denigrating comments about Russia. Returning to the Russian court after delivering Alexander's bombastic message to Napoleon, Balashov describes how his timely wit nonplussed the French. When Bonaparte described Russia as uniquely backward because it was the only European country with so many churches, Balashov replied, "I beg Your Majesty's pardon [...] besides Russia there is Spain, where there are also a great many churches and monasteries"—a "covert allusion to the defeats of the French in Spain" (III, 1, vii, 754/625). Tolstoy notes that although this exercise in political wit "was highly appreciated when he repeated it" at Alexander's court, it was not so much as noticed by Napoleon. We get the sense of Balashov as a shallow man very well pleased with himself and repeating his own words.

Witticisms as a genre express the power of mind over circumstance, especially social circumstance. Whatever surprise may arise from the insults of others, the challenge of fellow wits, or the sheer power of the unexpected, the wit immediately fabricates a clever response. Always capable of parrying thrusts with surprising deftness, the wit serves as a model of agility, style, and intelligence.

Dicta and wise sayings aspire to timelessness, but witticisms depend on timing. Without delay, the successful wit masters all the complexities of a set of social circumstances and formulates a perfectly apropos response that illuminates them. A surprising challenge seems to allow for no good response, but the wit instantly finds one. Lord Sandwich at the Beef Steak Club told liberal politician John Wilkes he would die either of a pox or on the gallows. "'My Lord,' replied Wilkes instantaneously, 'that will depend on whether I embrace your mistress or your principles.'"[7] Asked by a vicar what he would like his sermon to be about, the duke of Wellington immediately answered, "About ten minutes."[8] To a lady who told the painter James Whistler that "this landscape reminds me of your work," Whistler promptly responded, "Yes, madam, nature is creeping up."[9]

Instantly, instantaneously, without missing a beat, promptly: these words constantly recur in anecdotes about great witty responses. Like rescues in an adventure story, witticisms occur in the nick of time. It would not do to describe how someone insulted Dorothy Parker and, after scratching her head and pausing a while, Dorothy tried out a few replies until at last she found a good one. Diderot referred to the witty answers that occur to one a bit too late as "staircase wit."[10]

Speed matters not only in itself but also as a sign of effortlessness. The cleverness we so admire must seem to come naturally, without strain, as readily as shifting one's weight. Wit demands what Baldesar Castiglione called *sprezzatura* (nonchalance) and *disinvoltura* (ease). Successful wit is a sample of that "true art" that, as Castiglione explains, "does not seem to be art; nor must one be more careful of anything than of concealing it, because if it is discovered, this robs a man of all credit."[11] Anyone who has read Tolstoy's *Youth* knows that this was the sort of talent he both admired and despised.

For the wit, the value of values, if not the only value, is *cleverness*. Cleverness finds its home in the salon, and so witticisms transform any locale into a sort of salon. Since nothing could be less like a salon than the deathbed or the gallows, some of the most famous witticisms occur there as if to say, "By sheer power of mind I can make any occasion, even this, the occasion for cleverness." Told on his deathbed, "It must be hard," the British actor Edmund Gwynn allegedly replied, "It is. But not as hard as farce."[12]

For the wit, mental agility is all. Others may believe in God, principles, the afterlife, saintliness, or good and evil, but the wit recognizes all these objects of reverence as comforting delusions. As Oscar Wilde remarked, "There is no sin except stupidity."[13] Sometimes he added bad taste; thus his supposed last words were, "Either this wallpaper goes, or I do."[14] Is it clear why Tolstoy, a moralist obsessed with death, should have regarded witticisms as unspeakably shallow?

War and Peace opens with a salon scene, where guests compete to amuse each other with empty wit and well-bred insolence. Prince Andrei easily bests them while barely concealing his utter contempt for their shallowness. He seems to recall this and similar scenes when, as he dies, he dreams of a salon where he "continues to talk, astonishing them all with shallow witticisms" (IV, 1, xvi, 1175/984).

Wit: Bilibin and Speransky

At first, Andrei's search for an alternative to the world of wit leads him to war. Sent on a mission to the Austrian emperor, Andrei stays with Bilibin, a diplomat of immense verbal skill, social insight, and, above all, wit.

> Bilibin enjoyed conversation as he did work, only when it could be exquisitely witty. In society he was continually watching for an opportunity to say something remarkable, and took part in a conversation only when he found this possible. His conversation was always sprinkled with original, witty, polished phrases of general interest. These locutions, prepared in his inner laboratory, were of a transmissible nature, as if designed to be easily remembered and carried from drawing room to drawing room. [...] And, indeed, Bilibin's *mots*, circulating through the salons of Vienna, often had an influence on so-called important matters. (I, 2, x, 197–98/154)

In the references to Bilibin's premeditation—his "inner laboratory"—and to the "so-called important matters" that Bilibin's witticisms influence, we sense Tolstoy's scorn for this kind of intelligence. Nevertheless, Tolstoy acknowledges wit as a kind of intelligence and leaves no doubt about Bilibin's mental agility. Bilibin displays undeniable cleverness as he easily dispels the fog of self-justifications blinding others.

In so doing, he exemplifies a philosophy that we have come to call postmodern. For Bilibin, nothing is true except from some point of view that is disputable from other points of view. All perspectives seem equally convincing to those naive enough to believe them and equally absurd to those who regard them from outside. Thus, in the course of a sentence, Bilibin can switch from French to Russian to Germans speaking French, and from the speech of generals to the language of propagandists and diplomats, as he orchestrates a dialogue of perspectives. Each way of speaking, along with the assumptions on which it depends, mocks and is mocked by all the others.

Here is the philosophy of wit as Tolstoy understands it: nothing matters except the cleverness to rise above all languages and perspectives with exquisitely polished phrases uttered at just the right moment. Andrei, who still believes in heroism, respects Bilibin but returns from the salons to the endangered army. He still hopes to be what Bilibin can only pronounce with scorn, a hero. Kutuzov understands without being told the cynicism to which Andrei has been exposed and, in place of a serious debriefing, he questions

Andrei "with delicate irony [...] about the details of his interview with the [Austrian] Emperor, about the comments he had heard at court concerning the Krems engagement, and about certain ladies of their acquaintance" (I, 2, xiii, 214/169).

Disappointed in Napoleon, Andrei finds a substitute in Speransky. Speransky values nothing more than intellect, and his conversation consists almost entirely of witty remarks at the expense of more conservative or less thoughtful people. "Speransky told how at the Council that morning a deaf statesman, when asked his opinion, replied that he thought so too" (II, 3, xviii, 562/464).

In Speransky's circle, Andrei comes to appreciate how wit works by flattery and an implicit division of people into the clever and the dull. It seduces the right people

> with that subtle form of flattery that goes hand in hand with self-conceit, and consists in a tacit assumption that one's companion is the only man besides oneself capable of understanding all the folly of the rest of the world, and the wisdom and profundity of one's own ideas. [...] [Speransky spoke] with an expression that seemed to say, "*We*, you and I, understand what *they* are and who *we* are." (II, 3, vi, 523/431)

It does not take Andrei long to see Speransky as Kutuzov would. Arriving at one of Speransky's dinners, Andrei overhears the statesman's "precise" laugh—"a laugh such as one hears on the stage" (II, 3, xviii, 561/464). To Andrei, the dinnertime conversation now seems "to consist of the content of a joke book" (II, 3, xviii, 561). The gaiety of Speransky's inner circle "seemed forced and mirthless to Prince Andrei," and Speransky's "incessant laughter had a false ring that grated on him [....] There was nothing wrong or out of place in what they said: it was witty and might even have been amusing, but it lacked something that is the salt of mirth, something they were not even aware existed" (II, 3, xviii, 562/465). The salt of mirth depends on deeply shared feeling or experience. It is entirely possible to be humorous without genuine mirth.

For Andrei, as for Tolstoy, the world always contains more mysteries than we could ever discern, let alone solve. If there is one attitude that is unwarranted, it is smug self-confidence in one's mental superiority. That is just the attitude Tolstoy despised in progressives and intellectuals. "It was plain that it would never occur to Speransky, as it did so naturally to Prince Andrei, that it is after all impossible to express all one thinks; nor had it ever occurred to him to doubt whether all he thought and believed might not be utter nonsense" (II, 3, vi, 524/432).

Two Kinds of Aphorisms

Each of the genres mocked in *War and Peace* expresses pride in the human mind: for its capacity to summon the will to fight (the heroic pronouncement), for its discovery of the simple laws behind the apparent complexity of things (the dictum), and for its power to master artfully social circumstance (wit). The first and third exalt verbal mastery, the second and third intelligence.

Along with the narrator and author, the wise characters in *War and Peace* recognize words as a snare and intelligence as extremely limited in the face of the world's mysteries and complexities. Tolstoy's book develops the wisdom of another genre, which for the sake of convenience I will call the aphorism.[15]

Aphorisms regard the world as beyond words and as ultimately unknowable. "The way that can be spoken of / Is not the constant way," writes Lao Tzu. "The name that can be named / Is not the constant name [....] Mystery upon mystery / The gateway of the manifold secrets."[16] In *War and Peace* Kutuzov exemplifies such wisdom and can be seen as a sort of Taoist sage on horseback.

Tolstoy also loved the aphorisms of Pascal, the great mathematician and scientist who came to regard life's most important questions as beyond the grasp of reason. "The heart has its reasons, which reason knows nothing of" (*Le Coeur a ses raisons que la raison ne connait point*).[17] "To ridicule philosophy is to philosophize truly" (*Se moquer de la philosophie, c'est vraiment philosopher*).[18] No less famously, Pascal continually evoked the mystery of lonely selfhood, of consciousness trapped in a body that must die, and of a mind that can know others but must die alone. His famous line, "We shall all die alone" (*On mourra seul*),[19] probably shaped Tolstoy's masterpiece of mortality, "The Death of Ivan Ilych," and perhaps the dying of Prince Andrei.[20]

Aphorisms treat human attempts at knowledge not as worthless but as doomed to incompleteness. Each step takes us further, but the path ahead is infinite. Answers lead to more and more questions. That is the sense of Heraclitus's famous line "The Lord whose oracle is at Delphi neither speaks nor conceals, but gives a sign."[21] Apollo, the lord at Delphi, responds to a question not with an answer but with a sign, which must itself be deciphered. Asked for an interpretation, the oracle replies with something else to interpret. One question begets another, sign points to sign, and mystery gives rise to mystery.

Some aphorists regard the world as unknowable because it is fundamentally mysterious. The best we can hope for is "learned ignorance." Others attribute unknowability to the sheer complexity of things. George Eliot's aphorisms fall into this category. Tolstoy's most brilliant disciple, Ludwig Wittgenstein, produced both kinds: aphorisms of mystery in the famous conclusion to his *Tractatus Logico-Philosophicus* and aphorisms of complexity in the *Philosophical Investigations*.

Both kinds appear in *War and Peace*, although aphorisms of complexity tend to predominate. Taken together, the two kinds of aphorisms express the book's central philosophy. Sometimes the author voices the aphorism, and sometimes it is given to a character.

We have already encountered one aphorism of mystery: when the wounded Andrei, in the presence of Napoleon, thinks of "the unimportance of life, which no one could understand, and the still greater unimportance of death, the meaning of which no living person could understand and express." The "infinite heavens" that appear to Andrei at Austerlitz symbolize this view of the world. In much the same way, Pierre sees stars fading into infinity when he wonders how it is possible that he can contemplate the universe and yet be locked in a shed. He encounters Pascal's mystery of embodied consciousness.

When experience teaches Andrei that there can be no science of war because ineluctable contingency reigns, he voices aphorisms of complexity: "What science can there be in a matter in which, as in every practical matter, nothing can be determined and everything depends on innumerable conditions, the significance of which becomes manifest at a particular moment, and no one can tell when that moment will come?" (III, 1, xi, 775/643). Before Borodino Pierre presumes that a skilled commander can foresee all contingencies, but Andrei dismisses this view as sheer nonsense. "What are we facing tomorrow? A hundred million diverse chances, which will be decided on the instant by whether we run or they run, whether this man or that man is killed" (III, 2, xxv, 930/773).

Pierre discovers the infinite variety of human minds and souls, which exceeds all attempts to generalize beyond a certain point. When he delivers his speech to the Freemasons, Pierre grasps that even those who agree with him do not accept his point exactly as he does. "At this meeting Pierre for the first time was struck by the endless variety of men's minds, which prevents a truth from ever appearing the same to any two persons" (II, 3, vii, 528/436). By the end of the novel, this insight becomes the basis of Pierre's special wisdom and his ability to appreciate each person's "legitimate individuality" (IV, 4, xiii, 1323/1107).

Tolstoy himself formulates aphorisms in his trademark absolute language. Typically, he tells us what is *not* the case. The world and human emotions are never simple, clear, or pure: "But pure and absolute sorrow is as impossible as pure and absolute joy" (IV, 4, i, 1286/1076). In the epilogue, Tolstoy explains that if, as historians vainly hope, laws of history could be discovered, the meaning of human action would disappear. "If we concede that human life can be governed by reason, the possibility of life is destroyed" (Epilogue, 1, i, 1354/1131).

War and Peace orchestrates a symposium of the various short forms Tolstoy knew so well. It identifies the highest wisdom as aphoristic. Just as *The Importance of Being Earnest* can be described as a witticism expanded to a drama, *War and Peace* may be described as the longest aphorism in the world.

6

The Great Man
in *War and Peace*

———

JEFF LOVE

What is a great man? This central question in *War and Peace* folds into a venerable Socratic one: How should I live?[1] The former is perhaps merely the foremost public manifestation of the latter. For Tolstoy it seems that this public manifestation becomes clearest in the event of war—that is to say, in the presence of the possibility of imminent, violent death. It is a cliché to assert that the possibility of imminent, violent death is clarifying, but, like many such clichés, this one points to an inconvenient reality. What I mean is that war, by placing us face to face with the naked possibility of our own annihilation, shows us who we are as vessels of our own death, a harsh truth we may prefer to hide from ourselves. The ways in which we hide this elemental truth from ourselves form crucial motifs in *War and Peace* and provide us with the clearest insight into the notion of the great man.

Accordingly, I should like to nest my investigation of the great man within the context of the notion of deception and, in particular, of self-deception as opening up a useful point of view onto what the novel seems to consider great in the great man. My initial focal point is the brilliant description of Prince Andrei Bolkonsky at the battle of Austerlitz. I proceed from that description to a discussion of Napoleon and Kutuzov and finally to Pierre Bezukhov, Andrei's friend and foil in the novel, a distinctively Tolstoyan Sancho Panza. I conclude by hazarding a Tolstoyan definition of greatness as an ancient response to a modern problem, an intriguing turn on the wheel of tragedy and comedy proper to the Western poetic tradition.

My approach in this chapter is somewhat unusual. Tolstoy's concern with the great man in *War and Peace*, which plays a prominent role in the novel's historical essays, has typically been considered a polemical one, oriented to refutation of the so-called great-man view of history. That view, decisively shaped by responses to Napoleon himself, asserts that history is the product of exceptional human beings who determine the course of events in the same way that artists—or indeed, the divinity—shape their creations. This romantic view prospered in the first half of the nineteenth century and offers a ready justification for autocratic exercises of power, suggesting a fascinating and largely underappreciated political dimension to Tolstoy's novel.[2]

Prince Andrei and the Napoleon Myth

Prince Andrei Bolkonsky's experience of the infinite at Austerlitz, a seductive contradiction in terms, marks the high point of a major narrative and ideological sequence in the early part of *War and Peace*. This sequence sets out the Napoleon myth as refracted through Andrei's own fervent adherence to—and sudden awakening from—that myth, an awakening thrust upon him by failure and the ensuing proximity to death. This failure is worth examining in detail; it determines Andrei's subsequent narrative trajectory and brings to light a basic figure in the novel that repeats itself in a series of different contexts. Let me set out the salient points.

The Andrei whom we meet in the first pages of the novel is very much under the spell of Napoleon. He recognizes in Napoleon an avatar of those great conquerors of antiquity, Alexander and Caesar. But Andrei's admiration is of a distinctively modern sort, for it is not so much Napoleon's art as his science—his ostensibly superior knowledge, his "calculative" genius—that attracts Andrei: here *tekhnē* takes precedence over *poiēsis*. By this I mean that he shows himself to be an adherent of the modern belief in the power of mathematical physics to give us a complete picture of nature, one that should allow us to impose our will on nature in a way that the ancients might have imagined but never dared to realize.[3] On the eve of Schöngraben, for example, Andrei tries to work out a plan of battle. His approach is oriented to calculation of future movements "on a grand scale," an approach whose hidden affinity with modern mathematical physics will be exposed pitilessly in the descriptions of various German-speaking generals, culminating in that of General Pfühl at Drissa, as well as in the so-called essays, culminating in the second part of the epilogue.

The battle itself puts this approach in question, much to Andrei's dismay; it runs its course as a largely arrhythmic concatenation of events in which a wholly unexpected element, the incorrectly deployed artillery unit under the supple, spontaneous command of Captain Tushin, saves the day for the

Russians. "Concatenation"—literally, "chaining together"—may be still too strong a term for what happens in the battle, since the individual scenes fit poorly with each other, an effect sustained by Tolstoy's brilliantly disjointed narrative technique. This rather poor fit undermines the notion of battle as reflecting any kind of chaining together, whether causal or otherwise. The battle shows no pattern or predictability of outcome. In this respect, the fact that Andrei coolly considers a plan of engagement on the eve of the battle while the soldiers near him discuss the one great reality that may lie in store for them, death, hangs over the ensuing chaos of the battle with stinging irony.

If one cannot ascertain any laws of the battlefield, then what can a science of war be but a repository of illusion, a particularly pernicious one since it purports to assign perdurable form to violence, which undermines all form? Put in other terms, military science asks that form describe its own dissolution, a caustically ironic task that cannot possibly be carried out because of the contradiction at its heart.[4]

Yet Andrei refuses to accept what he sees at Schöngraben. To accept this experience would force an out-and-out confrontation with his image of Napoleon and thus of human grandeur itself. Making matters worse in this regard is the behavior of an important Russian commander, Prince Bagration, during the battle. Bagration presents to Andrei an unmistakable counterimage of the grand military leader. Andrei notices how Bagration does not direct the action of the battle but merely pretends to do so and through this pretense gives his soldiers a confidence they would not (and perhaps should not) otherwise have. To put this more bluntly, Prince Bagration resembles an actor who knows how to play his role well.[5] He is a man without illusions who creates a circumstantially effective illusion, and in this respect he is perhaps wiser than Napoleon.

Andrei remains essentially unconvinced of such a radical thesis—until Austerlitz. There he seeks to take hold of his destiny, to enact his Toulon just as Napoleon had done, and he fails miserably, if not yet fatally: history repeats itself as farce. Here is a snippet from this famous sequence, one of the greatest in world literature. Andrei lies wounded on the Pratzen heights. Supine, he looks up at the sky.

> But he did not see anything. There was nothing over him now except the sky—the lofty sky, not clear, but still immeasurably lofty, with gray clouds slowly creeping across it. "How quiet, calm, and solemn, not at all like when I was running," thought Prince Andrei, "not like when we were running, shouting, and fighting; not at all like when the Frenchman and the artillerist, with angry and frightened faces, were pulling at the swab—it's quite different the way the clouds creep across this lofty, infinite sky. How is it I haven't seen

Napoleon: an exalted destroyer. Paul Delaroche, *Napoleon at Fontainebleau* (1845, oil on canvas). The Royal Collection © 2011 Her Majesty Queen Elizabeth II.

this sky before? And how happy I am that I've finally come to know it. Yes! Everything is empty, everything is a deception, except the infinite sky. There is nothing, nothing except that. But there is not even that, there is nothing except silence, tranquility. And thank God!" (I, 3, xvii, 281)

Here is the great contrast between the fury of war and the overwhelming silence of a certain kind of peace, the bustle of action, necessarily finite, and its correlate, the immeasurable and infinite—in the language of Plato, the "really real" (*to ontōs on*).[6] This contrast turns more acidic when Napoleon spots Andrei lying on the battlefield and exclaims, "Voilà, une belle mort" (291).

Andrei barely perceives his former hero, whose voice, we are told, sounds like the buzzing of a carrion-loving insect—a fly.

Of course, the comparison is not subtle: set off against the infinite lofty sky is the wretchedly finite, carrion-loving Napoleon, stripped of the might conferred upon him by credulous followers and his own intransigent vanity. One has to think back to the description of Caesar in book VII of Lucan's *Pharsalia* to find similar malice regarding one of those exalted destroyers for whom, in the words of Gibbon, "military glory will ever be the vice."[7] But the key point here is that Andrei sees against the infinite emptiness of that sky the farce that had seemed so powerful, so immediate, so grand before.

The experience of emptiness or, indeed, of infinity in its elusiveness is one of illumination, to be sure, and it haunts Andrei for the rest of the novel: he fails to find any way of reconciling the lofty, infinite sky with the muddled finite paths of the world. This failure is a fundamental, constitutional figure that winds its way through the entire novel and leaves a trace in its title as well. As we shall see, the argument about the unpredictability of battles—and thus the impossibility of directing them—will turn on arguments based on the impossibility of imposing order on the infinity of possibilities that arise in them.

Indeed, it is well to emphasize that Andrei's quest and failure are but one signal variant of this basic figure in the novel, a figure that traces two radically opposed attitudes to the possibility of reconciling the infinite and the finite.

Reconciling the Infinite and Finite

This figure is dynamically embodied: two of the novel's most important characters give it flesh-and-blood form. On the one side stands Napoleon, the epitome of the modern will to mastery over all impediments to human power, the impetus of the finite being to overcome finitude, to wrestle with fate and win.[8] On the other stands Kutuzov, whose bumbling exterior conceals a subtle reticence: Kutuzov simply dismisses out of hand the elaborate science of war the Austrians employ against Napoleon. Indeed, on the eve of the battle of Austerlitz, at the council of war, Kutuzov famously falls asleep in front of all the key commanders (notably, Bagration is absent). Kutuzov claims, perhaps not without a hint of irony, that there is nothing more important than a good night's sleep before a battle. Is Kutuzov a fool? What does he know that allows him to ignore so blithely that very science of war the Austrian generals hold so dear?

Kutuzov seems to know what Andrei learns with distress at the battle of Schöngraben and with calm at Austerlitz: no one can possibly direct a battle and, by extension, master the course of events. Schöngraben of course seems to be a chaos. Moreover, Andrei observes that commands are often not given, and when they are, they are not carried out as they should be, or they result in wholly unexpected consequences. Zherkov, for example, is quite unable to convey an order to a senior general during the battle because his "strength failed him" when it came to placing himself in danger (I, 2, xix, 186). Hence the notion that one man or group of men can direct a battle seems problematic, to say the least, both in theory and in practice. Even with a sophisticated apprehension of the possibilities inherent in a battle, these are so multiple and contingent at any given moment that no method of prediction could grasp them all. They are indeed in this broader sense infinite or inexhaustible, as the narrator repeatedly affirms in the essays.

In these essays, two basic arguments emerge, both originating in Aristotle[9] and both dealing fundamentally with the problem of the infinite. (1) The causes of an event form an infinite chain or an infinite series of chains or an infinite series of infinite chains; there is consequently no way to isolate and identify any one chain as determinative of all the others, a finitizing move. (2) Motion is continuous, that is, a continuum, and thus potentially infinitely divisible—one would need something like a calculus of history to ascertain laws for events, and even then this calculus would be based on an extraordinarily fragile and complicated premise: that nature and history are one, and thus there is nothing distinctively human that creates history, a wonderfully ironic premise in a text like *War and Peace*. Even if we accepted that premise, the infinite as such would still be problematic, for no matter how precise one purports to be, there must always be room for more. The point of infinite divisibility is that there is an infinite excess over any given result, something the modern doctrine of limits merely mutes.

Kutuzov appreciates this infinite excess. Put in different terms, he appreciates the elusive quality of the kind of synoptic knowledge one must possess to decide with assuredness. Hence he takes a much more reticent approach to battle. He seems to react intuitively without stopping to think. As Andrei notes before the novel's greatest battle, Borodino,

> How and why it happened, Prince Andrei could in no way have explained, but after this meeting with Kutuzov, he went back to his regiment relieved with regard to the general course of things and with regard to the man to whom it had been entrusted. The more he saw the absence of anything personal in this old man, in whom there seemed to remain only the habit of passions, and, instead of intelligence (which groups events and draws conclusions), only the ability to calmly contemplate the course of events, the more calmed he felt over everything being as it had to be. "He won't have anything of his own. He won't invent, won't undertake anything," thought Prince Andrei, "but he'll

Kutuzov: an elusive master. R. M. Volkov, *Portrait of General Field Marshal M. I. Golenishchev-Kutuzov* (1813). Reproduced with permission, the Borodino Panorama Museum, Moscow.

listen to everything, remember everything, put everything in its place, won't hinder anything useful or allow anything harmful. He understands that there is something stronger and more significant than his will—the inevitable course of events—and he's able to see them, able to understand their significance, and, in view of that significance, is able to renounce participating in those events, renounce his personal will, and direct it elsewhere." (III, 2, xvi, 744–45)

This is a fascinating statement of a vision of mastery radically different from that associated with Napoleon and modern military science in the novel. Napoleon seeks to impose his will on events by grasping the patterns they follow such that will and intellect may become one, a combination which for our tradition is associated with the deity: the deity has only to think something to create it, to make it happen.[10] Kutuzov's approach assumes that this harmony is not possible for us: he suppresses will, a discipline that serves as the necessary precondition of obtaining an unclouded apprehension of events that cannot be reduced to strategy, formula, or method.[11]

What is at issue here? Two different views of theory and practice, one modern, one ancient, one distinctively Western, one having limited (but surprising) affinities with the East. The ancient view holds that theory and practice are incommensurable, whereas the modern view folds theory into practice—theory becomes *la méthode*—that is, theory becomes a kind of practice or practice a kind of theory; it makes no difference.[12] To put it in the terms I have just employed, for the ancients, intellect and will cannot be reconciled; no matter how extraordinary, every great conqueror comes to naught, his compensatory glory lying in the poets' willingness to make him immortal. For the moderns, however, this reconciliation becomes the highest end and the end of history. The force of modern striving is to dry up the very wellspring of ancient thought at its most tragic.[13]

Let me put this in a less cluttered way. To repeat: the basic argument against the notion of the great man is that no one man may shape events according to his will. This kind of freedom is impossible; it is an illusion that the tragic hero of the ancients embraces, if only in a monitory way and not as a matter of will but of *hubris,* the impetus to violence understood as a challenge to the hegemony of the gods.[14] The modern hero seeks to be free and free of tragedy. But, like his predecessor, he ends in ruin or defeat. Unlike his predecessor—and this is one of the potent innovations of *War and Peace*—this defeat is due not to the mysterious maleficence of the gods but rather to the inexhaustible openness of events, that they take place in a continuity that cannot be grasped in itself: no matter how much we learn, there is always more. It follows that we cannot be sure at any time that what we know is assuredly what we think it to be.

Thus we are never free to order things as we like; we do not possess our freedom. We take place in a whole whose identity is elusive: to declare that we can know that whole and what we are as belonging to that whole is necessarily reductive, a way of seeing unable to attain to the synoptic vision one would need to have, that disinterested view from nowhere which belongs to no one, the eye which sees itself. Hence to imagine that we can direct that whole according to our wishes or interests becomes utterly absurd, a sort of desperate defensive stance in the face of so much uncertainty and indeterminacy.

This problem plays itself out in the novel in a very complicated way. While Kutuzov's victory over Napoleon clearly indicates a preference for the kind of thoroughgoing cognitive humility I have associated with the ancients, Andrei appears unable to accept that preference. He perceives cognitive humility as a kind of punishment, and his death is a sharp comment on the intolerable oppression meted out by that punishment. Even Pierre, who takes quite a different path and appears to be so much more comfortable with humility, ends up in a very ambiguous position at the end of the novel.

The questions that these two central narrative paths raise seem unavoidable: Can one live in the face of such fundamental uncertainty? Can it be desirable to live in that way? Pierre's case is emblematic of the difficulty attendant on answering the latter question in the affirmative.

Pierre and Platon Karataev's "Teaching"

Pierre, like Andrei, is a follower of Napoleon at the beginning of the novel. At its end, having turned away from Napoleon in the great Russian war, he returns to Napoleon's revolutionary legacy as he plans to overthrow the Russian monarchy. How strange it is that Pierre comes full circle at the end of the text! Strange because Pierre, in contrast to Andrei, seems to have accepted the lessons of Kutuzov without rancor.

Pierre receives these lessons through his encounter with Platon Karataev at a crucial juncture in his life when, like Andrei at Austerlitz, he has faced his own annihilation, this time by firing squad. After this famous execution scene, brilliantly analyzed by Robert Louis Jackson, Pierre meets Karataev, who seems to embody a variant of the subtle reticence that characterizes Kutuzov.[15] Yet Karataev is a far more outrageous wisdom figure, a sort of Russian Zhuangzi, and Pierre is liberated from the notion of personal authority, the power of his own will, that he had sought to exploit in his domestic life as a great landowner in a way analogous to that of Andrei in the military sphere.

What does Platon Karataev teach? Strictly speaking, he does not teach at all. He merely is: he moves swiftly and easily, speaks in proverbs, freely contradicting himself, and shows not the slightest hint of reflective ratiocination. In this latter sense, he is beyond theory and practice; neither counts for him since both presuppose a separation between intellect and will that he does not and could not recognize. It is thus hardly surprising that Karataev is frequently described as "round" (IV, 1, xiii, 972); this is a transparent echo of an important Western image of the round as whole, integral.[16] Karataev misses nothing, needs nothing, wants nothing: he is as he is. There is no striving, no problem of will, no need for reasons to be. Karataev is disinterest incarnate, to engage a paradoxical expression.

If Kutuzov retains certain qualities of ancient reticence that would not be out of place in the pages of Thucydides' great history, Karataev connects them with Eastern traditions, our own and even those of the far Orient.[17] And this has a certain irony since his first name alludes to the most influential and important philosopher of the West. What Plato wrought is turned toward something akin to Eastern tradition, to an overcoming of the bustle and aimlessness of aims in life, to the elusiveness and mystery of being. As Zhuangzi, the sagacious Chinese, notes,

> Great understanding is broad and unhurried; little understanding is cramped and busy. Great words are clear and limited; little words are shrill and quarrelsome. In sleep, men's spirits go visiting; in waking hours, their bodies hustle. With everything they meet they become entangled. Day after day they use their minds in strife, sometimes grandiose, sometimes sly, sometimes petty. Their little fears are mean and trembly; their great fears are stunned and overwhelming. They bound like an arrow or a crossbow pellet, certain that they are the arbiters of right and wrong. They cling to their position as though they had sworn before the gods, sure that they are holding on to victory. They fade like fall and winter—such is the way they dwindle day by day. They drown in what they do—you cannot make them turn back. They grow dark, as though scaled with seals—such are the excesses of their old age. And when their minds draw near to death, nothing can restore them to the light.[18]

This remarkable passage describes well what Platon Karataev, as the foremost antipode to Napoleon, tends to represent in the novel, a manner of living that turns away from the everyday, the pressures of being among things that we identify with our interest or stake in them.[19]

Now one may well ask, what does this have to do with the great man?

It seems quite obvious that the Napoleonic figure is not great in any other sense than that he is greatly burdened by illusions, chief among which is that he has the power to determine events, a power that belongs ultimately to an absent god. It seems equally obvious that the great man in the novel is one resembling Kutuzov and Karataev as well as the frontline officer, Tushin, who saved the day at Schöngraben.

Wisdom resides with the latter, mere *technē* with the former. The Napoleonic general is a creature of *technē*, the technological approach to the world, and modern warfare is impossible without this adherence to technology. Kutuzov's impurity as a wisdom figure in the novel, an impurity marked in many subtle ways (his love of dreadful French novels supplying but one example), is clarified by Tushin and Karataev. But Karataev is not really a man of war, and this raises the other question: Can a man of war be a great man? Is Kutuzov not a hero?

Sage and Soldier?

These questions are central to the novel. For if the novel promotes the sage—and a very ancient or, indeed, non-Western version of the sage—as the great man, then there seems little room left over for Kutuzov or the soldier hero, no matter how the latter appears.

We should be careful to look at this issue from two perspectives. There is the exoteric praise of Kutuzov as the prudent general, which so many critics of the novel seem to have accepted without question, and of Tushin as the exemplary soldier.[20] But the prudence of Kutuzov and the spontaneity of Tushin owe most to the sage as presented in the novel; hence the notion of wisdom that seems to prevail in the novel is available, at best *in nuce,* in Kutuzov and Tushin. Kutuzov's involvement in the war, his placement as a general, is indeed corrupting: he is no Karataev, and one has to assume that his wisdom is not as pure as Andrei may have it—and it is safe to say that Andrei is not the purest witness—or that Kutuzov plays his role as an actor, as do so many other aged courtiers in the novel, just more wisely, more obliquely. Tushin is another matter: it seems clear that his heroism resides in his not succumbing to illusions of heroism—he is in this sense much closer to Karataev than Kutuzov: he is perhaps a most unmilitary military man.[21]

The novel thus seems to praise a model of behavior for the military man that is also put in question in its deeper recesses. On the one hand, one can construe the novel as a great patriotic effusion, not merely a history but also an explanation of Napoleon's military defeat in Russia that extols Russian virtues, a massive praise of one's own having few rivals.[22] On the other hand, the novel also seems to praise a much more radical position, that of the sage who subtracts himself from the ridiculous and short-sighted bustle of men who will do anything to promote or defend their own.

This discrepancy reveals one of the novel's more striking characteristics. If the life of the sage is truly the best life, the life that properly pertains to the great man, this greatness is hard if not impossible to achieve—or where it is achievable, as it apparently is in the case of Karataev, this is a life that maximally subtracts itself from the demands of the everyday.

But one must be careful to define the nature of this subtraction appropriately because the sage is at once deeply in and outside everyday life. Karataev's ability to deal with many different circumstances comes from his full commitment to none: he treats the demands of every situation with equanimity, equal attachment and nonattachment. Karataev's life is a life without partial commitments or ties. In this sense it is a sovereign life—and a most estranged and estranging one. He is, as noted above, disinterest incarnate, with all ironies intact.

No other character in the novel quite achieves this sovereignty. Even Pierre, who seems closest to Karataev, cannot imitate his life and falls, as if inevitably, back into the sorts of myths of will that the novel has attempted to debunk. Hence the hint that Karataev represents a wisdom hardly practicable in the world or, better, hardly tolerable in the world brings out the novel's ambiguous skepticism. For if striving to be wise in the manner of Karataev may be a high goal, it might also be both an impractical and undesirable one.

War and Peace presents a very mixed wisdom. The notion of the great man as one capable of determining the way things should be through planning is carefully exposed as an illusion, all the more attractive since it flatters human hopes in the greatest battle of our lives. To the extent one is stuck in this battle one is on the path of illusion: one is deceiving oneself. And who is not somehow stuck in this battle? Yet the novel also seems to suggest that illusion may well be preferable to wisdom. For if wisdom is not wholly impractical, it is also undesirable. As the extirpation of desire (or will), wisdom seems to bring us to an impossible indifference to things, a peculiarly quiescent state, that may seem to be merely another mode of dying or an end of history.

This mixed wisdom expresses a maxim of Greek tragedy as it has come down to us in mutilated form: that it is best not to have been born.[23] To advocate not having been born as the highest reward for us in the misery of life is to cherish being in its most negative aspect, as the excess or residue that haunts all things, having no definite character in and of itself. To be a great man is not to be—a delightful bit of Greek irony. To be a great man is in fact to welcome death as release from the sickness that is life. Perhaps there is a true warrior's credo in these words.

But there is another Greek way of looking at the novel's mixed wisdom that is perhaps more comprehensive, more sensitive to the book's competing currents. On the one hand, there is immensely heroic and tragic pathos in the desire for mastery, a desire that can arise only from terrible discontent with the way of finite life, its vulnerability to the vicissitudes of fate. On the other hand, there is an intensely comic aspect to that tragic pathos, to our inability to accept what seems inevitable. What is most serious for us is also in some way comical and stupid: what is it to spend one's entire life "outwitting" an ineluctable, inscrutable fate?

In *War and Peace* the wise man inhabits the point of indifference: he expresses the tragic and comic facets of the same striving and moves beyond them in doing so, a position that seems almost uninhabitable, beyond understanding and desire, intellect and will. And this is a position that appears in the novel most strikingly at the death of Andrei and in the life of Platon Karataev. Andrei discovers "divine love," which makes no differentiations finally, at the end and when it is too late; Karataev loves all and none. In either case, the point of indifference is a kind of affirmation and emptying out of interest, of all the myriad desires and needs that ennoble and enslave us, that give birth to the grandeur of tragic daring and the quiescence of comic reserve.

The one who is wise is neither great nor a man. Indeed, he is neither god nor man, neither master nor slave, neither active nor passive. He retains negatively the binary logic of either-or, of excluded middle, in setting that logic aside as undecidable.[24]

He is elusively.

In the words of Zhuangzi, "Be empty, that is all. The Perfect Man uses his mind like a mirror—going after nothing, welcoming nothing, responding but not storing. Therefore he can win out over things and not hurt himself."[25]

7

War and Peace from the Military Point of View

DONNA TUSSING ORWIN

Leo Tolstoy had firsthand experience of war and the military. He served almost five years in the army (January 1852 to November 1856), and during the Crimean War he even considered a military career. He chose literature over the army after the success of his first Sevastopol sketch, but his interest in the military and war did not disappear. When *War and Peace* began to appear a decade later, he was especially eager to hear the responses of military readers. These readers had a special stake in the novel, of course. They reacted to it not only as experts but also as objects of Tolstoy's analysis who questioned whether the author had done them justice.

With one partial exception, the four reviews that I consider in this chapter appeared after the publication of volume 4 of the novel, which described the campaign of 1812 from its beginning to the Battle of Borodino. The authors knew there was more to come—as it turned out, two more volumes—but they could no longer contain their excitement and irritation. The most prestigious Russian military journal, *Military Review* (*Voennyi sbornik*), published three reviews of the novel in 1868 alone and justified this by the extraordinary interest the novel had provoked.[1] Authors rushed to be the first to get their opinions in print. Interest was so high that the first review, by Captain N. A. Lachinov in the military newspaper *Russian Veteran* (*Russkii invalid*), was republished in slightly expanded form in *Military Review,* and A. N. Vitmer's two-part review came out as a book in 1869.[2] The most exhaustive review, that by M. I. Dragomirov, was republished in part in his selected works in 1881 and then in full in 1895 as a pamphlet.[3] This chapter, focusing primarily though not exclusively on Dragomirov,

explores the complex dynamics behind the reactions of military readers to *War and Peace.*

Just the Facts, Please

All the military reviewers criticized Tolstoy's performance as a historian. As
professional historians, Lieutenant-General M. I. Bogdanovich (1805–82)
and Colonel A. N. Vitmer (1839–1916) led the way here.[4] Bogdanovich
had won a Demidov Prize from the Imperial Academy of Sciences for the
first volume of his three-volume *History of the 1812 War of the Fatherland.*[5]
Determined to rely only on what he regarded as scientifically certifiable
sources, and in this sense a positivist, he had endured bitter criticism from
veterans for ignoring their memoirs as unreliable.[6] These attacks left him
undaunted, however, and he produced many more volumes on the period,
all in the same spirit. Bogdanovich brought this positivist spirit to his review. He compares *War and Peace* unfavorably to the novels of Walter Scott,
which, while fictional, are always true to the time and place of their settings.
Tolstoy, by contrast, distorts truth, not for any novelistic purpose, but "just
from the desire to say something new that had previously evaded historians."[7]
Although Bogdanovich agrees with Tolstoy that the official French and
Russian historians of 1812, Adolphe Thiers (1797–1877) and Lieutenant-
General A. I. Mikhailovskii-Danilevskii (1789–1848), were partisans of their
respective sides, he prefers even them to Tolstoy, whose "artistic feeling"
(*khudozhestvennoe chut'e*) is based on nothing objective at all, and who con-
jures up whatever facts are needed to support his opinions. If Tolstoy had
studied official documents of the period, he would never have so denigrated
the decisive importance of great men like Napoleon and Alexander I.[8]

Unbeknownst to Bogdanovich, Tolstoy had in fact consulted the former's
History of the 1812 War of the Fatherland. His annotated copy remains in the
Iasnaia Poliana Library. One of his marginalia, next to a letter from General
Bagration to Alexander's close adviser A. Arakcheev, provides a tiny but spe-
cific example of how Tolstoy interacted with the historical texts he consulted.

> On April 7, from his halting place [*scratched out,* Smolensk] at Mikhailovka on
> the Smolensk road, Bagration wrote the following. [There follows the printed
> text of the letter, and then Tolstoy's commentary resumes.] He wrote Arakcheev,
> but he knew that his letter would be read by the Sovereign, and therefore as
> much as he was capable of it he thought through every single word.[9]

The second sentence from this marginal comment appears in the text of the
novel exactly as Tolstoy wrote it here.[10] In this note we observe Tolstoy using

his artistic feeling to fill unavoidable gaps in documentary materials to which Bogdanovich as a positivist historian had limited himself. Of course there is no way to verify that Bagration acted from the motivation that Tolstoy ascribes to him, but in this case Tolstoy's artistic feeling served him well. The novelist appeals to the reader's sense of what he or she might have done in a similar situation, and we readily accept his psychological insight. In this way a particular incident of only antiquarian interest in the war is injected with a general (psychological and political) significance that preserves it for posterity.

If Bogdanovich's attitude toward Tolstoy's historical methodology was one of Olympian disdain, Vitmer objected to his theory of history and the errors of fact that supported it. He exposed sloppy dating in the novel and errors concerning the sizes of armies.[11] In one place, Vitmer shows how misdating distorts not only a sequencing of events but a proper understanding of their outcome. Had the dates been properly reported, the events would have demonstrated the historical importance of leaders, rather than, as Tolstoy would have it, their impotence.[12] The second installment of Vitmer's review detects one historical or tactical inaccuracy after another in Tolstoy's depiction of the Battle of Borodino.[13]

Sling enough mud and some of it should stick. However much a naive lover of literature may rely on novels to learn history, no one who has read the reviews of Bogdanovich and Vitmer, let alone modern histories of the period, can take *War and Peace* as unvarnished historical truth. Yet the accumulated power of so many errors detected did not even at the time (and does not now) destroy the power of the novel, not even for its military readers. Dragomirov explains why a soldier reader might well prefer the novel to history.

> The difference between his [Tolstoy's] descriptions of battles and historical descriptions is the same as that between a landscape and a topographical map: the first provides less, provides it from one point of view, but provides it in a way that is more accessible to the eye and heart of a human being. The second provides every object in the location from a great number of sides, it provides the locality from a distance of tens of versts, but it provides these within an artificial scheme that in its appearance has nothing in common with the objects being described; and therefore in it everything is dead, lifeless, even for the trained eye.[14]

It could have been predicted that even its military readers would forgive the novel its historical inaccuracies. *War and Peace* gave them a satisfying account of their own individual experience of war that the tools of history (maps, official documents, and chronologies) did not capture.

Fatalism in History

Tolstoy's contemporary military reviewers objected to the theory of history laid out in essay form in the opening chapters of the newly published two parts of the novel. These chapters bluntly assert that history is determined by "Providence," and that political and historical leaders are "history's slaves." This shocking declaration, if it did not spoil *War and Peace* for military readers, needed to be neutralized in some way or read out of the novel altogether. All of them performed this last, extreme operation by dividing the book into art and thought and claiming to accept the former and reject the latter.

It was not that the typical military reader thought of himself as an Alexander or a Napoleon. The readers were well positioned to appreciate Tolstoy's attacks on vainglory, and they did. Dragomirov calls braggadocio "the exploitation of war." He notes how at Bagration's command post after the Battle of Schöngraben, the adjutant Zherkov "has not yet fully managed to pull on his—before and after—battle mask." Although Zherkov already lies "boldly and gaily" about his supposed presence at an attack, he still looks around nervously to see if anyone might know he was not actually there; within a short while, he will gain confidence and will dine out on his lie ever after.[15] For Dragomirov, however, Tolstoy's text is a chiaroscuro in which hypocrisy is the tribute that vice pays to virtue. The darkness of a Zherkov or a selfish glory seeker like Dolokhov makes the too often unsung heroism of such frontline officers as Timokhin and Tushin shine all the more brightly.[16]

The problem for Tolstoy's military readers was the status accorded even genuine heroism within the context of his thought. If history was determined, this would affect frontline officers and soldiers as well as generals and staff officers at headquarters. Tushin and Timokhin, too, would be nothing but unwitting tools of history, and their behavior would be counted no more meaningful than that of Zherkov. According to Tolstoy's narrator, people as historical actors belong to "the unconscious, swarm-like life of mankind," which is not free (III, 1, i, 605). All "men of action," from the highest to the lowest, are "involuntary instruments of history" (III, 2, i, 682). Lachinov expresses the problem this raises for military readers very well. From the perspective of historical fatalism, public service is emptied of all meaning, and participants in an event are nothing but "labels" (*iarlyki*) dangling from it, but without any influence on it.[17] No soldier with any sense of self-worth could operate under such a supposition.

Ironically, all of Tolstoy's military reviewers were themselves historical determinists, for either religious or philosophical reasons, but they implicitly distinguished determinism of this sort from his "completely pure historical fatalism."[18] None of the military readers denied the existence of some grand design in life, which as soldiers they were defending. As a Hegelian, Vitmer jumps through hoops in his review to prove that while progress is preordained, in specific circumstances on the battlefield individuals determine how and when it will occur.[19] In his discussion of the second epilogue, Dragomirov criticizes Tolstoy's historical determinism as irrelevant in assessing the actions of practical men while not rejecting its validity outright. Modern historians, unlike the ancients, understand that ultimate truths are inaccessible to the human mind and therefore that they should "not waste time on cogitations about what they can never comprehend."[20]

Readers today may not like Tolstoy's historical determinism, partly for the same reasons as the military men, but as impartial judges they cannot wish away the conflict that he raises between the necessity of freedom in human psychology and of determinism in history. In the second epilogue he explains that if historical actors were free agents, then "the whole of history would be a series of incoherent accidents" (Epilogue 2, viii, 1200). Therefore, as Jeff Love puts it, "freedom challenges system, in this case a system of laws, and, ultimately, unity as well."[21] As Love goes on to show, in the second epilogue Tolstoy also argues for the existence of individual freedom.[22] Elsewhere in the novel, however, he reserves this for "personal life, which is the more free the more abstract its interests" (III, 1, i, 605).

Perhaps in response to the complaints of his military readers about his "historical fatalism," Tolstoy developed his argument about freedom and its limits further in the fictional narrative in what was volume 5 in the first edition of the novel (III, 1, and IV, 1–2), which came out in February 1869.[23] Platon Karataev, the freest man on the battlefield, was conjured into existence only then.[24] The fictional narrative demonstrates that freedom exists only *outside history*, in personal choices that individuals make whether on the battlefield or elsewhere. Once made, these decisions become part of the larger tapestry of history over which no individual has control. Napoleon, for instance, is enslaved to history because of his lust for power. A simple soldier participates in the swarm life of history when he kills an enemy soldier to save his own life. These acts are "free" of outside interference in that they come from internal impulses, while their consequences enter into what Tolstoy regarded as a "system" (to use Jeff Love's word) regulated by the laws of history. Of course, impulses and passions, though they may be internal, are not free. There are degrees of freedom within the individual, who is freer the more he acts independently of passions and according to the voice of moral reason. Platon Karataev chooses to stay outside history and free to the extent possible, and this is the lesson that he teaches Pierre Bezukhov. Even Platon's presence on the battlefield is his own choice, because he volunteered to be conscripted in place of a brother with children.

The idea of a separation between personal freedom and determined history that is preserved most robustly in folk wisdom as expressed by Platon Karataev may reflect the influence of the German thinker W. H. Riehl or the Slavophile K. S. Aksakov.[25] This protopopulism would not have mollified Tolstoy's military readers because it restricts freedom to private life, thereby denying that wars and those who plan them are anything more than tools of history.

Reasoning in War

Tolstoy emphasizes the emotional side of war, and this appealed to military readers like Lachinov and Dragomirov. Dragomirov agreed with Tolstoy that will is more important in battle than thought. "War and war alone summons that terrible and combined effort of all the spiritual sides of a man, in particular *will*, that reveals the full measure of his power and that is summoned up by no other kind of activity."[26] According to Dragomirov in an article published in 1861, there are dueling and equally natural psychological principles at play on the battlefield: a natural instinct for self-preservation and, on the other hand, a sense of duty based on honor as well as an "inexplicable, but totally human" and voluntary impulse to confront danger head-on and defeat it. This last impulse, felt by "very elite" (*izbranneishie*) soldiers only, "illuminates like blinding lightning mysteries of the human soul accessible to analysis and study in no other arena than the battlefield."[27] In an 1873 summary of these same principles, Dragomirov says that the mind serves "self-preservation" while the "self-sacrifice" that produces great deeds on the battlefield is the province of will only, which he defines as "moral energy."[28] Both principles are necessary in warfare: the first produces caution and the second, daring. Although it is necessary to protect the soldier and his comrades to the extent possible, thought, when it trumps will, can be the enemy of fortitude on the battlefield; therefore, will and daring must predominate in the successful army. Dragomirov may have learned these lessons in part from Tolstoy. As a cadet at the Nikolaevskii Military Academy he followed the Crimean War closely,[29] and he most certainly would have read Tolstoy's Sevastopol sketches. At the very least we can say that Dragomirov drew conclusions from the war similar to Tolstoy's as expressed in the sketches and then in *War and Peace*. In the first sketch, "Sevastopol in December (1855)," which so impressed the new tsar Alexander II that he had it translated into French and published in Brussels even before it came out in Russian, a soldier in the hospital after his lower leg has been amputated explains how to endure in war: "The most important thing, your honor, is *not to think a lot:* if you don't think, you're okay." The third sketch ("Sevastopol in August") uses the metaphor of fire to represent the soldier's will to fight, and this is then developed extensively in *War and Peace*. Dragomirov advocated tirelessly over his whole career for the importance of what Russians call the "moral" side of war and what Tolstoy in both the Sevastopol sketches and *War and Peace* depicted as the "spirit" (*dukh*) of the army. According to both Tolstoy and Dragomirov, this spirit determines the outcome of battles.

Despite his agreement with Tolstoy about the importance of will in war, Dragomirov believed that Tolstoy slighted the role of reason there. He did not agree that the decision to go to war was always and only illogical.[30] Nor did he agree with Tolstoy that war was opposed to human nature.[31] In other words, unlike Tolstoy in *War and Peace*, he did not reserve the ultimate reasons for war for God or Providence alone. This acceptance of war as a normal and even reasonable part of human life meant that Dragomirov, unlike Tolstoy, did not have to present warriors in combat as governed by feeling alone. Precisely because of the dominance of feeling on the battlefield, Dragomirov stressed the need for leadership in combat and for intensive training so as to minimize a soldier's sense of panic and helplessness there. Habits inculcated through training were needed to counter chaos inside and outside the soldier, and at the same time all soldiers needed to be prepared to respond to the unexpected. They must *understand* their role and be prepared to take the initiative where necessary. This required the kind of tactical thinking that Dragomirov defended in Nikolai Rostov.

Discussing Rostov's successful attack on French dragoons (III, 1, xv), Dragomirov argues that Rostov could not have been acting spontaneously, without thought or planning.

> Let's take, for instance, the attack by Rostov. It begins, "Rostov, with his keen hunter's eye, was one of the first to catch sight of the blue French dragoons chasing our uhlans." Then they come closer and closer; Rostov "felt by instinct that if the hussars were to strike the dragoons now, they would not be able to resist; but if they were going to strike, it had to be right away, that minute, otherwise it would be too late." The same Rostov very concisely explains his thought to his comrade and right afterwards they throw themselves into the attack. It all seems completely clear that Rostov's decision to attack comes not out of the blue, though quickly: the process of physical and mental work necessary for every attack is completely clear here. All the moments of this work—to see, to reckon, to decide, to carry through—are in plain view. But the author needs to revert to his beloved theme that everything happens by itself—and the next thing you know he transitions from the thoughts he has just uttered to "Rostov himself didn't know how and why he had done this. He had done all this the way he did things on the hunt, without thinking, without weighing pros and cons!" [...] At the beginning of the second part of volume four, the author goes even further: he reveals that Rostov had galloped into attack just because, allegedly, he couldn't resist the desire to gallop across an open field![32]

The episode discussed here is an example in the novel where, according to Dragomirov, the fictional narration contradicts the narrator's commentary on it. The fact that Rostov responds quickly and draws on skills and experience gained in hunting as well as war does not mean that he hasn't thought before he acts.

Dragomirov then refutes the narrator's contention that Kutuzov, listening skeptically "from the point of view of his age and experience" to Denisov's proposals for partisan warfare, would have "despised" his "intelligence" and "knowledge" (III, 2, xv, 742). What Tolstoy calls Kutuzov's experience is in reality nothing but conclusions that the mind draws from facts that, without the action of the mind, mean nothing in themselves; in other words, so-called experience is the very same combination of intelligence and knowledge that Kutuzov supposedly scorned in Denisov.[33] Quoting extensively from Prince Andrei's assessment of Kutuzov in the same episode (III, 2, xvi, 745), Dragomirov ridicules Andrei's impression of the commander in chief as a passive receptacle of mystical wisdom. Kutuzov embraces what is useful in the information that he receives and rejects what he considers harmful; this, Dragomirov says, is exactly the conduct recommended by Napoleon for a general in the midst of battle.[34]

Dragomirov also faults Tolstoy for either ignoring or misrepresenting the aspects of war that most require thought by commanders. He agrees with Tolstoy that a general's role in combat is limited to directing forces mostly beyond his control (as Kutuzov tries to do at Borodino) and to keeping up morale (Bagration at Schöngraben and Kutuzov at Borodino). But there are two phases in battle: "[I]n the first, the troops are fully under the influence of the senior commanders; in the second they themselves do their job to the extent that they are capable of it."[35] The battle plan that a general issues *before* combat can be decisive for success or failure. In mocking Napoleon's orders before Borodino because none are actually implemented, Tolstoy shows that he does not understand their function. They serve not as a rigid blueprint for action but as goals that the competent general knows cannot be fully realized unless the battle is over quickly, before it has time to develop beyond its first stage.[36] Once combat begins, the general must show the kind of flexibility that Tolstoy praises in Kutuzov and, for that matter, in Nikolai Rostov. At the same time, however, the orders of the general both before and during a battle provide guidelines to officers about how to proceed on their own.[37] Even during combat a general can often act to affect morale on the field. Dragomirov drives this last point home with an extended illustration from *War and Peace* itself, when Kutuzov in the Battle of Borodino aggressively rejects the pessimistic assessment of General Barclay de Tolly reported by Barclay's adjutant, Colonel Wolzogen, and even orders an attack for the next day (III, 2, xxxv, 806–8). Having quoted this passage, Dragomirov remarks scathingly that "the author himself is often his own best critic: as soon as he starts to depict events, he gives the lie to his own theoretical cogitations."[38]

Tolstoy and his spokesman, Andrei, also fail to appreciate the importance of logistics both before the battle and during it. Listening to the debates at the council of Drissa before the battle of Borodino, Andrei sneers to himself at those who define a military "genius" as the person who "manages to order a timely delivery of biscuits and tells this one to go right and that one to go left" (III, 1, xi, 644). To this Dragomirov retorts that logistics are vital: a commander must *foresee* where to send rations and troops.[39] And while, as we have seen, Dragomirov agrees with Tolstoy about the importance of morale in war, he makes the point that high morale depends on many factors, most definitely including the leader's ability to motivate troops,[40] but also on everything from weaponry, battle position, troop strength, "and even such factors as excessive cold or heat."[41] In other words, logistics affects morale.

In the first two installments of his essay, Dragomirov applauds Tolstoy's art for its accuracy and moral usefulness, while complaining that his mistaken philosophy and psychology lead him to distort a reality that he often portrays accurately in his narrative.[42] He even argues that Tolstoy's very strengths as a poet account for his mistakes as a theorist. The poet almost always speaks from a single, highly focused, and concentrated point of view, while the theorist must take all points of view into account.[43] Tolstoy, however, tends to generalize from a single perspective that, while valid in itself, does not capture the whole. In the third installment of his essay, where he discusses the final volumes of the novel, Dragomirov turns more critical simply because in these volumes Tolstoy's narrator insists in long digressions on those very generalizations to which Dragomirov and his fellow military readers so objected in volume 4. Sounding now like the sour Colonel Vitmer, Dragomirov presents Tolstoy's authorial commentator as a combination of ignorance and hubris. To explain war, this commentator relies upon a highly abstract and old-fashioned mathematical model much more systematizing than the modern military theory developed by Dragomirov and his comrades at the Nikolaevskii Military Academy.[44] The commentator proposes a straw-man version of contemporary theory, tears it to shreds, and then recommends the flexibility already built into that theory.[45] Meanwhile, the stupider Napoleon seems, the smarter the authorial commentator looks at his expense.[46]

These various thrusts by Dragomirov hit home. Tolstoy presents war as a kind of irrational, spontaneous human activity (though with a metaphysical dimension and rationale inaccessible to humankind). In keeping with this narrow definition of war, he systematically underestimates the role of mind in it, and in his review Dragomirov calls him to account for this. In his narrative commentary, Tolstoy represents officers like Nikolai Rostov as less rational in their actions than is plausible. As Dragomirov points out, the fictional narrative contradicts the narrator in this respect. The fact that Rostov does not stop and think before he acts does not mean that he does not act rationally; on the contrary, as Dragomirov tries to argue, Rostov employs the tools of practical reason as he calculates his advantage and rushes to seize it. Tolstoy's narrator denies even such figures as Kutuzov and Bagration the power of thought when, as Dragomirov interprets their actions, they draw on a lifetime's reflection on experience as they direct men in battle. Tolstoy does not say one word about the importance of training for officers and men. He depicts them before and after battle, foraging and sitting around campfires but never learning their craft. They just show up on the battlefield and perform.[47] He does caricature contemporary military theory, and he does denigrate Napoleon as a man, a thinker, and a soldier while adopting many of his thoughts about war.[48]

Because Tolstoy denies the rationality of behavior in war so completely, the narrator is the only source of reason left standing. His soldiers are said to act from pure impulse, whatever that might mean, and the narrator does the thinking for them. This is one explanation for the structure of the part of the novel on Borodino (III, 2), which begins and ends with lengthy digressions by the narrator. The digressions stand outside life, especially public life that includes war and politics, and give it a rational structure that it otherwise lacks. The author commentator provides the reasons behind a vision of life that is all flow, no self-determination. For the same reason, the novel ends with a long digression.

To Dragomirov and the other military reviewers of *War and Peace,* this explanation of their world was unacceptable. All of them were writers or scholars, and all were involved in military education. Dragomirov was a scholar soldier devoted to issues of training and tactics who aspired to be a fighting soldier and subsequently became a hero of the Russo-Turkish War (1877–78). If officers did not think or rationally maneuver on the battlefield, if wars made no rational sense from the human perspective—if they just happened by themselves and armies coalesced, fought, and died without any guidance from leaders—then Dragomirov and the others were simply wasting their time. Dragomirov counters Tolstoy's pernicious pronouncements about the uselessness of strategy and tactics by using Tolstoy's own fictional narrative to illustrate their existence and importance.

Reasoning about War

When it came to thinking about the psychology of war, Tolstoy was willing to analyze more deeply than were his military readers. Although Dragomirov himself studied and wrote about the psychology of war, he had the practical man's hostility to psychological analysis when it undermined his mission.

This helps explain his hearty dislike of Prince Andrei, to whom he devotes many pages of his review.[49]

Prince Andrei epitomizes the desire for glory of a young warrior, and Dragomirov should respect him for that reason. Dragomirov certainly admires Nikolai Rostov and, as we have seen, even defends Rostov from what he regards as Tolstoy's insufficient appreciation of this character. Yet Andrei in Dragomirov's reading is a vain young man who despises society but has no qualms about pulling strings to land himself a prestigious position on Kutuzov's staff in 1805. He has had no actual combat experience (and, like all of Tolstoy's soldiers, no evidence of field training). If he were serious about soldiering, he would have submitted himself to "the hard, laborious time as an apprentice that alone produces a master," but instead he expects his superiors to take him seriously as a tactician.[50] (This would have especially annoyed Dragomirov, who was already a specialist in tactics and eventually published the standard tactical manual for the imperial army.) Surveying the field from Tushin's battery before the Battle of Schöngraben, Andrei sketches a plan for the disposition of troops (I, 2, xvi, 177). He has been educated in the Prussian style of war in favor at the time, and so he is surprised at the actual course of the battle and the performance of officers like Bagration and Tushin. In interesting speculations about Andrei's education, Dragomirov brands him as a Russian Pfühl, "Pfühl as a dilettante."[51]

When Andrei's initial theories and plans are contradicted by facts on the ground, he does not adjust them, preferring to conclude that all detailed war plans are nonsense. Having attended the war council at Drissa, Andrei decides—and Dragomirov concurs—that the generals all bring different suggestions to the meeting, and so no conclusion about how to proceed could have been derived from it. But, Dragomirov explains, such councils are not intended to produce a plan and are used by a commander in chief to test and fine-tune a previously determined strategy. He says that Andrei ought not to be shocked by the practical reality that there can be many ways to achieve the same aim.[52] Andrei eventually decides that only the commander of a fighting unit can have any influence over a battle, and he requests to be made such a commander. In Dragomirov's interpretation, Andrei acts solely from vanity. Rather than admit his errors and learn from others, he prefers to throw in the towel altogether. "He nurses his boo-boo [*On lechit svoe bobo*]."[53]

Dragomirov's Andrei is "a little great man, capable of everything, but unfit for anything." He is too doctrinaire and stubborn to succeed as a military commander. Dragomirov recognizes Andrei's personal nobility, but asserts that he lacks the charisma, flexibility, and organizational skills of a true leader. Tolstoy seems to concede this last fact, Dragomirov snidely proposes, by never depicting Andrei as he directs reforms at Bogucharovo or as an active staff officer under Kutuzov at Bucharest. This happens only off stage.[54]

Dragomirov's criticisms of Andrei are all justified, and yet they leave out what should be most attractive to him in this character. He says nothing about Andrei's heroism at Austerlitz or, for that matter, his heroism at Borodino, when he is fatally wounded while modeling spirit and courage to his men. We know that as a character Andrei started out exactly as Dragomirov presents him: as a callow glory seeker who would get his comeuppance and die at Austerlitz. Tolstoy then realized that he was giving this character and his defining passion short shrift.[55] Tolstoy does not reject the desire for glory itself as low or inauthentic; it is the natural expression of the love of honor that distinguishes the true aristocrat and officer. In its purest incarnation in Prince Andrei, it is one stage in the quest of the mortal and imperfect self for validation beyond natural but ever-subjective animal self-love. The night before the Battle of Austerlitz, in one of the most beautiful passages in the novel, Andrei defines his own love of glory as the need to rule others through their unconditional love of him; this love will be won through great deeds like those performed by his hero Napoleon (I, 3, xii, 264–65). After his near death at Austerlitz, he seems to set aside his Napoleonic ambitions, and yet his love for glory, while at times silent, does not disappear from his soul. At Borodino he does not fall to the ground with his troops when he sees the spinning explosive shell because he "remembered that he was being looked at" (III, 2, xxxvi, 811). It is no accident that his appearance in the final lines of the fictional narrative is warlike and glorious in the imagination of his adolescent son Nikolenka. As his father before Austerlitz had imagined "mysterious power and glory hovering over me here in this mist," Nikolenka dreams of glory leading him and his Uncle Pierre at the head of a vast army. It is clear from the scene at Bald Hills preceding this last one that Nikolenka and Pierre will be involved in the Decembrist movement in some way and that his Uncle Nikolai Rostov will oppose them. Love of glory will play an important role in this historical drama even if only by seducing men into public life. Whether or not men control history and its wars, there would be no war without the desire for glory. There is irony but no sarcasm in this tender closing portrait of Nikolenka Bolkonsky. Himself a product of the Russian military aristocracy, the creator of *War and Peace* understood and sympathized with the need of such aristocratic natures to prove themselves worthy members of their clans and station on the battlefield. The near certainty of wounds or death was a small price to pay for glory, and indeed Iurii Lotman has maintained that gentry members of the generation of 1812 both courted death and often were ashamed to have survived the war.[56]

In *War and Peace* Tolstoy creates a gallery of characters who collectively represent the military type with its virtues, vices, and contradictions. Through Prince Andrei he explores glory and its origins in the human psyche. It is striking that although Dragomirov praises Tolstoy for creating so many types, he fails to sufficiently distinguish Andrei from the usual run of glory seekers in the novel. As we have seen above, he criticizes the vainglory of a Zherkov, yet nowhere in his review does he analyze the dynamics of true love of glory as manifested in its purest form in Andrei. Surely this is the passion that motivates supreme acts of courage on the battlefield that Dragomirov himself praises so highly and tries to encourage through training. Perhaps he prefers to think of such acts as more selfless than they appear from the point of view of psychological analysis. Perhaps he does not want to hear that lovers of glory care so much what others think of them. That psychological explanation would seem to undercut the magnificence of glorious deeds by making heroes less godlike and more human in their neediness.

Tolstoy may not have agreed with the attacks on him by his military readers, but he took them seriously and even tried to anticipate them. In an article, "A Few Words Apropos of the Book *War and Peace*," that came out at the same time as the original volume 4, he defends his depiction of historical figures and events as all true to historical sources that he claims to be able to produce on demand. At the end of the article, he also summarizes his philosophy of history and war as laid out in the opening chapters of the two parts of volume 4.[57]

Emphasizing chaos in war and the moral will of human beings to counter that chaos to the extent possible, Tolstoy goes too far in *War and Peace* when he claims that this is all war is for the human beings who wage it. His military readers rightly call him to account for his neglect of the importance of tactics, strategy, and training in warfare, and Dragomirov rightly points out contradictions between the implications of the fictional narrative and the pronouncements of the narrator in this regard. Yet Tolstoy's military readers have their blind spots too. Their own love of glory and sense of honor are emotional pillars on which their soldierly resolve and even patriotism rest, and they are averse to probing these too deeply. Like the humble soldier amputee in the hospital in "Sevastopol in December," they can't afford to think too much. So Tolstoy, who so admired Russian soldiers and was one himself, parts company with them in this respect. As a novelist, he is free to perform the abstract work of philosophizing about the psychological bases of soldiering in a way that his military readers do not. He does this partly through the digressions of his didactic narrator but also, and more effectively, through character development. His military readers, however rational their analysis in other respects, do not do justice to his greatness here.

8

Tolstoy and Clausewitz

The Duel as a Microcosm of War

——

RICK MCPEAK

On the eve of Borodino, Prince Andrei Bolkonsky bears the onerous burden of battle command. He is understandably anxious about leading troops in combat for the first time. He also frets about the fate of his sister, Princess Marya, and his son, Nikolenka. Grieving the recent death of his father, Prince Andrei seriously contemplates his own mortality as well. His thoughts of loss lead to regrets about the failure of his loving relationship with Countess Natasha Rostov. In this gloomy mood, he produces one of the most troubling passages in *War and Peace*: "One thing I would do if I had the power [...] I would take no prisoners. What are prisoners? It's chivalry" (III, 2, xxv, 774). With these ominous words, Prince Andrei contends that there is no room for "chivalry" on the battlefield. He thus advocates the prosecution of violence devoid of virtue. Specifically, he verbally condones the annihilation of all his foes, even those who are unable or unwilling to continue the fight. Perhaps we could attribute Andrei's cynicism, at least in part, to the extenuating circumstances recounted above. We can rest assured, however, that his creator will intervene before this young warrior turns his threatening words into actual atrocities on the battlefield.

As practitioners and philosophers of war, Leo Tolstoy (1828–1910) and Carl von Clausewitz (1780–1831) grappled with the nature and employment of violence.[1] Both Tolstoy and Clausewitz attempted to explain war to their uninitiated readers by employing the metaphor of the duel, a violent tradition connected to chivalry.[2] The Russian cultural historian Iurii Lotman defines the duel as "two-person armed conflict conducted in accordance with defined rules and designed to restore honor."[3] Some similarities between the duel and war are readily apparent. Duels, whose violent and destructive potentials are circumscribed, and wars, whose levels of violence and destruction vary widely, aim to right perceived wrongs. Duelists issue challenges, and communities declare wars. Diplomats, representing communities, are obliged to promote or restore peace, and seconds, representing duelists, are duty bound to promote reconciliation. Wars and duels allegedly conform to explicit or implicit rules of conduct such as laws of war and codes of honor. All duels and wars eventually end, often with unexpected results.

Clausewitz and Tolstoy, whose readers were familiar with the conventions of dueling, described war as an extension of the duel. In his seminal treatise, *On War,* Clausewitz depicts war as a "duel on a larger scale."[4] Just prior to the battle of Austerlitz, Prince Andrei establishes a comparable connection between individual and collective violence. The brash young hussar, Count Nikolai Rostov, disparages the reputations of all staff officers, including, by inference, the influential adjutant Prince Andrei Bolkonsky. Andrei deflects this potential insult, which would normally oblige him to challenge Nikolai to a duel, by observing, "One of these days we'll all [line and staff officers alike] take part in a big, more serious duel" (I, 3, vii, 243). For Prince Bolkonsky, then, the impending collective battle resembles individual combat expanded in space and time with graver consequences.

Tolstoy first considered the war-duel connection in the opening chapter of "Sevastopol in May." Beginning with an obverse perspective from the war as duel-on-a-larger-scale paradigm, he portrays the duel as war-on-a-smaller-scale model. His narrator explores a minimalist version of armed conflict as an unlikely substitute for war. This admittedly "strange" alternative to extensive ongoing carnage entails diminishing the opposing forces from hundreds of thousands to just two, with one on each side. According to Tolstoy's narrator, this reduction in force pits an individual soldier defending Sevastopol in a "duel" against an individual soldier attacking the city.

Throughout the narrative of *War and Peace,* Tolstoy maintains the association between war and the duel. Pierre challenges Dolokhov to a duel during a feast to honor Prince Bagration's leadership on the battlefield. The drafts of *War and Peace* indicate that Tolstoy originally intended to make this linkage between Austerlitz and the duel even more explicit. In 1805 and 1806, Moscow is abuzz with news of the stunning military defeat at Austerlitz. A nobleman of Count Bezukhov's stature, despite—or perhaps because of—his lack of military experience, is naturally intrigued by the campaign against Napoleon. In the drafts, an obsessed Pierre pores over campaign maps and reflects on strategy. During the banquet for Bagration, Count Bezukhov opines that the military leaders erred because they did not attack Napoleon with the forces on their own right flank. The seasoned warrior, Dolokhov, replies to the naïf, Pierre, with dripping sarcasm, "Yes, you would have been good at war fighting."[5] Tolstoy originally intended these scornful words about Pierre's lack of martial experience to initiate Dolokhov's goading, which would lead eventually to their duel. On the morning of the duel, Pierre returns to his maps and imagines a scenario in which Napoleon is defeated at Austerlitz.[6] Thus the large-scale battle of Austerlitz constitutes the milieu for small-scale combat between Pierre and Dolokhov. Although these scenes did not survive editing, they underscore the author's continuing conceptual correlation between war and the duel.

In the final text of the novel, after Prince Anatole Kuragin besmirches the honor of Countess Natasha Rostov, Prince Andrei contemplates fighting him. Back in uniform and bound for Turkey, Andrei seeks a way to avenge Kuragin's villainy without causing any more damage to Natasha's reputation.

> Prince Andrei considered it improper to write to Kuragin and challenge him. Without giving him a new pretext for a duel, Prince Andrei considered that a challenge on his part would compromise Countess Rostov, and therefore he sought to meet Kuragin personally with the intention of finding a new pretext for a duel. (III, 1, vii, 627)

Kuragin leaves Turkey soon after Bolkonsky arrives, so Prince Andrei misses this opportunity to confront his foe.

In this chapter, I analyze Clausewitz's and Tolstoy's use of the duel to explain their own philosophies of war as expressed in the former's masterwork *On War* and the latter's *War and Peace*. I then show how Tolstoy employs fictional duels, virtual and actual, to challenge the rationality and morality of individual and, by inference, collective combat (II, 1, iv–vi, 311–320).[7] I also explore points of convergence and divergence between Tolstoy's and Clausewitz's ideas about unrestricted and constrained violence.[8]

Readers who take Clausewitz's and Tolstoy's musings about the relationship between duels and wars at face value could conclude that a battle involving two armies, each with one hundred thousand troops for a total of two hundred thousand combatants, simply consists of one hundred thousand separate duels (number of combatants divided by two). In fact, Tolstoy's and Clausewitz's theories indicate that warfare is exponentially more complicated than a mere compilation of one-on-one engagements. For Tolstoy, combat entails an ever more complex and unpredictable interaction of freedom and necessity producing a potentially infinite number of contingencies; for Clausewitz, it involves the intricate interaction of violence, chance, and reason.[9]

On War begins with a treatise about the enduring nature of war. Clausewitz acknowledges that the character of individual armed conflicts changes with the passage of time, the qualities of the opponents, the advent of technology, and other variables. He argues, nonetheless, that the nature of war remains constant throughout the ages.[10] Clausewitz portrays war as "an act of force to compel the enemy to do our will" and employs the image of the duel to describe an individual attempt to impose one's own will on an opponent.[11] In Clausewitz's extended duel, every violent and destructive action by friendly troops elicits a forceful response by the enemy. Naturally, according to Clausewitz, this struggle between opposing forces trying to have their way with each other escalates toward maximal violence. Indeed, he contends, there are "no logical limits"[12] to the "primordial violence"[13] unleashed when one community attacks another. Clausewitz first explores ideal war, devoid of strictures on violence, so he can understand and explain the constraints inherent in actual war.

In the realm of absolutes, where Clausewitz formulated his maximalist description of war, armed conflict is imposing a community's will via unconstrained and uninterrupted violence. In the real world where Clausewitz practiced his craft, however, both physical laws and political considerations restrict the application of absolute force. Theoretically, a state's armed force is a material and organic mechanism for killing and destroying everyone and everything in its path. In reality, resistance prevents this machine from operating at maximum capacity. Clausewitz observes that "action in war is like movement in a resistant element."[14] His scientific term for constant resistance, "friction," emphasizes the human factors that preclude peak efficiency on the battlefield. In Clausewitz's framework, friction includes fear, the natural response to danger; fatigue, the inevitable byproduct of physical exertion; and ambiguity, the consequence of risks taken during armed conflict.[15]

In addition to friction, the sum of all nonrational limitations, Clausewitz addresses rational constraints on absolute violence. His most famous maxim, an antithesis to his theses about primordial violence and irrational forces, defines war as "a continuation of political intercourse by other means."[16] Identifying war as a tool for pursuit of national policy, Clausewitz acknowledges the validity of the instrumental approach to the application of violence. Specifically, he contends that national leaders must carefully consider stakes and objectives so they can decide what kind of war, on the scale from absolute to limited, their armed forces will wage. Then, in order to ensure that the instrument of policy, armed conflict, achieves the established political aims, all leaders must ensure that military objectives are consistently subordinated to political ones.[17]

Clausewitz's "paradoxical trinity" is the synthesis of all rational and nonrational forces influencing the prosecution of violent conflict. According to the Prussian theorist, violence, chance, and reason "are like different codes of law, deep-rooted in their subject and yet variable in their relationship to one another."[18] The duel, which combines the potential for escalating violence with the unpredictability of human reactions and the rational constraints of honor codes and rules of etiquette, proves an ideal trope for illustrating this intricate theory of war. Clausewitz thus presents the duel as a microcosm of armed conflict with circumscribed violence on a scope accessible to his readers. Consequently, he invokes the duel primarily for its explanatory power.

Tolstoy probably never read *On War*; nonetheless, his fictional depictions of war and the duel sometimes seem to echo and at other times contradict Clausewitz's theory.[19] For example, early in his literary career, Tolstoy rejected the instrumental approach to war fighting. In the opening rhetorical flourish of "Sevastopol in May," he depicts war as a tragic waste of resources and a costly failure of diplomacy. According to Tolstoy's narrator, when diplomats stop talking, cannons start firing, and people, with all their aspirations and potential, begin to die in droves. Tolstoy, who actually participated in the artillery barrages at Sevastopol, proclaims "the question unresolved by diplomats is even less likely to be resolved by powder and blood."[20] For this young artillery officer, then, war is not an instrument of policy but rather proof positive that diplomacy has failed to prevent conflict. In contradistinction to Clausewitz and other advocates of the instrumental approach, Tolstoy portrays war as an unpromising option of last resort.

In *War and Peace* Tolstoy advances his argument and further contradicts Clausewitz by categorically renouncing the rationality of war. Tolstoy's description of Napoleon's 1812 invasion defines the resulting war as an activity "contrary to human reason and to the whole of human nature" (II, 1, i, 603). Tolstoy thus classifies Napoleon's act of aggression, symbolic of all warfare designed to achieve national objectives, as inhumane and irrational. Tolstoy also enlists Prince Andrei to buttress his case against the instrumentality of war. On the eve of Borodino, Andrei begins his diatribe about the horrors of war by disparaging excessive German reliance on reason:

> Tomorrow these German gentlemen won't win the battle, they'll only muck things up as much as they can, because all there is in a German head is reasoning, which isn't worth a tinker's damn, but in their hearts they haven't got the one thing needed for tomorrow [...] They gave *him* [Napoleon] the whole of Europe and came to teach us! Fine teachers! (III, 2, xxv, 774)

Tolstoy's narrator identifies one of those "fine teachers" as Carl von Clausewitz, the inveterate Prussian who actually served on Kutuzov's staff in 1812.[21] According to Prince Andrei, Clausewitz and his ilk pursue their rational theories and plans but lack the tenacity necessary to defeat Napoleon. The Russian people, on the other hand, possess the requisite resolve, primarily because they are fighting for their own survival. Prince Andrei opines that nations should fight to advance their interests but only when the stakes are "worth going to certain death, as now" (III, 2, xxv, 775). This existential threat, Prince Andrei predicts, will motivate the Russian forces to "fight hardest," "spare themselves least," and ultimately defeat Napoleon's army (III, 2, xxv, 773–74). Consequently, Prince Andrei counters Napoleon's and Clausewitz's rational instrumental approach with an emotional existential approach to war fighting.

In his influential military theory, Clausewitz employs the duel to exemplify his paradoxical trinity. Tolstoy's fictional depictions of duels illustrate his own theory of war and also dispute the rationality and morality of violence in general. The obvious similarities between duels and wars have already been enumerated above. One evident difference, addressed by Tolstoy's narrator in "Sevastopol in May," is the duel's relative economy of scale. In the worst of circumstances, the maximum number of casualties during individual combat is two and the amount of collateral damage minimal. Consequently, in his quixotic musings about a minimally destructive duel as a possible alternative to the maximally destructive Crimean War, Tolstoy's narrator wonders whether the duel might be more "rational" (*logichnee*) and "humane" (*chelovechnee*) than war (PSS 4:19).

The duel is, after all, a violent practice traditionally regulated by and designed to preserve the virtue of honor. In his recent study about this principle, Kwame Anthony Appiah concludes that honor is inexorably linked to respect: "A man of honor must be ready to defend his honor—to risk his life, in fact, to ensure that he gets the respect that is his due."[22] According to the calculus of the duel, when one member of a community fails to show appropriate respect to another, the offended party is obliged to resolve this affront to his honor by challenging the offender to a duel. The code of honor requires the offender to respect the offended party's challenge by issuing a public apology or agreeing to fight. In theory, then, individual combat is violence prosecuted in consonance with a universal principle, human dignity; in reality, however, inherent contradictions undermine the credibility of the duel.

Designed to protect a collective principle, the duel was traditionally practiced only among a select group, the nobility. Appiah argues that rising nation-states consolidated and centralized their power, in part, by forcibly reducing the influence of the nobility. In her definitive work on Russian dueling, Irina Reyfman notes that the tsarist regime promoted order through threats of force against all servants of the tsar, including noblemen.[23] According to Reyfman, the Russian nobility responded to these threats from above and to the widespread and arbitrary violence characteristic of nineteenth-century Russian society by adopting a code of honor (principles) enacted through duels (practice). Paradoxically, the extraordinarily violent Russian duel "served as a strong—although largely symbolic—gesture to counter the state's violence against the individual."[24] In the Russian context, individual combat was "largely symbolic," because the Russian nobility's small-scale acts of violence were designed to regulate the endemic brutality in Russian society. According to Reyfman, the Russian honor code focused on the nobility's reputation and promoted their individual and collective class identity and self-worth. Duels promoted conflict resolution and self-policing by resolving disputes among the nobility about reputation, identity, or dignity.[25]

At Austerlitz, one member of the Russian nobility, Count Nikolai Rostov, impugns the honor of another, Prince Andrei Bolkonsky, who justifiably could have fought the younger officer. Nonetheless, Prince Bolkonsky deliberately and honorably avoids a duel with Count Rostov and resolves a potentially violent confrontation by appealing to their impending cooperative effort against a common enemy.[26] Tolstoy's first prospective duel in *War and Peace*—a fight that could or should have transpired but did not—points to some critical differences between the duel and war.

Opponents in a duel, who generally live in the same "honor world," subscribe to a singular code of honor.[27] Enemies in war emerge from different honor worlds and social strata; therefore, they rarely follow the same conventions of etiquette. Near the end of *War and Peace*, Tolstoy illustrates this point with a concrete connection between war and the duel. Napoleon, whose military prowess was founded on violating the established methods of waging war, nonetheless expected the Russians to play by the rules, especially after the Grand Armée captured Moscow. Tolstoy compares France and Russia to participants in a duel with swords. The French insist on compliance with the rules of etiquette for the sword fight; the Russians, realizing the ultimate stakes of this existential struggle, abandon the sword and pick up a club (Tolstoy's symbol of the Russian folk engaged in a national war).

> [F]rom the moment he [Napoleon] stopped in Moscow, in the correct position of a fencer, and instead of his adversary's sword, saw a club raised over him, he never ceased complaining to Kutuzov and the emperor Alexander that the war was being conducted against all the rules (as if there existed some sort of rules for killing people). (IV, 3, i, 1033)

Tolstoy's sarcastic parenthetical remark refutes the rationality of individual and collective combat. Even if the Russians and French had played by the allegedly nonexistent rules, personal offense, an essential element of the justification for the duel, was often absent on the battlefield.

As a practitioner and philosopher of war, Tolstoy attempted to comprehend and explain a warrior's willingness to attack, and potentially even kill, a foe who had never personally offended that warrior. In the concluding

chapter of "Sevastopol in May," French and Russian troops, who are devoted to killing each other, arrange a truce during which they set aside hostility and celebrate humanity. Their exchange of pleasantries briefly replaces
the exchange of cannon fire. Clearly, there is no genuine personal animos-
ity between these opposing forces, yet they return to their brutal exploits.
Immediately before the Battle of Schöngraben, the banter between Russian
soldiers, including Dolokhov, and their French counterparts culminates in
mutual uproarious laughter. These momentary reprieves fail to convince the
French and Russians at Sevastopol and Schöngraben to behave logically and
"unload their guns, blow up their munitions, and all quickly go back home"
(I, 2, xv, 177).

Count Nikolai Rostov's poignant encounter at Schöngraben reinforces
this line of thought. Galloping toward the French forces, Nikolai intends
to "cut them to pieces" (I, 2, xix, 189). After he is thrown from his horse,
however, he grapples with the similar aims of the approaching troops. "'Can
it be they're running to me? Can it be? And why? To kill me? *Me*, whom
everybody loves so?' He remembered his mother's love for him, his family's, his friends', and the enemy's intention to kill him seemed impossible"
(I, 2, xix, 189). Nikolai, a naive participant in war, assumes that if these un-
identified people could only get to know him, they too would certainly love
him. These fellow humans, whom he has never even met, seemingly have no
discernible motive for depriving Nikolai of life and love.

Tolstoy's second duel, this one implicit, transpires on the eve of Borodino,
when Prince Andrei conflates the personal offense characteristic of the duel
with the impersonal malice typical of war. During his agonizing psychological preparation for the battle, Andrei describes the impact on individuals of
the French threat to Russia's survival. When he overhears Wolzogen and
Clausewitz advocating expansion of the war irrespective of the resulting loss
of civilian property and lives, the Russian regimental commander angrily
retorts, "Yes, *im Raum verlegen* [extend the war in space], *Im* this *Raum*
[in this space] I had a father, and a son, and a sister in Bald Hills. It's all
the same to him" (III, 2, xxv, 774).[28] Prince Andrei puts human faces, including his own, on the potential victims of absolute war prosecuted with
no restrictions on violence. By recasting the French army's invasion as a
personal affront, he blurs a traditional dividing line between war and the
duel. Soon after he catalogs personal offenses perpetrated by the enemy, he
recalls the treachery of Anatole Kuragin. The offenses of both Napoleon's
forces and Kuragin motivate Prince Andrei to seek revenge. In fact, the realization that Anatole remains alive and unharmed agitates Andrei "as if someone had burned him" (III, 2, xxv, 777). His profound sense of personal
offense and renewed desire to fight Kuragin—personal elements related to

dueling—combine to fuel the malevolence he deems requisite to success on the killing fields of Borodino.

The actual duel between Pierre and Dolokhov begins with an unconfirmed personal offense. Pierre receives an anonymous note about Dolokhov's alleged indiscretions with Helene. At the banquet, Dolokhov engages Pierre in a verbal duel, deliberately insulting him and fueling his suspicions, by raising a toast to "the health of beautiful women, Petrusha [a diminutive of Count Bezukhov's first name that would be insulting in this setting], and their lovers" (II, 1, iv, 313). Despite the insult and the implication, Pierre is not convinced of Dolokhov's guilt; nonetheless, in a fit of rage, he challenges the experienced fighter to a duel.[29] Once Pierre finally convinces himself that there was an affair, he blames Helene and exonerates Dolokhov. Pierre then challenges himself by asking, "Why this duel, this murder?" (II, 1, iv, 314). After his second, Nesvitsky, offers a particularly compelling argument for reconciliation, Pierre dismisses his own behavior as "terribly stupid" (II, 1, iv, 314); yet he inexplicably fails to reconcile with Dolokhov.[30] Pierre's irrational and dishonorable behavior conforms to Tolstoy's dynamics laid out in his own theory of history.

According to Tolstoy's ideas, once the challenge is issued, Dolokhov and Pierre become pawns of violence. The same unseen force (*sila*) that, according to Tolstoy, drives opposing forces to fight in war even though they typically have no genuine quarrel with each other impels Pierre to confront Dolokhov. "It was obvious that the affair, having begun so lightly, could no longer be prevented by anything, that it was going on by itself, independent of men's will and would be accomplished" (II, 1, v, 315).[31] Despite Pierre's serious misgivings, he exercises his own freedom by engaging in the duel. Then violence takes on a dangerous life of its own, and the outcome is both uncontrollable and unpredictable.

This fictional duel between Pierre and Dolokhov depicts the influence of Tolstoyan contingency and Clausewitzian friction and fog on individual combat.[32] Mist from the snow significantly reduces visibility. Pierre, who has never fired a weapon, grasps the pistol as if "afraid of killing himself with it" (II, 1, v, 315). He fires aimlessly, is startled by the retort, and, surprising himself and all observers, seriously wounds Dolokhov. As Dolokhov takes aim at Pierre, the violence escalates to the level of two possible casualties. Unexpectedly, the experienced duelist misses the large target presented by Pierre's massive frame. Reduced visibility, blood loss, and sheer luck probably contribute to Pierre's fateful emergence as the victor instead of the victim.

After Pierre wounds his opponent, he immediately regrets his own aggression and attempts to come to Dolokhov's aid. Dolokhov, upon discerning Pierre's intention to provide assistance, commands his opponent to return

The decisive moment in the duel between Pierre and Dolokhov (1953) from Dementii A. Shmarinov's illustrations for *War and Peace*. Reproduced with permission, Tolstoy State Museum, Moscow.

to the barrier so Dolokhov can take his shot. Pierre resists his own better instincts and, in compliance with etiquette, obeys his opponent and stands calmly in the sights of an accomplished duelist. The seconds are convinced that Dolokhov, even under duress, will mortally wound his opponent. To the seasoned warriors observing the duel, this scenario resembles butchery more than bravery.[33] Consequently, Pierre's second, Zaretsky, and even Dolokhov's second, Denisov, try to mitigate the situation, encouraging Pierre to protect himself by turning sideways and covering himself with his pistol (*zakroites'*!). Although this protective measure seems humane, the duel's culture of violence typically proscribes displays of compassion.

According to Clausewitz and Prince Andrei, there is also no room for benevolence in war. Although Clausewitz argues that we should apply only the amount of violence appropriate to achieve political aims, he also claims we must remain deadly serious during the prosecution of that measured violence. "War is such a dangerous business that the mistakes which come from kindness are the very worst."[34] In Clausewitz's rational construct, well-meaning attempts to minimize suffering could unintentionally prolong conflict and thus paradoxically inflict more casualties and destruction than would the application of maximum available combat power to subdue the enemy rapidly.

Contemplating Borodino, Regimental Commander Bolkonsky begins his discourse with a seeming non sequitur: "Take no prisoners [...] That alone would change the whole war and make it less cruel" (III, 2 xxv, 775). How could the mass execution of enemy combatants possibly reduce the brutality of combat? According to Prince Andrei and reminiscent of Clausewitz, war is a lethally grave affair that should be prosecuted without sentimentality. "If there was none of this magnanimity, we'd go to it only when it was worth going to certain death, as now" (III, 2 xxv, 775). Stated differently, communities should not go to war when they simply want to pursue policy objectives but only when their very existence and way of life are at stake. Prince Andrei argues that war is no game, so we should prosecute it solely for existential reasons and abandon the charade of noble behavior. He advocates a maximalist response when a community faces a threat to its way of life, like Napoleon's invasion of Russia. In one of the most cynical passages from *War and Peace*, he describes total war, which, in his opinion, leverages every human vice (e.g., deception, cheating, stealing, cruelty, and murder) to win by capitalizing on death and destruction (III, 2, xxv, 774–76).

After Dolokhov's shot misses, Pierre pronounces his immediate judgment on the duel, which sounds very much like Prince Andrei's characterization of total war: "Stupid...stupid! Death...lies...(II, 1, v, 316)." Pierre declares individual combat irrational, destructive, and deceptive. His duel, which is both illogical and inhumane, does not ameliorate any personal offense or give him any satisfaction. From Tolstoy's perspective, "powder and blood" solve nothing on the battlefield or the dueling field.

Pierre, after reflecting on the duel with Dolokhov, tells Prince Andrei, "The one thing I thank God for is that I didn't kill the man." Andrei, a Tolstoyan seeker near his moral nadir, retorts, "It's even very good to kill a vicious dog"

(II, 2, xi, 383).[35] Once again near bottom just before Borodino, Prince Andrei seriously contemplates a chance to eliminate his own "vicious dog," Anatole Kuragin. Tolstoy employs extraordinary measures to disabuse Andrei of the notion that he will receive any satisfaction from a duel with Kuragin. A well-placed artillery round prevents Prince Andrei from avenging his enemies, Prince Anatole Kuragin and the entire Grand Armée alike. In a repeat of his experience at Austerlitz, serious injury leads to epiphany.[36] After Andrei is wounded at Borodino, he notices Kuragin suffering on a nearby stretcher and empathizes with him just as Pierre had done during his duel with Dolokhov. Andrei weeps and finally grasps the ultimate value of "love for our enemies" (III, 2, xxxvii, 814). This virtue, incompatible with all forms of violence, is Tolstoy's antidote to blood vengeance on the dueling field and atrocities on the battlefield.

Tolstoy's celestial intervention and philosophical objections notwithstanding, powder and blood eventually drive Napoleon from Russian soil and remove the existential threat to Mother Russia. Prince Andrei's exhortation to take the gloves off for Borodino and Tolstoy's endorsement of the "club" of partisan warfare result in a historic victory, which the author unapologetically celebrates. When Kutuzov, who had assured Prince Andrei that the French would eat their own horses, observes his prophecy come true, he praises the assembled Russian warriors for securing a total and immortal victory over the French. Then the venerable Russian commander in chief quips, "While they were strong, we took no pity on ourselves, but now we can pity them. They're also people. Right, lads?" He gives his perplexed followers a moment to process this noble notion and adds, "But, that said, who invited them here? It's their own doing, [expletive deleted] the French" (IV, 4, vi, 1089). The Russian people's unabashed "Hurrah!" indicates they, perhaps more than any philosopher of war, understand the spirit and substance of virtuous violence.

9

The Awful Poetry of War

Tolstoy's Borodino

—◆

DONNA TUSSING ORWIN

The account of the Battle of Borodino in *War and Peace* is Leo Tolstoy's most extensive treatment of a single day's action. At the same time, as A. A. Saburov remarks, it includes very few of the actual events in the battle.[1] What generalizations unify this fragmented narrative and make it so compelling? Although it is a brilliant demonstration of the psychology of war, a celebration of Russian patriotism in a crucial battle, and an illustration of Tolstoy's theories, it also depends for its lasting influence on a literary dimension of the text as yet not sufficiently appreciated by literary critics. In this chapter I first briefly demonstrate how Tolstoy mixes war psychology with his theories of war in his description of the battle, and then I turn to a discussion of the awful poetry of war that permeates and unifies the whole segment.

The Individual Experience of War

The battle is described in volume 3, part 2, chapters 30–39 of the novel, where it is focalized through different participants in it. We view it first of all through the eyes of the two commanding generals, Napoleon and Kutuzov. Although I am aware of the controversy surrounding Tolstoy's representation of these historic figures, I treat them here purely as imaginary characters to be judged by the psychological and, to a lesser extent, historical criteria to which we submit all of Tolstoy's fiction.[2] Napoleon experiences his first major defeat even though, as Tolstoy's narrator says, he does everything he has done before and even does it better (III, 2, xxxiv, 803; PSS 11:244–45). At Austerlitz Napoleon had stood on top of the world like a god commanding its actions; at Borodino that realization of a heroic fantasy is replaced by a nightmare. Tolstoy deliberately uses the language of fantasy and dreams to describe Napoleon's state of mind during both battles.[3]

Kutuzov, who is more modest than Napoleon about what he can accomplish in battle and at the same time is said to be in touch with Providence, plays to perfection the role of morale builder assigned him by Tolstoy's theory of leadership.[4] Tolstoy attributes what we might call Kutuzov's restrained style of leadership to his extreme old age. Although he still enjoys "passions" associated with the body, he has outlived the "personal" (lichnoe) when it comes to the desire for glory, a passion related to mind and will. Unlike Napoleon, he does not seek to impose his will upon events through that aggressive faculty of mind (*um*) that "groups events and draws conclusions" (III, 2, xvi, 745; PSS 11:174).

> "He won't have anything personal. He won't invent, won't undertake anything," thought Prince Andrei, "but he'll listen to everything, remember everything, put everything in its place, won't hinder anything useful or allow anything harmful. He understands that there is something stronger and more significant than his will—the inevitable course of events—and he's able to see them, able to understand their significance, and, in view of that significance, is able to renounce participating in those events, renounce his will and direct it elsewhere. And the main reason why one believes him," thought Prince Andrei, "is that he's Russian, despite the Genlis novel and the French proverbs; it's that his voice trembled when he said, 'See what they've brought us to!' and had a catch in it when he said he'd 'make them eat horseflesh.'" (III, 2, xvi, 745; PSS 11:174–75)

Andrei uses the verb "understand" (ponimat') twice in this reflection; Kutuzov "understands" because he, unlike Napoleon, has discarded the personal to the extent possible in a living human being. He stands outside the fray in a way that more engaged participants (including Napoleon) do not. Kutuzov therefore is as close as possible to the point of view of the contemplative narrator who opens and closes volume 3, part 2 of the novel.[5] He differs from this narrator in one respect noted by Andrei in this same passage and crucial to the success of the Russian side. He has been roused to anger by the French invasion. This anger felt by every Russian fuels the patriotic "spirit" (*dukh*) that keeps the outmanned Russians standing against repeated French assaults. Kutuzov's focused anger makes him the proper leader for the Russian forces and also, though opposed by courtiers, the unanimous choice as commander in chief of the "people" (III, 2, xvi, 745; PSS 11:175). At Borodino, in keeping with this mandate, Kutuzov in fact does more than just contemplate the battle.[6] From his perch on Gorki, to the extent possible, he actively manipulates the mood of the Russian forces. He rejects the pessimism of General Barclay de Tolly as expressed through his emissary Wolzogen, and without even waiting for General Raevsky to finish his upbeat report, he commands his adjutant to write orders for an attack the next day. The attack turns out to be impossible because the Russian troops are too exhausted to mount it; in this respect Kutuzov's order is an expression of the willful mind that he mostly lacks. It communicates itself across the battlefield in a way that none of Napoleon's orders do that day and has the positive effect of motivating flagging Russian troops (III, 2, xxxv, 808; PSS 11:251).

The representation of Kutuzov at Borodino is more abstract and less purely psychological than that of Napoleon. Through the latter, Tolstoy shows us how it feels to lose control of the battlefield. Although none of Tolstoy's contemporary military readers confirmed from personal experience the truth of this particular insight, there is no reason to doubt its veracity, which none of them denied either. Tolstoy does not similarly admit readers into the mind of Kutuzov at Borodino. We do not know whether he acts out of calculation in preferring Raevsky's report to Wolzogen's, nor do we know whether he really intends to attack the next day. (At Fili he does seem genuinely distraught that he must order the continuation of the retreat through Moscow, while he remains resolved to defeat the French [III, 3, iv, 831; PSS 11:278–79]. Kutuzov is faithful to a willed goal, not to any one action for achieving it.) Our lack of direct access to Kutuzov's thoughts allows Tolstoy to sidestep the issue of tactics and strategy, which, his military readers agreed, he systematically undervalues in his theory of war. Even if Kutuzov does turn briefly aggressive, Tolstoy need not accuse him of manipulating others. Since at this moment he ostensibly so perfectly represents the will of the people he leads, he does not impose himself on them even in his own willfulness. This allows Kutuzov to lead without assuming the hubristic and power-hungry vices of the other great men whom Tolstoy attacks so ferociously in the novel.[7]

Frontline officers are more directly involved than staff officers in the crucial leadership act of motivating troops. Pierre observes one young officer marching backward as he leads his infantry into action (III, 2, xxxi, 795; PSS 11:235); his "lowered sword" and uneasy gaze may communicate panic to his men. Prince Andrei, on the other hand, as at Austerlitz, instinctively performing his leadership role, remains on his feet as a shell falls near him, (III, 2, xxxvi, 810–11; PSS 11:253–54). His act costs him his life and may be useless in the short run in affecting the course of battle, but it models courage and resolve to his men and fellow officers just as Kutuzov's order to reengage the enemy on the next day does.[8]

In a battle won or lost, in Tolstoy's opinion, by a collective act of thousands of wills, even a frontline officer is only one actor in it. Tolstoy conveys the experience of the individual soldier (whether conscript or officer) mostly through Pierre Bezukhov. Both here and elsewhere eyewitnesses are necessary because, as one of his military readers, General M. I. Dragomirov, observed, the engaged fighter rarely understands what is actually happening to him.[9] Pierre finds himself at an artillery battery that, though he does not know it at the time, is the famous mound, subsequently named Raevsky Redoubt or the Kurgan Battery, at the very center of the struggle.[10]

At the end of chapter 33, we are told by the narrator that men in the heat of battle do what they can to save themselves but that salvation seems to take different forms depending on "the mood of the moment"—that is, they are influenced by what others are doing around them. In accordance with this mood, they may run forward or backward. Men do more in battle than just run for their lives, however. They find ways to protect themselves and steady their nerves, and it is in pockets where they do this that Russian resistance hardens and surprises the French. In the artillery battery on the Raevsky Redoubt, Pierre discovers a home and seeming safe haven in a space separated from the surrounding field by its height and by trenches on three sides (III, 2, xxxi, 793; PSS 11:232). Busy soldiers joined in a mood of "family animation" accept him into their "family-like circle" and dub him "our master" (794; PSS 11:232–3). Readers have already seen such a battery from Captain Tushin's perspective during the battle of Schöngraben (I, 2, xx, 191–94; PSS 9:233–36), and they, like Pierre, understand its family dynamics. It is here and at this stage of battle that Pierre sees the "fire" of aroused patriotic energy burning in every face (III, 2, xxxi, 795; PSS 11:235). Every such family has a head, in this case not the senior officer who is on the scene but a junior officer whose enthusiasm Pierre admires.

Suddenly and unexpectedly, the young officer is killed, the imaginary home collapses, and Pierre sees—what he did not notice before—the chaos and deadly and random violence threatening him and others on the battlefield. "Everything became strange, vague, and bleak in Pierre's eyes" (III, 2, xxxi, 796; PSS 11:236). The battery runs out of ammunition and Pierre volunteers to bring some from the rear. While he hesitates momentarily by the caissons, they are hit directly by a shell and explode. "Suddenly a terrible shock threw him backward onto the ground. At the same instant the flash of a big fire lit him up, and at the same instant a deafening roar, crash, and whistling rang in his ears" (III, 2, xxxii, 796; PSS 11:237). All of Pierre's senses—sight, hearing, touch, and also command of his own body—are overpowered as an enormous impersonal force overwhelms him. In chapter 32, he returns to the battery "forgetting himself from fear," and briefly struggles with an enemy combatant in a similar state of mind (797; PSS 11:237–38). In this episode we see men at their most free from others and even themselves, not even encumbered with any sense of self while they fight for survival like beasts.

Here the narrator must step in to explain what is happening to Pierre, who cannot bear witness to his own behavior. The eyewitness becomes himself a subject of a battle state known to warriors but described by no one before Tolstoy. As Pierre distances himself from the killing fields, they seem to boil, and the noise of firing intensifies "to the point of despair, like a straining man calling out with his last strength" (798; PSS 11:238). Whereas in the opening moments of the battle Pierre had been enticed onto the field by its painterly symmetry and grandeur (III, 2, xxx, 789; PSS 11:228–29), he (and the reader through him) now experiences its hellish reality expressed metaphorically in the image of the suffering body of one individual. By the end of the chapter, Pierre has come to himself again and thinks, wrongly, that surely the inhuman melee will soon cease. Thinking can neither comprehend nor manage the irrational human experience of war, and this is why the rationalizing voice of the author cannot fully convey it.

A special example of how men cope on the battlefield occurs in chapter 36, in the reserves (808–11; PSS 11:251–54). Prince Andrei and his regiment lose hundreds of men without firing a single shot as they wait behind the lines. Individuals obsessively fiddle with their clothing or equipment; they shout out cautions and advice to a passing artillery battery as a horse steps over a trace; they construct "little dwellings" from scraps on the ground; Prince Andrei himself, with no orders to give, measures and counts his footsteps as he paces the field. These activities and others keep the men centered on themselves rather than on the uncontrollable horrors around them. The use of the word "dwellings" (*domiki*) links these strategies to what occurs in the battery on the Raevsky Redoubt. The reserve troops huddle individually in provisional, tiny homes of their own devising.

Making Sense of Borodino

The different episodes with their focalizers in the description of the Battle of Borodino add up to a compelling psychology of the warrior that I have sketched here and that can stand on its own. Vsevolod Garshin (in "Four Days" and "From the Reminiscences of Private Ivanov") was one of the first authors influenced by Tolstoy's psychology of war, and all subsequent war writers are indebted to it directly or indirectly. As I noted earlier, however, since the fictional narrative on its own does not comprise a coherent military historical account of the battle, Tolstoy's narrator intervenes as historian or philosopher in four different chapters in volume 3, part 2 to provide one. In chapter 1 he discusses the role of Providence in history and the way it decisively influenced events in 1812 despite the intentions of all the actors

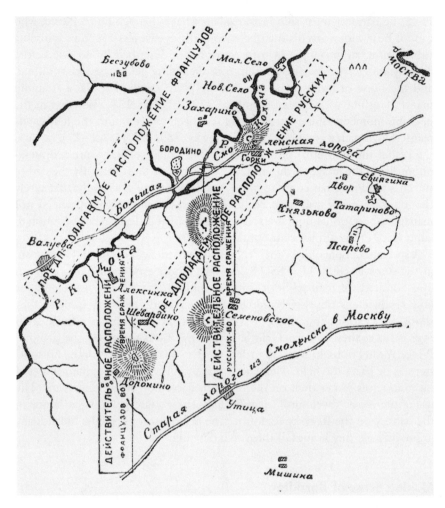

Tolstoy's map of the opening positions of the battle, based on his own trip to the battlefield on September 26–27, 1867. Published in the first edition of *War and Peace* (PSS 11:188).

involved. In chapter 19 he corrects previous historical accounts of the initial positions of the warring sides. In chapter 33 he gives an overview of the beginning of the main action of the battle, and in the final chapter of the book (39) he summarizes the battle's outcome and its consequences for the continuation of the war.

But while the historical and philosophical conclusions of the narrator in these chapters do supplement the fictional account of the battle, they are not the only generalizing context within which it should be viewed. (Indeed, if they were, the battle description would be of less general interest and lasting value than it is.) As I have just demonstrated, it offers unparalleled psychological insight into the individual experience of war. Furthermore, in literary terms and without recourse to cloying rhetoric, it makes a compelling case for Russian patriotism that has been tapped in subsequent military crises in Russia ever since.[11] All of this takes place in a setting that is both specific to the time and place of the actual battle and also universalized through the power of literature.

All the different episodes occur in a geographic location that, as is well known, Tolstoy himself toured on September 26–27, 1867. He wrote his wife afterward that "God should only grant me health and quiet, and I will write a battle of Borodino the likes of which has not been known before. Listen to me brag!" (PSS 83:152–53). Tolstoy was rightly pleased with himself for what is probably his major accomplishment as a historian. Previous historians had misrepresented the opening positions of the opposing sides. Comparing his examination of the site with accounts he had read, Tolstoy discovered that two days before the battle the Russians had retreated on the left, and as they had done so, the front lines of the enemy had also shifted. To make this argument in the novel and to underscore his bone fides as a historian, he included a map in chapter 19 that illustrated both the supposed and the real initial positions of the two armies. The map has other polemical purposes as well. The most ferocious fighting of the conflict took place on the left side of the battlefield, between the so-called Bagration flèches and the town of Borodino. Once the Russians had retreated on August 24 from the Shevardino Redoubt that they themselves had built, they were no longer separated from the attacking French by the Kolocha (or Koloch') River, and had to depend upon the flèches, which were thrown up hastily after the retreat. The map, which sketches in the flèches, supports the argument of Tolstoy's narrator in chapter 19 that the Russian army's poor field position made its performance in the battle all the more remarkable, and he attributes this performance to morale rather than tactics or strategy. It is also significant that neither the flèches nor the Raevsky Redoubt is named on the map, though other features are. The map therefore underscores Tolstoy's polemical point that those defensive points were subsequently named—wrongly in his opinion—after leaders rather than the anonymous thousands of men who defended them.

In addition to buttressing Tolstoy's theories of war and history, the map has a literary function.[12] It appears in the text *before* the fictional episodes set on August 25, when, although in Tolstoy's account Russian commanders did not fully grasp the consequences of this, the lines had already shifted as a consequence of the French occupation of Shevardino. In chapters 20–23, Pierre visits the battlefield on that day. He drives down from Mozhaisk and

The Borodino battlefield today. View of the Raevsky Redoubt. Photograph by Andrey Kartavenko, 2007. Reproduced with Permission of the State Borodino History and War Museum and Reserve.

then past the village of Tatarino to the heights of Gorki, where he surveys the "amphitheater" of the upcoming battle. He notes the terrain and the villages of Bezzubovo and Zakharyino to the right, and he then joins Benigson and other generals for an inspection of the left side of the front line. The group descends from Gorki to the Kolocha River, crosses into the village of Borodino, and turning left, rides to a mound that will later be known either as Raevsky Redoubt or Kurgan Battery.[13]

They ride through the burned-out village of Semyonovskoe and on to the flèches that are still being dug facing the Shevardino Redoubt, where they see French officers in the distance, including, they speculate, possibly Napoleon himself. After accompanying the group to the far left flank (near Utitsa, mentioned not here but in chapter 33), Pierre returns to Gorki, where he spends the night. On the way back to Gorki, on the evening of August 25, he visits Prince Andrei in the village of Kniaz'kovo (chapters 24–25). The next day, having viewed the opening moments of the battle at Gorki from above and at a distance, Pierre follows a general down into the fray (chapter 30), and then, in the company of General Raevsky's adjutant, ends up at the center redoubt, where he settles himself in the artillery battery (chapters 31–32).

Sketch of the battle from the French perspective by German artist Albrecht Adam. Based on a lithograph that Adam created from the sketchbook he kept during the 1812 campaign, when he served as an artist in the French army. Postcard from late nineteenth or early twentieth century as part of the Ermolov Jubilee Edition series, V. E. Apukhin. Reproduced with Permission of the State Borodino History and War Museum and Reserve.

Except for Mozhaisk, which is off the map, every single town or battle feature that Pierre sees from the heights or that he visits is marked on Tolstoy's map. Conversely, the map includes very few features that are *not* mentioned in the text. Since readers have access to this map, and they have also toured with Pierre, they know exactly where Pierre has his battle experience on Raevsky's Redoubt. Behind Semyonovskoe, also on the map, Prince Andrei and his regiment wait for hours to back up the infantry protecting the artillery battery on Raevsky Redoubt. On the French side, Napoleon's camp at Valuevo (chapter 26) and, of course, the Shevardino Redoubt are on the map. The crucial Kolocha River is included, as are other important topographical features like roads and unnamed streams. Readers who are so inclined can accurately locate every fictional episode of the battle on Tolstoy's map. The interaction between the map and Tolstoy's text is so exact that a reader can visit the battle site today—it is a national park with a museum— and find the locations of various fictional episodes there. I did this in August

1812 г. Бородинское сраженіе. 26 Августа. Послѣ полудня.   Изд. М -Б. ж. д.
Bataille de la Moskowa. le 7 septembre. Après midi.

Sketch of the battle after midday by Russian artist and participant A. I. Dmitriev-Mamonov. Photo of lithograph of the sketch made in 1822 by S. Shchifliar. Photo by Fototipiia Sherer, Nabrol'ts I Ko. Postcard (Moscow: Izd. M.-B. zh. d., 1903). Reproduced with Permission of the State Borodino History and War Museum and Reserve.

2010. To further concretize the setting of the action, the narrator's summary of the main action in chapter 33 supplies distances (from the flèches to Borodino and from Shevardino to both, 798–99; PSS 11:239). The map and these measurements, as well as repeated mentions of the exact time of day at which an action occurs—all tools borrowed from history—confer legitimacy on Tolstoy's fictional narrative independent of any idea it is intended to illustrate or underpin.[14] Surely when Tolstoy wrote to his wife that he would "write a battle of Borodino the likes of which has not been known before," he had this specificity of setting partly in mind.

The very same strategy that makes the setting of the battle so realistic also moves real space and real time into the world of the poet, where it becomes susceptible to his artistry. Tolstoy takes full advantage of this potential while being careful not to overplay his hand and diminish the realism of the setting. Underemphasized but omnipresent in the description of the Battle of Borodino is poetic imagery that links it in various ways to nature, to elevated war poetry, and to epic.[15] We know that while he himself was at the battle site, Tolstoy paid special attention to the position of the sun (PSS 13:40), and subsequently the appearance of sun and sky is carefully noted in his description of various phases of the battle.[16] Attention to such details can be understood as yet another way that he locates his narrative in real space and time. At the same time, Tolstoy's notes at Borodino (partly dictated to his brother-in-law S. A. Bers, who accompanied him on the trip) hint at the literary use to which he was already planning to put the data he was gathering.

> Black shadows from the forests and buildings in the east and from the kurgans.
> The sun rises to the left, from behind.
> The sun is in the eyes of the French. (PSS 11: 40)

In the novel, the sun in Napoleon's eyes impedes his ability to follow the battle (III, 2, xxxiii, 799; PSS 11:239). As the sun had seemed to have favored Napoleon at Austerlitz when he stood bathed in its full rays above the fog, here at Borodino it blinds him. At one point in the narrative, the sun seems to Pierre to be an actor in the battle itself.

> Pierre ran down.
> "No, now they'll stop it, now they'll be horrified at what they've done!" he thought, aimlessly following behind the crowds of stretchers moving off the battlefield. *But the sun, veiled in smoke, was still high, and ahead, and especially to*

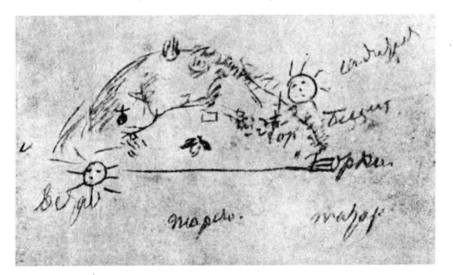

Tolstoy's sketch of the position of the sun during the battle. The sketch is in a fold-out embedded in notes that include the observations quoted above (PSS 13, between pp. 40 and 41).

the left near Semyonovskoe, something seethed in the smoke, and the roar of gunfire, musketry, and cannonades not only did not abate, but intensified to the point of despair, like a straining man crying out with his last strength. (III, 2, xxxii, 798; PSS 11:238 [emphasis mine])

The shrieking individual as an image of battle locates it firmly within the human sphere. Yet whereas in most cases in Tolstoy's war writing the regular movement of the sun is contrasted to chaos on the battlefield, at this moment the sun seems to become part of the atmosphere of the battle. Though Pierre wills an end to the fighting, the sun seems to stand high and still over the battle as it did in the Bible for Joshua at the Battle of Beth-Horon. Whether the sun aids fate in bringing about a Russian victory or is simply a portent of and chance contributor to the victory, it takes on symbolic value in the text.[17]

D. S. Likhachev has suggested that the symbolic use of sun imagery here and elsewhere in *War and Peace* may be associated with Russian medieval military tales.[18] A source closer in time to Tolstoy would be the eighteenth-century ode. Neither in volume 3, part 2 nor elsewhere does Tolstoy associate war with natural disasters the way Russian odic poets do, but he does use the physical elements constitutive of such disasters to describe fighting at Borodino. The boiling and smoke on the battlefield to the left of Semyonovskoe bring to mind traditional odic comparisons of warfare to an active volcano.[19] Neither Tolstoy nor his odic predecessors prettify war in these images. For Lomonosov and Derzhavin (the latter a longtime officer in the Russian army), as for Tolstoy, war, as Tolstoy memorably characterized it in "Sevastopol in December" (1856), is "blood, suffering, and death." It is precisely this reality of war that both constitutes its awful grandeur and gives full measure to heroism in it. War tests people in ways that no other human activity does, and in the process it arouses energy that Tolstoy uses the natural metaphor of fire to characterize. The fire that a retreating Pierre sees on the battlefield comes from weaponry that, the narrator informs us, inflicts most of the casualties (III, 2, xxxiii, 800; PSS 11:241). At the same time, the metaphoric spark in the eye of each Russian soldier on the day before the battle stands for internal energy available and needed to withstand chaos.[20] Fight fire with fire. Earlier in his time on the battlefield, the combined energies of Russian troops seem to Pierre like a thunder cloud (III, 2, xxxi, 796; PSS 11:236). When the battlefield seems to boil as Pierre retreats from it, it is with those combined energies of men fighting to conquer one another and save themselves.

Perhaps the most wide-ranging and complex epic imagery in book 10 is that of grain, fields, and harvest. This imagery virtually saturates the entire book. The colloquial word for grain (khleb; хлеб) appears twenty-three times in it, and those for various specific grains (mostly rye and oats)—another eighteen times. Twelve of these appearances (хлеб plus the other grains) are directly related to the Battle of Borodino and the rest to yoked events at the Bolkonsky estate Bald Hills and Smolensk. There are many references to fields and harvest as well. The book's events all take place around harvest time, allowing Tolstoy to "naturalize" the traditional epic association of harvest and grain with peacetime activities. Furthermore, no one who has visited the actual site of the battle can avoid the overwhelming sense of it as idyllic and pastoral rather than warlike.[21] Not a single mention of grain and harvest by itself in the text feels merely literary, and yet taken all together the motif allows and even forces the reader to interpret it symbolically as well as literally.

Tolstoy also disguises this poetic dimension of the text by giving it a satisfying complexity. War interrupts the harvest. At the same time, however, the harvesting of grain can stand for war. This commonality emerges indirectly from the interweaving in the text of the words for field (pole; поле), which appears twenty-one times in the Borodino section, and for battlefield (pole srazheniia; поле сражения), which appears twenty-five times there, including one instance in French. Tolstoy seizes upon a linguistic fact in Russian (as in several other languages, including English) to make another connection common in epic. The fact that the Russian for "battlefield" is two words rather than one intensifies the possibility for wordplay that Tolstoy proceeds to exploit so effectively. In chapter 19, introducing his map of the battlefield, the narrator uses the word "pole" four times to characterize the physical space in which the battle occurs.[22]

Перейдя на левую сторону Колочи, влево от дороги, Наполеон передвинул всё будущее сражение справа налево (со стороны русских) и перенёс его *в поле* между Утицей, Семёновским и Бородиным (в это поле, не имеющее в себе ничего более выгодного для позиции, чем всякое *другое поле в России*), и *на этом поле* произошло всё сражение 26-го числа. В грубой форме план предполагаемого сражения и происшедшего сражения будет следующий. (PSS 11:187–88)

By crossing to the left side of the Kolocha, to the left of the road, Napoleon shifted the whole future battle from right to left (viewed from the Russian side), and transferred it to *the field* between Utitsa, Semyonovskoe, and Borodino (a *field* no more advantageous as a position than *any other field in Russia*), and the whole battle of the twenty-sixth took place *on that field*. In crude form, the plan of the supposed battle and actual battle is as in the map opposite. (III, 2, xix, 755–56)

In this instance, there is no distinction drawn between the broader meaning of the word "поле" (pole) as any open, treeless space, and the more specific meaning of it as an agricultural space. The potential for symbolism and also for various parallels and comparisons is inherent in the broad semantic field of the word itself, but for the time being it remains untapped. It stands in relation to what is to come as the introduction does in a fugue.

In the opening section of chapter 21 (PSS 11:193), Pierre surveys the "поле сражения" (pole srazheniia) from the heights of Gorki. This is the first use of the term in volume 3, part 2 (where it occurs twenty-three more times), but in this case, the physical space that Pierre scrutinizes looks more like grain fields than like a battlefield.

Налево местность была ровнее, были *поля с хлебом* [....] Всё, что видел Пьер направо и налево, было так неопределенно, что *ни левая, ни правая сторона поля* не удовлетворяла вполне его представлению. Везде было *не поле сражения,* которое он ожидал видеть, а *поля,* поляны, войска, леса, дымы костров, деревни, курганы, ручьи; и сколько ни разбирал Пьер, он в этой живой местности не мог найти позиции и не мог даже отличить ваших войск от неприятельских. (PSS 11:194)

To the left the terrain was more level, there were *grain fields* [....] Everything Pierre saw to right and left was so indefinite that *neither the left nor the right side of the field* fully satisfied his notions. Everywhere there were *fields,* clearings, troops, woods, smoking campfires, villages, barrows, streams. But not *the battlefield* he had expected to see; and much as he tried to make it out, on this living terrain he could not find a position and could not even distinguish our troops from the enemy's. (III, 2, xxi, 761)

War and peace, battlefields and grain fields are contrasted. At the same time, however, in the phrase "ни левая, ни правая сторона поля" (neither the left nor the right side of the field; ni levaia, ni pravaia storona polia), "field" is used here in the more neutral sense of the word as treeless space as opposed to "grain fields" (pole s khlebom; поле с хлебом) specifically identified as such. The contrast between war and peace continues as war invades and disrupts peaceful activities. When Pierre accompanies the inspection party in chapter 23, they pass through "*broken rye, beaten down as if by hail,* along a road newly made by the artillery across the furrows of a *plowed field* to the flèches, which were still being dug" (*polomannuiu, vybituiu, kak gradom, rozh',* po vnov' prolozhennoi artilleriei po kolcham *pashni* doroge na fleshi, tozhe togda eshche kopaemye; *поломанную, выбитую, как градом, рожь,* по вновь проложенной артиллерией по колчам *пашни* дороге на флеши, тоже тогда ещё копаемые; 767–68; PSS 11:201). In chapter 24, Prince Andrei on the night before the battle looks out "at a *plowed field* with stacks of oats on it (na *pashniu* s razbitymi na nei kopnami ovsa; *на пашню* с разбитыми на ней копнами овса; 769; PSS 11:203). Here Tolstoy uses the unambiguous term for a plowed field, "пашня" (pashnia).

Once the battle begins, the phrase "pole sraszheniia" predominates, but its relation to grain fields is not necessarily opposing.

[О]собенно левее по всей линии, по лесам, *по полям*, в низах, на вершинах возвышений, зарождались беспрестанно сами собой, из ничего, пушечные [. . .] клубы дымов [. . . .] (PSS 11:228)

[E]specially to the left, along the whole line, over the woods, *over the fields,* in the hollows, up on the heights, puffs of cannon smoke were ceaselessly born of themselves out of nothing [. . . .] (III, 2, xxx, 789–90)

Казалось то, что дымы эти бежали, то, что они стояли, и мимо них бежали леса, *поля* и лестящие штыки. С левой стороны, *по полям* и кустам, беспрестанно зарождались эти большие дымы [. . . .] (PSS 11:229)

It seemed that these puffs of smoke now raced along, now stood still, and past them raced woods, *fields,* and gleaming bayonets. On the left side, *over the fields* and bushes, these big puffs of smoke were ceaselessly being born [. . . .] (III, 2, xxx, 790)

Все точно так же, как и он [Pierre], и, как ему казалось, с тем же чувством смотрели вперед, *на поле сражения.* На всех лицах светилась теперь та *скрытая теплота* (chaleur latente) чувства, которое Пьер замечал вчера и которое он понял совершенно после своего разговора с князем Андреем. (PSS 11:229)

Everyone was looking ahead at *the battlefield,* as he was, and, it seemed to him, with the same feeling. On all faces there now shone that "hidden warmth" (*chaleur latente*) of feeling which Pierre had noticed the day before and which he had understood perfectly after his conversation with Prince Andrei. (III, 2, xxx, 790)[23]

In these distant views, fields of peace and war are not contrasted, mostly because the war element seems more harmonious than it is in fact. Down on the battlefield with Pierre and in the midst of battle, in one key passage the words are used, if not interchangeably as they had been in the opening paragraph of chapter 21, then without reference to any moral contrast between war and peace.[24]

[Н]о это были два отдельные и слабые действия в сравнении с тем, что происходило в середине *поля сражения. На поле* между Бородиным и флешами, у леса, на открытом и видном с обеих сторон протяжении, произошло главное действие сражения, самым простым, бесхитростным образом [. . . .] Потом, когда дым застлал *всё поле,* в этом дыму двинулись (со стороны французов) справа две дивизии [. . . .] (PSS 11:239)

[B]ut these were two separate and weak actions compared with what was happening in the middle of *the battlefield.* On the *field* between Borodino and the flèches, by the woods, on a stretch open and visible from both sides, the main action of the battle took place in the most simple, artless way [. . . .] Then, when smoke lay over *the whole field,* from the right (on the French side), the two divisions [. . . .] (III, 2, xxxiii, 798)

Here "поле" (pole) refers simply to a flat treeless space on the battlefield rather than to grain fields. Neither here nor anywhere else does the intermixing of "поле" (pole) and "поле сражения" (pole srazheniia) explicitly make the connection between death in battle and harvest. On the contrary, the opening lines of the final chapter (39) of the book again draw an ironic contrast between peacetime agriculture and the slaughter of war.

> Несколько десятков тысяч человек лежало мёртвыми в разных положениях и мундирах *на полях и лугах,* принадлежавших господам Давыдовым и казённым крестьянам, *на тех полях и лугах,* на которых сотни лет одновременно сбирали урожаи и пасли скот крестьяне деревень Бородина, Горок, Шевардина и Семёновского. (PSS 11: 263)
>   Several tens of thousands of men lay dead in various positions and uniforms in *the fields and meadows* that belonged to the Davydov family and to crown peasants, on *fields and meadows* where for hundreds of years peasants of the villages of Borodino, Gorki, Shevardino, and Semyonovskoe had at the same time gathered crops and pastured cattle. (III, 2, xxxix, 818)

Only in one place, and in a different way, is war directly linked to harvest. During the battle, Prince Andrei and his men wait for hours as reserve troops in a field of oats (mentioned twice the first time as "trampled," III, 2, xxxvi, 808, 809; PSS 11:251–52), and it is here that Andrei receives his fatal wound. He is evacuated to a dressing station in a nearby wood, where there are baggage carts and horses.

> Лошади в хребтугах ели *овёс,* и воробьи слетали к ним и подбирали просыпанные *зёрна.* Воронья, чуя кровь, нетерпеливо каркая, перелетали на берёзах. (PSS 11:255)
>   The horses in nosebags were eating *oats* from them. And sparrows flew down to them, pecking up the spilled *grain.* Crows, scenting blood, crowing impatiently, flew about in the birches. (III, 2, xxxvi, 811).

The language in this passage is utterly concrete. One word especially stands out in this regard. Хребтуг (Khrebtug), the word translated as nosebag, is defined in Dal's famous dictionary of Russian as a sack made of various coarse materials "that drivers tie to the upraised shafts to feed oats to their horses."[25] It is a sign for a particular material object. The pronunciation of some of the words themselves in this passage seems to imitate the sounds they describe: the pronunciation of the phrase "лошади в хребтугах" (lóshadi v khrebtúgakh; horses in nosebags) imitates the action of chewing; "каркая" (kárkaia; crowing) sounds like crowing. We imagine birds flying about, and we smell blood. It is perfectly natural that the idle cart horses would feed while the battle raged and that the feed would be oats, perhaps even grown in the field where Andrei's regiment had lain in reserve. Oats rather than wheat (the grain of choice in classical poetry) are appropriate for a Russian setting, as is rye, which appears elsewhere in book 10. Still, such related imagery invites us to associate the battlefield and the field hospital poetically, and the seed pecked at by sparrows reminds us of the wounded and dying men crowded around the operating tents. To make sure that we draw this connection, Tolstoy adds the traditional epic motif of crows attracted by the scent of blood. Men are the grain mowed down on the killing fields of war. At the same time, readers are continuously aware of the irony of the comparison of men to grain as another way that war invades peace in the novel. Realism becomes epic here, infused with poetic meaning but not transformed from material reality into symbolism.

Tolstoy approached the description of the Battle of Borodino as a historian, a philosopher of war and history, a psychologist, and a poet. Poetry is fundamental to his task because only it can unify what from all the other perspectives is incomprehensible. War as we conceptualize it after the fact is an act of the human imagination. The devices of realism alone are not sufficient to describe it as human beings experience it. Only imagination can supply the images that make sense of the indescribable. Tolstoy's quest to show war in its true grandeur and horror therefore led him to the necessity of remythologizing it. In *War and Peace* the mapping of the fictional narrative of war onto real space seems to ground it in history and in a specific geographical place, while discrete recourse to epic metaphor poeticizes history and the places where it occurred. The poetic devices that Tolstoy employs have their own extension in time if not in space; he draws on genres and metaphors that are part of the Russian cultural imagination and of Western art in general. The result is a mythologizing of the battle and the battlefield of Borodino, which become part of an epic that *War and Peace* bequeathed to the Russian people and to the world.

10

Tolstoy and Clausewitz

The Dialectics of War

———

ANDREAS HERBERG-ROTHE

In *War and Peace* Tolstoy narrates how on the eve of the battle of Borodino, two German staff officers in the Russian service ride past Prince Andrei, who recognizes them as Count Wolzogen and Carl von Clausewitz. Prince Andrei overhears their conversation.

> "*Der Krieg muss im Raum verlegt warden. Der Ansicht kann ich nicht genug Preis geben*" [War must be extended in space. I cannot put too high a price on this view], said one.
> "*O ja,*" said the other voice. "*Da der Zweck ist nur den Feind zu schwächen, so kann man gewiss nicht den Verlust der Privatpersonen in Achtung nehmen*" [Oh, yes...The aim is to weaken the enemy, so one cannot pay attention to the loss of private persons]
> "*O ja,*" the first voice confirmed.
> "Yes, *im Raum verlegen,*" Prince Andrei repeated, snorting angrily, when they had ridden by. "*Im* this *Raum* I had a father, and a son, and a sister in Bald Hills. It's all the same to him. There's what I was saying to you—tomorrow these German gentlemen won't win the battle, they'll only muck things up as much as they can, because all there is in a German head is reasoning, which isn't worth a tinker's damn [....] (III, 2, xxv, 774)

This is the initial point in *War and Peace* from which any interpretation concerning the relation of Tolstoy and Clausewitz must emanate. We must ask why Tolstoy chose Clausewitz and why he portrayed him in such a way. Obviously he knew that Clausewitz had served not only in the Prussian but also, during Napoleon's Russian campaign of 1812, in the Russian army.

Portrait of Carl von Clausewitz (with permission of Clausewitz.com). Carl von Clausewitz served nearly three years in the Russian army in order to fight Napoleon. This portrait by an unknown artist shows Clausewitz in Russian uniform with a Swedish medal given in fall 1813, suggesting that this picture was made between fall 1813 and Clausewitz's reentry into the Prussian army at the beginning of 1815.

Tolstoy seems to know Clausewitz's writings well enough to be able to judge that those German gentlemen have nothing in their heads but useless theories.

Is Tolstoy right that Clausewitz was merely a theoretician? Clausewitz fought as a Prussian officer against the French army in the Napoleonic Wars and the wars of liberation, abandoned his service in the Prussian army as a kind of resistance against the king, and joined the Russian army in order to fight Napoleon. His horse was shot dead beneath him during this campaign. He suffered frostbite and wrote to his wife that he had seen ghastly scenes that would have driven him mad had he not been hardened by what he had seen before them.[1] Contrary to Tolstoy's portrayal of him in this scene in *War and Peace,* Clausewitz's theory is based on his personal experience of war, much of it in the Russian army. Clausewitz's contribution during Napoleon's Russian campaign was significant. Perhaps most significantly, he mediated the Convention of Tauroggen between General York of the Prussian corps and General Diebitsch from the Russian army, and he may even have formulated its final version. He was able to persuade General York to withdraw his allegiance to Napoleon and declare his corps neutral. Because Clausewitz had abandoned the Prussian military for three years to serve with the Russians, the Prussian king removed him from active duty and appointed him an administrator at the Prussian war academy. This forced retirement led him to write a book that would bring him the glory he had been denied on the battlefield.[2] He wrote not only his famous *On War* but seven additional volumes analyzing war campaigns of his own times and particularly those of Napoleon and earlier great commanders like Swedish king Gustavus Adolphus Magnus (1594–1632). His analysis of Napoleon's Russian campaign for his book on the subject convinced him that defense is the stronger form of war, and Clausewitz incorporated a large part of this analysis into the final version of *On War.* As this chapter explains in detail, his participation in the Russian campaign prompted a fundamental shift in Clausewitz's understanding.

Great theoreticians often drastically change their minds at some point in their lives. Just as with Kant, Hegel, Marx, and Tolstoy, there is an early and a late Clausewitz. Even the famous first chapter of *On War* that is his main legacy and that concludes with the wondrous trinity evolves from an early to a later stage. The early Clausewitz favored an existential view of war comparable to the one of Tolstoy in *War and Peace.* The later Clausewitz favored an instrumental view, and it is precisely this position that Tolstoy criticizes in the scene in which Clausewitz appears. In existential warfare, one or both sides fight for their identity and survival; in instrumental warfare they fight for their (material) interests. Clausewitz's final legacy is neither an existential nor an instrumental view of war but his wondrous trinity, in which he summarizes his different and even conflicting war experiences and analyses.

So-called trinitarian war is a concept assigned misleadingly to Clausewitz but in reality developed solely by Harry Summers and Martin van Creveld.[3] Clausewitz understood force, violent struggle, and the affiliation of the combatants to a community as the three fundamental tendencies of any war. Though particular historical and societal circumstances and events arranged these tendencies differently in each case, none could be absent. It is always a great problem to explain the terms *Gewalt* (which means both force *and* violence) and *Kampf* (struggle *and* fight) to an English-speaking audience.

In Clausewitz's definition, *Gewalt* expresses the asymmetrical relationship of action and suffering, while *Kampf* indicates a symmetrical relationship of action and counteraction. Differing translations for the German term *Gewalt* indicate the difference between Clausewitz's initial definition and the trinity. Whereas Michael Howard and Peter Paret translate it in Clausewitz's initial definition as "force," they translate it as "primordial violence" in the trinity. Clausewitz's wondrous trinity (*wunderliche Dreifaltigkeit*) represents his ultimate idea of war as a floating balance between conflicting tendencies, particularly between war as an instrument and war as an existential phenomenon in its own right. In this context, *Gewalt* can't be translated just as force because this term is inextricably connected with an instrumental understanding.

Like John Keegan today, Tolstoy criticized the later Clausewitz's instrumental view of war and the interpretation of *On War* in Russia during his lifetime.[4] He overlooked his own agreements with the early Clausewitz and his existential view of war. As Raymond Aron and Olav Rose have pointed out, Tolstoy must have been aware of Clausewitz's writings to some extent, but our comparison of the two authors does not depend on which specific parts of *On War* or Clausewitz's analysis of the Russian campaign Tolstoy knew.[5]

Tolstoy's Knowledge of Clausewitz

Clausewitz and his work were well known in Russia even to the general public between 1836 and 1847. Up to the Crimean War, Russians regarded Clausewitz as one of the foremost military strategists. Authors like General of the Artillery N. V. Medem (1798–1870) and Colonel P. A. Iazykov, who both taught at the Imperial Nikolaevskii Military Academy, as well as the military historian Lieutenant General M. I. Bogdanovich (1805–82) accepted his theories. Baron Henri Jomini (1779–1869), trying to make a reputation in his newly adopted fatherland, was forced to take a firm stand against Clausewitz in order to press his claims on the Russian generals and public opinion. Clausewitz's *On War* was extensively quoted. After the Crimean War, there evolved an ever-growing criticism of Clausewitz: starting with A. I. Astaf'ev (1861), he was criticized for his "metaphysics." Nonetheless, General G. A. Leer (1829–1904), one of Russia's most eminent military theorists, was indebted to Clausewitz's historical writings.[6]

Although Tolstoy certainly knew of Clausewitz's status in Russia, we cannot be sure whether he read any works by him. He may have read only excerpts of his writings, even only interpretations of them. There are similarities between passages of *On War* and *War and Peace*,[7] but I disagree with Aron and Rose that this proves Tolstoy actually read *On War*.[8]

Although Clausewitz's analysis of the Russian campaign of 1812, incorporated into his posthumously published works, was not translated into either French or Russian until the twentieth century, Tolstoy may have known it, or parts of it. There Clausewitz mentions that he became an adjutant of General Pfühl through the recommendation of Colonel Wolzogen.[9] Tolstoy portrays both German officers in the service of the Russian army, and if he had read the history of the campaign, this might explain why in the novel Clausewitz is talking with Wolzogen rather than Pfühl, whose adjutant he has been. In the history of the Russian campaign, a few pages after Clausewitz reports on how he joined Pfühl's staff, he criticizes Wolzogen for the same reasons Tolstoy does. "Whoever wishes to engage in an activity like war should have a trained intellect but not be bound by book learning; [...] He will always remain unintelligible to men with instinctive abilities and will never gain the confidence of the most gifted among them, who know exactly what they want to do. This was the case with Colonel Wolzogen."[10]

Clausewitz's description of the episode portrayed in Tolstoy's novel is very similar to it. The night before the battle of Borodino, General Barclay sent Wolzogen while Pfühl sent Clausewitz to get instructions from Kutuzov and to inform him about the condition of the Russian army.[11] Tolstoy and Clausewitz had the same opinion of General Pfühl. It seems reasonable to conclude from all this that Tolstoy knew parts of Clausewitz's history of the Russian campaign. Herfried Münkler has even argued that *War and Peace* could be understood as a repudiation of Clausewitz's version of the battle of Borodino.[12]

Instrumental and Existential Warfare

Tolstoy attacks Clausewitz because he seems to combine the instrumentality of war with its escalating effects. In other words, Clausewitz in Tolstoy's view seems to view the escalation of violence in war as a means to gain victory. It is possible to respond to these charges by returning to the above-mentioned differences between the instrumental and the existential view of war. In the first, war is primarily a means of policy to pursue goals, whether political ones or some other kind. According to the second, the warring parties are fighting for their very existence, either as a political body or for their physical existence or their identity.[13] When Prince Andrei says before Borodino that one should fight only for a cause for which one is willing to die, he is expressing the existential concept of war.

In his "Political Declaration" (*Bekenntnisdennschrift*) of 1812 Clausewitz takes the same existential view of war as does Prince Andrei after the Prussian defeats at Jena and Auerstädt. Here he finds existential meaning in war, understanding it not simply as an act in which a nation pursues its interests but as an act of self-realization. At this point in his intellectual development, Clausewitz does not yet define war as an instrumentally rational act of violence that forces the enemy to conform to one's will. Rather, war is a way of proving to oneself that one actually has a will. Clausewitz and the Prussian army reformers believed that even a defeat, if only it were honorable, would generate the moral strength to create a better society. In their eyes, resuming the war against Napoleon was not just a moral obligation; it also expressed their historical experience that the lost war of 1806 had alone cleared the way for a fundamental transformation in Prussia.

Although there are of course intersections and transformations from one tendency to the other, one has to distinguish between them. In a letter to the Prussian Field Marshal August Gneisenau from January 1811, Clausewitz stressed that his view of politics remained the same. Sooner or later Prussia would become embroiled "in a new catastrophe" and would have "trouble saving itself from total collapse." In this same passage, however, he reiterated the primacy of honor over life in his philosophy: if Prussia "perishes with honor, [. . .] I hope to perish honorably with it, or at least to sacrifice my existence." In another letter to Gneisenau toward the end of the year, Clausewitz wrote that "the double curse of a dishonorable demise is resting upon us."[14] He thus distinguished between Prussia's political existence as a state and an apolitical form of existence that remained bound to Prussia's honor and recognition.

Once a war is understood as existential, a distinction must be drawn among totally different forms of existence:

1. Direct "physical," objective or substantial existence[15]
2. Existence as the identity of an existing political subject—a community, society, nation, etc.
3. Existence in the sense of an identity to be created, one that has yet to be instituted
4. "Moral" existence, recognition as an equal state among states, an equal citizen within a state

The early Clausewitz attempted a clear ranking of these forms of existence: at the very top he placed the moral, which was followed by the political. For the sake of these first two forms, he was prepared to risk his own immediate physical existence and that of the state. It isn't clear how much value Clausewitz placed on the creation of an as yet nonexistent political subject—in concrete terms, the German nation. It's impossible to know whether the transformation of the Prussian state sought by the army reformers was only a means to successful warfare or an end in itself. Army reformers differed on this. For Clausewitz's military teacher and friend Scharnhorst and for Gneisenau, the lost battles of Jena and Auerstädt were the necessary prerequisite for sociopolitical renewals. In contrast, Clausewitz's analyses focused more on the aspect of transforming Prussian politics and society so as to conduct a successful war. His existential view of war can be characterized as being in the interface between these concepts of existence.

Simultaneously, to a certain extent the early Clausewitz believed that dying in the struggle for recognition was the most exalted form of death. For him, the Prussians' own blood would not be spared when the fight for honor was resumed after their defeats. "Was blood shed in vain? Will this glorious hour of our death not bolster the courage of our descendants?" The king who "dies gloriously ennobles the nation, and his glorious name is a balm for their wounds!" In this sense, Clausewitz's "Political Declaration" states that even the destruction of liberty "after a bloody and honorable struggle assures the people's rebirth. It is the seed of life, which one day will bring forth a new, securely rooted tree."[16]

Finally, his reflections on the Russian campaign and then Napoleon's defeat at Waterloo turned Clausewitz's attention to the instrumental view of war, which became famous in his formula of war as a continuation of policy. This last was not his final position, however. Eventually, mulling over his different war experiences, he arrived at a dialectical concept of war that is most fully expressed in his wondrous trinity. The dialectical understanding of war expressed in the trinity supersedes the instrumental view of war because the latter becomes just one tendency within the wondrous trinity.[17] Taken individually, instrumental as well as existential concepts lead to absurdities, miscalculations, and misunderstanding of the dynamics of war. Nevertheless both are fundamental to each war, both are present in each war and together constitute its totality, and at the same time both conflict with each other in every war. Clausewitz came to this complex understanding only at the end of his life, so he was able to rework his great book only in part, most fully in his famous first chapter of the first book. Tolstoy also realized that an existential view of war as well as heroism was not the solution to the problems of modern warfare, but he drew other conclusions from this. He became a pacifist. Clausewitz and Tolstoy battled with the same problems, even if their solutions were different, and indeed Tolstoy saw no solution. In Clausewitz's final understanding, the two approaches coexist in war like two poles of a magnet.[18]

Tolstoy rightly criticized the instrumental, modern view of war and he introduced Clausewitz as the symbol for it. Unlike modern critics of Clausewitz, he realized that it was not sufficient to change from one pole (on the magnet that is war) to the other in viewing war's essence. He became a radical paci-fist,[19] while Clausewitz developed a dialectical approach.

Napoleon's Failure in Russia and Its Consequences for Clausewitz's Theory

Clausewitz drew quite different conclusions from the failure of Napoleon's Russian campaign in 1812 than he did from the Prussian defeats at Jena and Auerstädt. There was no fundamental difference between Napoleon's strategy in Russia and the one he had employed in the earlier campaigns that Tolstoy, like Clausewitz, admired. In Clausewitz's view, Napoleon had wanted to wage the war in Russia in the same way he had always done. He would commence with decisive blows, use the advantage thus gained in order to strike further blows, and use the winnings to stake everything repeatedly on one card until he had broken the bank. This was Napoleon's method, without which, as Clausewitz wrote in his history, he would not have achieved his earlier enormous successes.[20]

The decisive factor in the Russian campaign was that the enemy behaved quite differently. It was difficult to engage an opponent who sought to avoid all fighting. Second, Russia's almost limitless space presented an insuperable obstacle to Napoleon's strategy.[21] From the purely military point of view, it was right to destroy the Russian army, occupy Moscow, and then negotiate with Tsar Alexander.[22] But the Russian army's evasive actions, its scorched-earth tactics, and the great spaces of Russia meant, according to Clausewitz, that Napoleon's army perished as a result of its own efforts.

Napoleon's campaign in Russia did not fail because he advanced too far and too fast but because the only methods that could have brought success failed. As Clausewitz stated in book 8 of *On War*, the Russian Empire could not be conquered in the conventional way. Such a country could be van-quished only as a result of its own weakness and the effects of internal divi-sions. Napoleon could hope to shake the courage of the Russian government and the loyalty and steadfastness of its soldiers only if he could reach Moscow. In Moscow he hoped to find "peace," and this was the only rational war aim he could set himself.[23]

Napoleon succeeded in reaching Moscow, but in what circumstances! In Clausewitz's view, he could have attained peace only if a further condition had been met: he would have had to continue to inspire dread once he had arrived in the city. Of the 280,000 soldiers who started the campaign under his leadership, only 90,000 made it to Moscow. Clausewitz argues that if Napoleon had taken better care of his army, the losses would have been much

Der

Feldzug von 1812 in Rußland,

der

Feldzug von 1813

bis

zum Waffenstillstand

und der

Feldzug von 1814 in Frankreich.

Hinterlassene Werke

Generals Carl von Clausewitz.

Berlin,
bei Ferdinand Dümmler.

1835.

Carl von Clausewitz wrote not only *On War* but a total of ten volumes about war and warfare. (*Hinterlassene Werke des Generals Carl von Clausewitz*, 10 vols. [Bonn: Duemmler, 1832–38]). The first three of these books were later combined to become *On War*. In volume 7, the cover of which is shown here, he analyzed mainly Napoleon's Russian campaign. This volume became the basis for the most extensive section of *On War*, his descriptions of the defense.

lower. As it was, he arrived there with a shrunken army of exhausted soldiers and worn-out horses to face a hostile army of 110,000 men on its right flank, surrounded by a people in arms. He was forced to set up defenses facing in all directions, without magazines and with insufficient stores of ammunition, connected with the outside world by a single, completely devastated road. A French army in this condition and situation could not have survived the Russian winter in Moscow.[24]

There had surely been no other case in which "the evidence is so clear that the invader was destroyed by his own exertions."[25] But if Napoleon was unsure whether he would be able to hold his ground through the whole winter in Moscow, he should have returned to France before its onset. As Clausewitz saw it, Napoleon's retreat was inevitable from the moment Tsar Alexander refused to sue for peace. The whole campaign had been based on the assumption that he would do so.[26] Regardless of whether the Russian government planned to set fire to the city deliberately or the Cossacks did so unintentionally, Moscow in flames symbolized the vanity of the hope that peace could be found there.[27]

The Russian campaign demonstrated in the most vivid way imaginable the superiority of defense over attack, as Clausewitz asserted repeatedly from this moment on. Every attack loses impetus as it progresses, as he put it in the final words of one of his last texts.[28] The superiority of Russian defensive operations led him to qualify his previous view of the exemplary character of Napoleon's strategy because the offensive way of waging war was inappropriate when Russia, rather than Prussia or Austria, was the opponent. Previously the French had been victorious everywhere, and therefore their aggressive form of war was regarded as a "true arcanum," the holy of holies in the waging of war. Clausewitz drew the following conclusions from the Russian campaign:

> Anyone who thinks this matter through carefully will say to himself that attack is the weaker form of war and defense the stronger form. He will also see, though, that the former is the positive form, that is to say the greater and more decisive, and that the latter has only negative purposes; this brings about a balance, and makes it possible for the two forms to exist alongside one another.[29]

This change in Clausewitz's assessment of Napoleon becomes especially clear in one of his late texts, where he no longer sees Napoleon's boundless violence as a consequence of his genius. He now treats it as a strategy to which Napoleon had to resort in an emergency, an indication of his tendency to "gamble." The exceptional circumstances in which France and Bonaparte had found themselves almost everywhere had made it possible to "overthrow the enemy" and to render him defenseless. Plans that had arisen on this basis, and the execution of those plans, became the general norm in military theory, but this amounted to a summary dismissal of the entire history of war up until that point, and that would turn out to be foolish.[30]

The tension within Clausewitz's assessment of Napoleon can be seen in the final words of his account of the Russian campaign: "We repeat, everything that he was he owed to his daring and resolute character; and his most triumphant campaigns would have suffered the same censure as this one had they not succeeded."[31] Napoleon conducted this campaign as he had conducted all his others. This was how he had made himself the master of Europe, and it was the only way he could have achieved this. Anyone who had admired Bonaparte in all his earlier campaigns as the greatest of commanders should not, therefore, despise him now. Clausewitz's positive appreciation of Napoleon's achievements must be seen in the context of the fact that in the course of the Russian campaign Napoleon and his army were not really defeated in a single skirmish or battle. "In every battle the French were victorious; in each they were allowed to achieve the impossible—but when we come to the final reckoning, the French army has ceased to exist."[32] While continuing to admire Napoleon's military genius, Clausewitz realized as a result of the Russian campaign that even this genius could not be successful under all conditions. "It could not be foreseen with certainty, it was perhaps not even likely, that the Russians would abandon Moscow, burn it down, and engage in a war of attrition; but once this happened the war was bound to miscarry, regardless of how it was conducted."[33] Clausewitz's later thought and his hesitant abandonment of the view that Napoleon's strategy was exemplary reflects the tension between his continued admiration for Napoleon and his insight, which was the consequence of the failure of the Russian campaign, into the inevitable variability and historical specificity of strategy. In fact, Clausewitz (like many later Germans) always remained under Napoleon's spell. He never realized that there was a contradiction between his own definition of military genius and Napoleon's genius in that Napoleon lacked the higher virtue needed by a statesman like Frederick the Great: not to rely solely on military capabilities but to take into account the political circumstances before and after the war.[34]

In *War and Peace* Tolstoy practically repeats this judgment concerning Napoleon. At the beginning the narrative presents Napoleon as someone who possesses a military flair that could be taken for genius. Later, after the crossing of the Niemen in June 1812, Napoleon is described more like a criminal lunatic.[35] Hegel took the same view. When he wrote *The Phenomenology of the Spirit* during the campaign of 1806, which resulted in the Prussian defeat at Jena, he thought he had experienced the absolute mind described in his *Philosophy of Mind* when Napoleon was riding past him in the streets of Jena. In his later writings, especially in *Elements of the History of Rights*, Hegel changed his mind about Napoleon. So Clausewitz as well as Hegel and even Tolstoy in their early writing all first admired Napoleon, then changed their opinions. Although they shared to a certain degree their admiration for Napoleon, they viewed him from different standpoints: Clausewitz saw him as a strategist, Hegel as a philosopher, and finally Tolstoy in his description of Prince Andrei's assessment, as an existential warrior.[36]

Whereas Clausewitz emphasized the failures of Napoleon and his army in the 1812 campaign, Tolstoy, while acknowledging the problems of the Russian general staff, maintained that it was the Russian people themselves who defeated Napoleon. Clausewitz's main objective was to understand and explain why Napoleon's previously successful new kind of warfare failed in Russia. For Tolstoy the Russian victory over Napoleon was to stand as model for the regeneration of the Russian army after its failure in the Crimean War.

In Clausewitz's view, the strategy derived from Jena and from Napoleon's early successes reached its limits for the first time in Moscow. After Jena, Clausewitz had initially adopted an existential notion of war. In this conception, the transformation of the political subject, the modernization of the army, and limited changes in Prussia's political conditions were supposed to provide the means by which warfare could be waged successfully. The new way of waging war had been modeled on the example of Napoleon, but it was the limitations of this very model of warfare that were revealed in Moscow.

This had two consequences for Clausewitz's military theory. First, he recognized that Napoleon's strategy could not be applied, as he had previously thought, in all conceivable circumstances. Second, he began—despite his admiration for Napoleon—to criticize him for sticking to his established strategy in spite of changed circumstances and thereby trying to bend fate to his will. What Clausewitz had formerly seen purely as Napoleon's genius he now reevaluated as thoughtlessness and negligence. While Napoleon's goal of defeating and dispersing the Russian army and occupying Moscow was a feasible objective for a campaign, in order to achieve this something else would have been needed: sufficient strength in Moscow. Bonaparte had neglected this, however, "solely out of the arrogant recklessness that was characteristic of him."[37]

The most conspicuous lesson of the Russian campaign was the superiority of defense to attack. A less obvious lesson, but one fully developed and repeatedly stressed by Clausewitz in his later writings, was the primacy of policy over warfare. The Russian campaign could not have been won as it had been waged. Here Clausewitz drew attention to a fundamental limit of warfare. In his view, in the circumstances of the time Russia could not be militarily defeated, not by any conceivable strategy and not even by Napoleon. It is true that in later years, Clausewitz returned repeatedly to the subject of the conditions under which Russia could in fact have been defeated (especially in book 8 of *On War*). These reflections seem to have been prompted, however, by the possibility of a new war between Prussia and Russia and thoughts about Prussia's prospects of success, rather than by any renewed change of mind on Clausewitz's part about the significance of politics for warfare in the light of the limits of what was militarily possible. While the Prussian defeats had demonstrated the superiority of military force over "inadequately armed ideals" and over politics in the form of diplomacy, in Moscow the limits of attempts to achieve political goals by military means became clear. It was this experience of the immanent limits of even Napoleon's strategy that prompted Clausewitz to develop a new basic idea of his political theory, the primacy of policy over warfare.

Tolstoy was neither the first nor the last to emphasize a direct connection between Clausewitz's instrumental view of war as a tool of policy and a tendency toward absolute war and therefore an escalation of violence as a means of war. Jomini (perhaps for the first time), followed by Liddell Hart as well as Keegan, is a prominent example. René Girard has taken a similar stand in our times.[38] Most unfortunately, the German general staff from the war of unification up to the Second World War drew this same connection.[39] Nevertheless, this assessment requires serious scrutiny. Martin van Creveld, one of the most eminent contemporary Clausewitz critics, argues that an instrumental war would be by definition limited and that with such an approach one could not win any battle or war against an opponent who was fighting for his survival and identity.[40] While Tolstoy, Liddell Hart, Keegan, and all the others criticize Clausewitz for the supposed connection between his instrumental view and total war, van Creveld takes the opposite view. In my opinion, none of these critics of Clausewitz is right because each of them concentrates on only one pole of a dynamic tension.

Jena, Moscow, and Waterloo in Clausewitz's Political Theory

The lost battles of the Prussian army at Jena and Auerstädt were, without doubt, the most significant events in Clausewitz's life. They demonstrated the superiority of military power over policy and also of the strategies of unleashing violence, attack, and decisive battle over the existing belief in the equal status of maneuver and giving battle. After Jena and Auerstädt Clausewitz developed an existential construction of war according to which the state, as the actor waging war, should be replaced by the nation and the people, as had happened in France. Clausewitz's thought began to evolve again after Moscow. The superiority of defense over attack, the military value of avoiding a decisive battle, and the immanent limits of what could be achieved by military action at least suggested that policy should be accorded primacy over military aims. Waterloo in turn demonstrated the primacy of policy in a situation where the two sides were waging war in very similar ways and at the same time showed the negative side of Napoleon's strategy of unrestrained violence, which—as could now be seen—had led to self-destruction.[41]

Once Clausewitz had drawn from this battle the conclusion that Napoleon should have tried to limit his defeat, it was not difficult to take the next step and begin to treat strategies for limited wars as no less important than Napoleon's strategy of maximum force. As we have already seen, even after Waterloo Clausewitz's attitude to Napoleon remained a mixture of admiration and criticism. We can therefore identify four fundamental antitheses in Clausewitz's theory, which were based on his experience and examination of war campaigns and can be found in his analyses of Jena, Moscow, and Waterloo. These include the expansion or limitation of violence, an existential or an instrumental understanding of war, the primacy of military force or policy, and the priority of the attack or the superiority of the defense.

As I have been arguing, Clausewitz shared a common belief with Tolstoy in what Münkler calls existential warfare. The difference is that Clausewitz made this argument after the Prussian defeat at Jena, while Tolstoy made it in the context of the Russian resistance against Napoleon. In response to the fictional dialogue between Wolzogen and Clausewitz, Prince Andrei insists in *War and Peace* that "[i]f there was none of this magnanimity in war, we'd go to it only when it was worth going to certain death, as now. Then there would be no war because Pavel Ivanych offended Mikhail Ivanych. But if there's war like now, then it's war. And then the intensity of the troops would be something quite different" (III, 2, xxv, 775).[42] Ironically, given the negative representation of him in the novel, Clausewitz's justification of the existential construction of war may even shed light on Tolstoy's (and Andrei's) conception of it.

After the Prussian defeats at Jena and Auerstädt, the focus of Clausewitz's analysis was no longer the Prussian state but the German nation as a subject waging war. "We wander, orphaned children of a lost fatherland, and see that the luster of the state we served, the state we helped to form, has been extinguished."[43] During these years his goal was, in Paret's words, "the ideal of German freedom." "We nourished the loftiest hopes; never can an army have purchased more noble glory with its blood than we would have done had we saved the honor, the freedom, and the civic happiness of the German nation."[44] Clausewitz realized that the French victories had been made possible by the mobilization of the entire nation. For the first time in history, conscript armies had been put into the field whose numbers alone made them superior to the armies of the military powers that had been dominant up to that point.[45]

The mobilization of the nation did not just affect conscripts. The *levée en masse* decreed that *all* French citizens were considered part of the contingent called upon to perform military service. Young men would join the ranks, married men would forge weapons and be responsible for supplies, women would make tents and clothing and work in the hospitals, children would make bandages, and old people would go to the public squares, where they would keep up the soldiers' fighting morale and declare their hatred of the enemy. The decree stated that "[f]rom now on, until the moment when all enemies have been driven from the territory of the Republic, all French citizens are called upon to perform permanent military service."[46] In his obituary of Scharnhorst, Clausewitz stressed the military potential of the concept of the nation. With their revolutionary measures, he argued, the French had freed the terrible element of war from its old financial and diplomatic restraints. He now saw war marching onward in the form of raw violence, carrying with it the great forces it had unleashed.[47]

Clausewitz combined this orientation toward a German nation realized outside state institutions with what Münkler calls an "existential construction of war." According to this conception war is not a direct way of pursuing policy goals but a medium through which a political entity is constituted, transformed, and changed. Through it man can rise above his normal condition, go beyond his everyday egoism, and attain for the first time the condition in which the body politic becomes conscious of its identity.[48]

This existential construction of war as a means of constituting or transforming a political identity is apparent in a letter Clausewitz wrote in 1806. "You want a revolution. I am not opposed to this, but will it not be much easier to bring about this revolution in the civic constitution, and in the constitution of the state, in the midst of the movement and vibration of all parts that is occasioned by war?"[49] In a letter from 1809 he once again states his belief in the need for a revolution in Europe. "Whoever is victorious, Europe cannot escape a great and general revolution. [...] Even a general insurrection of the German peoples [...] would only be a precursor of this great and general revolution."[50] Here Clausewitz advocates more than just a revolution of civil society and the state constitution. He is also saying that it will be easier to bring about this revolution by waging war. We should not allow ourselves to be deceived by Clausewitz's revolutionary choice of words, however. At this stage of the development of his thought, he supports the idea of a revolution and orients himself strongly toward the "German nation" as a political subject. But he uses these ideas only as the means to the desired end of military success. From Clausewitz's perspective, the achievements of the French revolutionary armies necessitated a fundamental transformation of the political subject if Prussia (or Germany) were to be able to offer effective resistance to Napoleon and his army, which had so far been victorious in all its battles. Prussia's old army and its old political structures would not be able to do this. However, for Clausewitz the apparently total preoccupation with and privileging of military success also places limits on the extent to which man can rise above his normal condition through war and violence, since this process remains tied to the instrumental value of his actions. By way of contrast, no real limits are set by Ernst Moritz Arndt and Theodor Körner at the time of the wars of liberation and later by Ernst Jünger and Max Scheler in World War I and by Frantz Fanon in the period of decolonization in the 1950s and 1960s to what I shall call the disinhibition of man through war and violence.[51]

Clausewitz's new ideas, like those of the Prussian military reformers after Jena, were a double-edged sword. As a reaction to Prussian defeats, military reforms were introduced that were oriented simultaneously toward the example provided by the victorious Napoleonic armies and specific Prussian conditions. The result was a particular kind of tension. On the one hand, the whole of society was to be mobilized to support the waging of war, with the goal of creating a *soldat citoyen* who would always be ready for patriotic action and prepared to sacrifice himself. On the other hand, the political transformation had to remain limited, as there was no intention of doing anything to endanger the existing structure of rule. Prussia did not have a sovereign nation of citizens, and it did not even have a constitution restricting the powers of the monarch and making it possible for citizens to participate in drawing up legislation. But how could national enthusiasm and a readiness to sacrifice oneself for the nation-state be brought about in accordance with the French model without the necessary social basis—equality of all citizens and the opening up of opportunities for them to participate in political life?

The military reforms were therefore self-contradictory, even though there can be no doubt that they contained many positive elements—in particular, the abolition of degrading and inhumane punishments. The only way the reformers could mobilize the whole of society for war without changing any part of the existing social structure was through an "educational dictatorship" (*Erziehungsdiktatur*).[52] Before the Prussian defeats, the army had been an institution characterized by internal brutality, an absence of freedom, and strict separation between different social ranks. The reformers took the view that it needed to become the "main school of the entire nation," for war and also for peace, as the minister of war, Herrmann von Boyen, put it in the

1814 Prussian Law on Defense. In taking this step the reformers went much further than requiring the whole nation to serve during the restricted period in which war was actually being waged. From now on, this kind of service was to be a goal in peacetime as well. The military was supposed to become more civilized, but the nation was to be militarized. The second of these points was understood by Councillor of State von Raumer as the "beneficial sense of order, subordination, and honor" acquired by citizens during their military service and then applied in the civil context.[53]

It would be a mistake to see Clausewitz as a revolutionary. In reality, his 1809 letter expresses the contradiction experienced by all conservatives in revolutionary times (as Aron puts it). If the "raging turmoil among the people" were one day to endanger the king, he would unquestioningly lay down his life for the monarch. He could not hope to delay a revolution or to reverse it by doing this; that would require very different measures, and heroic self-sacrifice would not be enough. But he would do whatever he could, and proudly. At the same time, he emphasized that the king would be lost if he had to rely on such actions. While continuing to manifest unconditional loyalty to the state as embodied in the king, or rather an almost feudal submissiveness to the person of the king, Clausewitz clearly realized the extent of the revolutionary crisis, and it was this that placed him in the reformers' camp.[54] Clausewitz's existential construction of war thus expresses the tension between loyalty to the old order and the revolutionizing of warfare based upon the French model. It must also be seen in relation to changes in those areas of politics and society that presented obstacles to military modernization.

The Dialectical Conception of *On War*

Tolstoy, like Clausewitz, uses a lot of contrasts. *War and Peace* itself, starting with the title, is organized around antitheses, and this is related to the Hegelian intellectual climate of nineteenth-century Russia. The novel opens with opposites that will have to be compared if not reconciled: city versus country, reason versus feeling, Russian versus French, and so on. Very different thinkers, on different sides of issues, nonetheless organized their thought in terms of antitheses and (sometimes but not always) synthesis. Tolstoy makes moral contrasts that seem multidimensional and in fact create all kinds of nuances that the reader must note in order to understand the novel—for instance, the contrast between Petersburg and Moscow. Tolstoy had read little if any Hegel, but he made brilliant use of the Hegelian structure. He is more interested in expressing the subtleties of existence through two seemingly opposed positions than he is in striving for either synthesis or duality. Wholeness is important but rarely achievable and always unstable.[55]

Clausewitz developed another kind of dialectics. For him the conceptualization of war in terms of antitheses was a problem that he made some attempts to solve. Though he was never able to do this, as was the case with so many of the plans he had at the time of his death, he even intended to write a separate chapter on the principle of polarity.[56] In an article written shortly before he died, Clausewitz wrote that the "whole of physical and intellectual nature" is kept in balance by means of antitheses.[57] When he dealt with the relationship between attack and defense, he wrote of the "true logical antithesis" between them, which was of greater significance than a simple logical contradiction.[58]

Aron and Paret, the authors of some of the most important studies of Clausewitz published to date, have both emphasized his dialectical method, and Aron assumes that Clausewitz would have disclosed the secret of his method in the above mentioned chapter he intended to write about polarity. He draws attention in particular to the fact that none of the commentators on Clausewitz has so far undertaken any further investigation of the significance of this remark. The planned chapter on polarity would, says Aron, have covered the different kinds of antitheses, which is to say that it would have dealt with the particular features of Clausewitz's method.[59] It is this question, the secret of Clausewitz's dialectics, to which we now turn.

Nevertheless, Aron argues that the *narrow* concept of polarity could not become a fundamental concept for Clausewitz because it is tied to the idea of a zero-sum game. As Clausewitz put it, the principle of polarity is valid only in cases where "positive and negative interests exactly cancel one another out." In a battle, both sides are trying to win; only this is "true polarity," since if one wins the other must lose.[60] Aron distinguishes between the zero-sum game of the duel and the diverse forms of antitheses typical of the pairs of concepts employed by Clausewitz.[61] In these antitheses, each concept can be seen as a pole: theory and practice, the scale of success and the risk taken, attack and defense. Aron concludes that if one wanted to identify a fundamental concept in Clausewitz, it would be that of the antithesis.

Paret argues that Clausewitz's general approach is dialectical in character. This was, he says, characteristic of Clausewitz's generation, all of whom thought in terms such as contradiction, polarity, the separation and connection of the active and passive, the positive and the negative. The principle of polarity seemed to be the only thing that could overcome the infinite distance between the positive and the negative. Clausewitz's treatments of polarity and of the relationship between attack and defense were, according to Paret, variations on this contemporary theme.[62] In Clausewitz's time polarity was a fundamental principle of Goethe's understanding of nature as a force that could be divided into polar opposites that would then reunite. In Goethe's conception expressed in 1828, polarity and growth were the two great wheels driving the whole of nature.[63] Clausewitz's remarks at the beginning of his first chapter are in accordance with this methodological principle. He introduces the escalating effects of violence, fear, and power in war (the so-called intensification of force) and deduces these, like Hegel, from the interactions that are common to both his own and Hegel's understanding of polarity.[64] Hegel stressed that the contemporary discovery of polarity had been of "enormous significance."[65]

During this time of fundamental changes in ideas, habits of thought, and political conditions, the question of whether an antithesis should be thought of as a unity or whether it could do no more than emphasize the contrast between old and new, was an issue of paramount importance. In 1811 Rahel Levin described this problem in the following terms: "In this new world that has been broken into pieces, the only thing left to a man who wishes to understand [...] is the heroism of scholarship."[66]

Different aspects of polarity need to be distinguished from one another. Schelling, for example, stressed that behind what appeared to be contrasts there was a hidden identity that must be sought, and he understood polarity as a law of the world: "It is a priori certain that [...] real principles opposed to one another are at work throughout the whole of nature." If these opposing principles are united in one body, they give that body polarity, according to Schelling. Goethe, on the other hand, placed more emphasis on the lively tension between opposites: "The life of nature divides what is unified and unites what is divided."[67]

The most important influences on Clausewitz were the currents of rationalism, enlightenment, idealism, romanticism, and the natural sciences. Clausewitz learned about rationalism at an early age from J. G. K. Kiesewetter, a follower of Kant. During Clausewitz's time in Berlin, the idealism of Fichte and Hegel was the dominant current of thought in intellectual circles. In addition to reading the Goethe-Schiller correspondence in 1829, Clausewitz also attended the lectures of the romantic philosopher Heinrich Steffens during the winter of 1824–25 and those of the naturalist Alexander von Humboldt, which were the start of a new flowering of the natural sciences in Germany, in 1827.[68]

One can say that Clausewitz's theory of war floats within the field formed by these five currents of thought. Each of them provided him with stimulation, but his own position cannot be traced back to any single one of them. By floating in this way, Clausewitz was able to develop a position of his own, which is more than a mere variation on the theme of the significance of antitheses and their unity so widely discussed at the time.

Clausewitz developed a theory of war deeply rooted in his historical experiences and analyses and containing a dialectical essence, whereas Tolstoy highlights only one extreme in a pair of opposites. Clausewitz's final word, therefore, is his trinity, which consists of the three tendencies of violence/force as well as fight/struggle and finally the affiliation of the combatants to a cohesive community. Clausewitz's last word, his legacy, is neither the instrumental nor the existential construction of war but his wondrous trinity.

Tolstoy's view is also valid and important, however. It reminds us that each war is a tragedy, that it is dangerous when violence becomes an independent force in war, and that violence in war is not only a means for politics. Given Tolstoy's negative representation of Clausewitz in *War and Peace,* it is ironic that the two men agree about all these matters. The very late, dialectically inspired, Clausewitz portrays these ideas in a theoretical and Tolstoy in his novel in a literary manner.

11

The Disobediences
of *War and Peace*

ELIZABETH D. SAMET

Zoltan Korda's film *The Four Feathers* (1939), based on the eponymous 1902 novel by A. E. W. Mason, tells the story of Harry Faversham (John Clements), an ambivalent British soldier from a prominent military family accused by his friends and fiancée of cowardice after he resigns his commission on the eve of his regiment's taking ship to join Kitchener's army in North Africa. Presented by his accusers with four white feathers—the shaming emblems of his seeming cowardice—Harry redeems three with acts of extraordinary bravery in the Sudan. He saves the life of one friend struck blind by the sun and left for dead after an attack by Dervishes, and he rescues two more by liberating the prison at Omdurman.

In the film's final scene, Faversham, dining with his comrades, his reconciled fiancée, and his future father-in-law, the bullying General Burroughs (C. Aubrey Smith), enacts a rather different kind of heroism by rewriting the history of Balaclava. He returns the fourth feather to his fiancée by correcting her father's embroidered account of the battle. The positions of both armies are established on the table: from behind a row of guns (walnuts) the Russians await the enemy's charge. On the right is the British infantry (a "thin red line" of wine). In the center, at the head of the Sixty-Eighth Regiment, astride his horse, sits Burroughs (a pineapple), while behind the Sixty-Eighth waits the commander in chief (an apple). According to the general, the attack was launched by his command: "The Sixty-Eighth will move forward!" Burroughs's account reveals a conventional understanding of military action as organized and directed by a leader's command. Faversham, however, tells rather a different story involving the general's spirited horse, Caesar (represented in this war game by a fork).

You never said it, Sir [....] No, Sir, you never had time. At that moment, Caesar [...] startled by a stray bullet, took the bit between his teeth and dashed straight to the Russian lines. Away went Caesar, away went you, away went the Sixty-Eighth, away went the commander in chief, away went everybody. And another magnificent mistake was added to an already magnificent record. But nobody ever said the Sixty-Eighth will move forward. Unless it was the horse.[1]

Conveniently ignoring the fact that the British lost at Balaclava, the film thus ends with the suggestion that history has been made not by a general but by an insubordinate horse. Replacing the logic of command and control with a narrative of battle as the haphazard result of a stray bullet and the premature charge of a spirited animal, Faversham's revision offers a portrait of battle as the sum total of acts of chance rather than a plan engineered by human agency.

As this vignette intimates, my theme is obedience—or, more exactly, disobedience—my premise that Leo Tolstoy's *War and Peace* is in several senses a disobedient book. Playful though it is, *The Four Feathers* offers a version of cause and effect that should feel familiar to readers of Tolstoy's novel: one in which accident often triumphs over human design, in which invisible patterns of action and consequence refute a heroic narrative dramatizing events as authored by great men, and in which the only obedience can be the obedience perforce surrendered to chance. In his chief example of the illusory agency of individuals, Tolstoy calls it a mistake to imagine that Napoleon actually superintended the retreat from Moscow. In fact, "during all this time of his activity," the French emperor "was like a child who, holding the straps tied inside a carriage, fancies that he is driving it" (IV, 2, xi, 1008). Examining Tolstoy's novel by considering the concept of obedience—understood as compliance with, or submission to, customs, norms, rules, laws, or another's will—exposes not only the degree of the novel's nonconformity but also Tolstoy's expression through it of what could be called a doctrine of disobedience.

The disobedience of *War and Peace* is manifold. It operates not only within the narrative itself in individual, communal, military, and political senses but also beyond it—in the historiography and ideology that informed its composition and in the very manner of its telling. Yet it is by no means easy to separate discrete strands. What is the significance of Tolstoy's disobedient representation of a world that is itself so disobedient to its initial readers' prevailing expectations about the workings of the universe?[2] What, moreover, does *War and Peace* have to say to a twenty-first-century reader who encounters it in an era often characterized as one of persistent, decentralized, and increasingly unpredictable warfare?

Although they have not always used the word "disobedience," various readers of Tolstoy's novel have responded forcefully to the book's fundamental recalcitrance. Percy Lubbock complained, for example, that the novel's constituent parts refused to "coalesce" and came to seem more "disparate and disorganized" at each successive reading.[3] And what, after all, is Henry James's often quoted description of *War and Peace,* together with Dumas's *The Three Musketeers* and Thackeray's *The Newcomes,* as one of the age's "large loose baggy monsters," if not a recognition of the book's disobedience of established formal principles? James's allusion to monstrosity occurs in his preface to the New York edition of *The Tragic Muse,* in the context of an argument about aesthetic value, specifically the centrality of "composition," by which James means organization, to art. Exuberant and full of "life" as it is, *War and Peace* nevertheless lacks the "deep-breathing economy" and "organic form" James associates with beauty. What, he asks, can a novel dominated by "queer elements of the accidental and the arbitrary, artistically *mean?*"[4]

In an essay on the Englishness of Turgenev, James offers a more expansive assessment of this quality of arbitrariness in Tolstoy. Here James differentiates between Turgenev's "method" and Tolstoy's exuberance.

> The perusal of Tolstoy—a wonderful mass of life—is an immense event, a kind of splendid accident, for each of us: his name represents nevertheless no such eternal spell of method, no such quiet irresistibility of presentation, as shines, close to us and lighting our possible steps, in that of his precursor [Turgenev]. Tolstoy is a reflector as vast as a natural lake; a monster harnessed to his great subject—all human life!—as an elephant might be harnessed, for purposes of traction, not to a carriage, but to a coach-house.[5]

The all-encompassing fidelity of Tolstoy's fiction, which reflects life in the manner of a natural lake, eschews the policing design in which James locates the essential difference between world and art. The same fundamental lawlessness characterizes at once the novel and the experience of reading it. A similar understanding of the vertiginous quality of Tolstoy's fictional universe animates the claims of English critics from Matthew Arnold to Virginia Woolf that Tolstoy creates life, not art, and, more generally, that Russian literature unsettles English readers trained up on Victorian novels by denying them the closure they have come to expect.[6]

Tolstoy himself readily—even defiantly—acknowledged his novel's generic slipperiness. "What is *War and Peace?*" he reflected in "A Few Words Apropos of the Book *War and Peace*" (1868). "It is not a novel, still less an epic poem, still less a historical chronicle. *War and Peace* is what the author wanted and was able to express, in the form in which it is expressed."[7] By this tautology I suppose Tolstoy meant that *War and Peace* is what it is. In being what it is, the novel resists not only "conventional forms of artistic prose" but also—notwithstanding that it is drawn from actual events—historical narratives of cause and effect. "A historian has to do with the results of an event," he explains, "the artist with the fact of the event."[8]

Tolstoy proposes that his "disregard" for convention is in fact part of a larger Russian trend, and he goes even further by linking the disregard for convention with artistic excellence: "[T]here is not a single work of artistic prose in the modern period of Russian literature, rising slightly above mediocrity, that would fit perfectly into the form of the novel, the epic, or the story."[9] The production of disobedient novels was by no means unique to Russia during the period. Among *War and Peace*'s monstrous cousins we might number Melville's *Moby-Dick,* with its abundant prefatory matter, digressions on the skeletal structure of whales, and philosophical interludes; Charles Dickens's *Bleak House,* an experiment in double narrative one reviewer faulted for an "absolute want of construction"; and George Eliot's *Daniel Deronda,* a novel with a double plot, which James likened to "a looking-glass which had fallen upon the floor [...] and was lying in fragments."[10] Each of these books posed structural problems for its earliest readers; each seeded the ground for various twentieth-century implosions of the genre.

The aforementioned novels could all be said to have a political dimension; in none, however, does generic instability necessarily constitute a philosophical statement. In *War and Peace,* by contrast, hybrid form is inseparable from Tolstoy's rejection of a dominant worldview, especially of the idea that war is an enterprise through which a few latter-day epic heroes shape the ends of history. In his seminal Tolstoy criticism of the 1930s, Boris Eikhenbaum discerned an epic style and structure in *War and Peace.* George Steiner likewise perceived affinities of "temper and vision" between Tolstoy and Homer.[11] But what does it mean to understand *War and Peace* as an epic? Surely it signifies more than the presence of periodic digressions, more than the subject matter of war. In fact, *War and Peace* seems the antithesis of epic, at least as defined by M. M. Bakhtin, in its rejection of a "commonly held evaluation and point of view" and its embrace of the "openendedness, indecision, indeterminacy" Bakhtin associated with the novel.[12] Emphasizing the epic's inertness, Bakhtin asserted a contrast between its inexorable teleology and the more elastic, unstable structures of the novel. Even more germane to the question of epic lineaments in *War and Peace* is David Quint's reexamination in *Epic and Empire* of the "old opposition between epic and romance" through a study of the tradition of the defeated.

> While the narrative romances that we are most familiar with [...] contain seemingly aimless episodes of wandering and digression—*adventures*—they also characteristically are organized by a quest that [...] will finally achieve its goal. But the romance that Virgilian epic sees as the "other" of its teleological plot is almost pure adventure [....] The Virgilian linking of this kind of romance

narrative to the condition of defeat remains normative even for Lucan's rival tradition of the losers' epic, in which narrative structures approximate and may explicitly be identified with romance. Such epics valorize the very contingency and open-endedness that the victors' epic disparages.[13]

Quint's analysis of the losers' epic, which embraces contingency and resists the linear march of victory, offers a lens through which to view the tension animating *War and Peace* between a misguided belief in human agency—in the power of individuals to initiate events and to bring about particular ends—and what Tolstoy perceives to be our fundamental instrumentality, subject as we are to the invisible forces that actually shape historical narrative.

Tolstoy borrows epic motifs only to subvert the presumed authority of what Hegel called "[w]orld-historical men—the Heroes of an epoch, [...] its clear-sighted ones."[14] Among the techniques Tolstoy exploits is that of beginning in the middle of things. *War and Peace* opens in medias res with Anna Pavlovna Scherer in the act of accosting Prince Vassily as he enters her salon with what is effectively a demand for war: "Eh bien, mon prince, Gênes et Lucques ne sont plus que des apanages, des estates, de la famille Buonaparte. Non, je vous préviens, que si vous ne me dites pas que nous avons la guerre, [...] je ne vous connais plus." Through Anna Pavlovna's threat that she will not "know" Prince Vassily in the future if he does not agree with her that Russia is at war, Tolstoy establishes the very definition of war as a subject of contention within the novel. Vassily comments on the belligerence of this greeting: "Dieu, quelle virulente sortie!" (I, 1, i, 3) But he does not respond to its substance. The question of whether a state of war exists remains undecided.

Tolstoy reaffirms this initial inconclusiveness in ways large and small.[15] In the very next scene, for example, Pierre picks up Caesar's *Commentaries* at random from a shelf in Prince Andrei's study—it is "the first book that caught his eye"—begins "reading it from the middle," and is almost immediately interrupted by the entrance of Andrei himself (I, 1, v, 24). This introduction of an ancient war story in progress, denied both beginning and end, emblematizes the drift of the entire novel, which depicts a world in perpetual motion. The search for the beginnings, or "causes," of historical events plunges the investigator into a vertiginous, unending quest: "[A] countless number of causes present themselves. The deeper we go in search of causes, the more of them we find." Yet each, Tolstoy continues, proves "equally false" (III, 1, i, 604).[16] To believe otherwise is to embrace what Gary Saul Morson calls "the fallacy of the decisive moment."[17] In contrast to the Caesarian conclusiveness of "Veni, vidi, vici," Tolstoy offers only the fiction of purpose: "When a man finds himself in motion, he always thinks up a goal for that motion" (IV, 2, xix, 1028).

War and Peace twice tries to conclude—in part 4, volume 4, and again in the first epilogue—where it began, in medias res. In the first instance, Tolstoy breaks off a conversation between Natasha and Princess Marya about Pierre's imminent departure for St. Petersburg: "'Only what's he going to Petersburg for!' Natasha said suddenly, and hastily answered herself: 'No, no, it has to be so...Right, Marie? It has to be so...'" (IV, 4, xix, 1125). Princess Marya does not answer; the chapter ends in an ellipsis, its inconclusiveness not subsequently resolved. The first part of the epilogue also ends elliptically, as Nikolenka Bolkonsky drifts off to sleep after being awakened by the "terrible dream" in which he and Pierre are "marching at the head of a huge army" (Epilogue, 1, xvi, 1177–78).

When the novel finally does end, it leaves us with an astronomical, historical, and metaphysical map that defuses the epic tension between heroic will and the incorrigible force of war through a recognition of the ultimate "subjection of the person to the laws of space, time, and causes" (Epilogue, 2, xii, 1214). One of the differences between the novel's resolution and that of epic is the absence of conclusive heroic action, even if the vain desire to become a hero persists in Nikolenka (and perhaps Pierre). Broad though its sweep may be, classical epic ends with a focus on the individual act: Priam retrieving and burying Hector's miraculously healed corpse, the dea ex machina of Athena enforcing peace in Ithaca, Aeneas ending the war in Italy by plunging his sword into the breast of Turnus. But in *War and Peace,* the mass of humanity replaces the individual figure, contingency dislodges agency, and Tolstoy insists in the epilogue's final sentence that we must "renounce a nonexistent freedom and recognize a dependence we do not feel" (Epilogue, 2, xii, 1215).

The title of Tolstoy's novel promises a kind of balance—a contrapuntal architecture of order and disorder—but it is war that dominates the narrative by threatening always to break out again. We certainly cannot settle the point at which it begins. We cannot even settle the moment at which it ends: Anna Pavlovna asserts war as a preexisting condition, while Andrei's son dreams it into the future. The book thus stands in opposition to an Enlightenment understanding of war itself as unnatural interruption rather than habitual condition: "millions of men set about killing each other," Tolstoy tells us in his 1868 commentary, because in doing so they were simply "fulfilling that elementary zoological law which the bees fulfill by exterminating each other in the fall."[18]

The disobedience of the plot of *War and Peace*—one contemporary reviewer suggested the novel had no plot at all[19]—is an inevitable symptom of Tolstoy's theory of history. By the time Tolstoy published the first, abbreviated version of the work in the 1860s, conventional approaches to history were already coming under attack, just as new theories of social science were coalescing. There is a parallel between Tolstoy's representations of events and the historiography of, for example, Leopold von Ranke, who in 1824 offered a critique of traditional humanist methods that molded the past into coherent narratives to serve didactic ends. Historians traditionally aspired to "the office of judging the past, of instructing the present for the benefit of future ages," but Ranke announced in the preface to his first book that his historical project had a different aim entirely: "It wants only to show what actually happened [*wie es eigentlich gewesen*]."[20] Historians influenced by Ranke also shared Tolstoy's suspicion of "biographical historians" (Epilogue, 2, ii, 1182). They dismissed this style of history writing—and other forms of life writing along with it—as a corrupt genre that had more in common with literature than with history because of its tendency to cast great men as the agents of historical change. In the twentieth century, E. H. Carr argued that such work was animated by the "Bad King John theory of history," in which individual actors eclipse the social forces that actually drive events. Carr found something "childish, or at any rate, childlike, about" the need "to postulate individual genius as the creative force in history."[21]

Tolstoy has no interest in anointing a Bad King John. Even Napoleon, Anna Pavlovna's "Antichrist" (I, 1, i, 3), gives way before a version of history animated by unseen causes and sometimes by chance or Providence. In her desire to affix blame on Napoleon, Anna Pavlovna resembles what Tolstoy later calls the "savage" who "imagines that the figure carved on the prow of a ship is the force that guides it" (IV, 2, xi, 1008) or the "muzhik" who believes that "the devil moves" a locomotive (Epilogue, 2, iii, 1186). The pathos of *War and Peace* arises from its unstinting representation of man's ignorance—or, in the case of Andrei, the dawning consciousness—of his own subjugation to the laws of necessity. Furthermore, acceptance of such subjection is not synonymous with knowledge of the particular forces that work on the individual. That knowledge, Tolstoy tells us again and again, is impossible. Even though human beings are at the mercy of a "law of predetermination" that "governs history," he argues in "A Few Words," we seem paradoxically hardwired to imagine "a whole series of retrospective conjectures aimed at proving [our] freedom to [ourselves]."[22] It is from the collision between the unarticulated laws of necessity and the elaborate fictions human beings weave to explain their own behavior that the counterpoint of war and peace—of *War and Peace*—grows.

Given its author's philosophy of history, *War and Peace* in some sense demands the fiction of disobedience. In Andrei's case, going to war is itself an act of disobedience or a rebellion against a life that, he tells Pierre, "is not for me" (I, 1, v, 25). Military culture, regimented though it may be, effectively liberates

Andrei from the constraining disappointments of an unhappy marriage and the emptiness of society life. If Andrei's dissatisfactions lead him to go to war, however, once there he discovers that he has simply traded one world of contingency for another. All the novel's dissections of battle work to expose the chasm between what is supposed to happen—all those plans devised by the new German scientists of strategy mocked by Tolstoy—and what actually does happen. "[N]ot everything," Andrei wryly informs Bilibin when the latter asks him why the Russians failed to capture the French marshal Mortier, "goes as it's supposed to, and with such regularity as on parade" (I, 2, x, 155).

Even parades do not go according to plan in *War and Peace*. Tolstoy foreshadows the confusion that will characterize the novel's battles by explaining that the order to prepare for Kutuzov's review of the troops is somehow "unclear." Kutuzov wishes to show the Austrians "the sorry condition" of his soldiers by presenting them in their traveling uniforms. A council of commanders, however, determines that the regiment will show to better advantage "in parade uniform," thus inadvertently foiling Kutuzov's plan (I, 2, i, 112–13). As the army crosses the Enns River soon thereafter, the confusion only intensifies. The scene on the bridge reveals soldiers not maneuvering but herding and dispersing like animals or like the river itself: "Prince Nevitsky saw the swift, noisy, low waves of the Enns, which, merging, rippling, and swirling around the pilings of the bridge, drove on one after the other. Looking at the bridge, he saw the same monotonous living waves of soldiers" (I, 2, vii, 139). These early scenes of confusion set the stage for the wholesale chaos of the battles of Schöngraben, Austerlitz, and Borodino, to say nothing of the guerrilla warfare that follows.

It is Andrei's encounter with the artillery captain Tushin at the battle of Schöngraben that begins to crystallize the sardonic frustration he displays with Bilibin into a more determined cynicism. "No one," Tolstoy records, "had given Tushin any orders about where to shoot or with what." On his own initiative, in consultation with his sergeant major, Tushin decides "it would be good to set fire to the village" (I, 2, xvii, 181). Defying two orders to retreat, as well as the French, the odds, and his own instinct for self-preservation, Tushin carries on with his four cannons in a kind of delirium of martial labor (I, 2, xx, 193–94). When Andrei arrives to deliver a third order for the battery's retreat, he overcomes his own fear of the flying cannonballs, surveys the carnage of horses and men, and dismounts to assist Tushin in bringing away whatever guns he can.

For his pains, of course, Captain Tushin is later reprimanded by Prince Bagration for leaving two pieces of artillery behind. It is Andrei who defends the captain to his superior. "And if Your Excellency will allow me to voice my opinion [...] we owe the success of the day most of all to the operation of

this battery and the heroic endurance of Captain Tushin and his company."
Bagration finds himself unwilling to contradict Andrei "and at the same time
[…] unable to believe him fully" (I, 2, xxi, 199). Perhaps Bagration cannot
conceive of one unit having such a decisive impact, for as Andrei's observations of his commander's behavior during the battle reveal, Bagration's understanding of the way in which battle unfolds is less like that of the German
strategists and more like Tolstoy's own.[23]

> Prince Andrei listened carefully to Prince Bagration's exchanges with the com-
> manders and to the orders he gave, and noticed, to his surprise, that no orders
> were given, and that Prince Bagration only tried to pretend that all that was
> done by necessity, chance, or the will of a particular commander, that it was
> all done, if not on his orders, then in accord with his intentions. Owing to
> the tact shown by Prince Bagration, Prince Andrei noticed that, in spite of the
> chance character of events and their independence of the commander's will, his
> presence accomplished a very great deal. Commanders who rode up to Prince
> Bagration with troubled faces became calm, soldiers and officers greeted him
> merrily and became more animated in his presence, and obviously showed off
> their courage before him. (I, 2, xvii, 182)

Within the Russian high command, Bagration's ability to interpret events is
second only to Kutuzov's.

Only the latter, according to Tolstoy, has a full comprehension of the war's
significance. It is Kutuzov, after all, who insists that Borodino is a victory, that
to lose Moscow is not to lose Russia, that the key to winning is the readiness of the people, not the anticipation of Napoleon's every move (IV, 4, v,
1086). Kutuzov's credo, "*patience and time*"—the "two warriors" than whom
"there's nothing stronger" (III, 2, xvi, 744)—expresses his policy fully and
succinctly and also illuminates his understanding that there is, as Andrei comes
to understand, "something stronger and more significant than his will—the
inevitable course of events—and he's able to see them, able to understand
their significance, and, in view of that significance, is able to renounce participating in those events, renounce his personal will and direct it elsewhere" (III,
2, xvi, 745). Instead of cloaking his instrumentality in a Napoleonic rhetoric of
heroic destiny, Kutuzov, Andrei realizes, discerns "the will of Providence" and
embraces his obedience to the spirit of the Russian people (IV, 4, v, 1085). For
Tolstoy, this is the only kind of obedience that makes any sense.

Kutuzov's self-awareness is antithetical to the personal allegiance and fervid
patriotism of a soldier like Nikolai Rostov. It promotes none of the "[t]errible
doubts" (II, 2, xxi, 416) that beset Rostov at the news of Alexander's truce
with Napoleon. With the "feeling of self-forgetfulness" and "passionate at-
traction" for the emperor that surged through him at the review still fresh in

his mind (I, 3, viii, 245), Nikolai angrily insists on the necessity of absolute obedience to the tsar: "And if we start judging and reasoning about everything, then there'll be nothing sacred left [...] Our business is to do our duty, to cut and slash, not to think, that's all" (II, 2, xxi, 416–17). Nikolai's confusion stems from his belief in Alexander as a motor of history. Rostov gives voice to the very worldview Tolstoy sets out to discredit; the confused young officer is vital to the author's project of exposing the seductive fictions whereby we ascribe historical agency to individual actors.

Rostov's desperate pronouncement reveals the stereotypical enthusiasm of a blindly obedient Old World soldier. Nikolai's brand of faith in the tsar as the author of history may not be unique to, but it is perhaps especially characteristic of, a military mindset. The distinguishing features of military life—a chain of command that makes visible the unseen causal links that exist everywhere throughout society; a rigid hierarchy that explicitly fixes place, purpose, and responsibility; an obsessive attention to ritual and routine; an emphasis on absolute obedience—have conditioned Nikolai to internalize the view that the world is controlled by powerful human agents like Alexander and Napoleon, who likewise imagine their own omnipotence.

Yet this model of military obedience was being called into question during the very period of the novel's composition and revision in the latter half of the nineteenth century. In contrast to this view of the Old World automaton, Americans were cultivating a different theory of obedience founded on democratic principles rather than on the personal allegiance motivating Rostov. Soldiers, the theory went, could execute orders with a thoughtful, willing obedience harmonious with both the political conditions out of which they had grown as citizens and also the causes for which they fought.[24] Some American commanders embraced this new model more readily than others. Perhaps no one perceived its importance more thoroughly than Ulysses S. Grant, who celebrated the Union army as a thinking machine. Of the army that Sherman marched through Georgia, Grant wrote, "[H]e had sixty thousand as good soldiers as ever trod the earth; better than any European soldiers, because they not only worked like a machine but the machine thought. European armies know very little what they are fighting for, and care less."[25]

This philosophy of command and obedience had military and political implications; moreover, its articulation of the role of human compliance and agency in the unfolding of battles offers a revealing contrast to the assumptions dominating the Old World Tolstoy depicts. In fact, the confusion Tolstoy introduces to the European battlefield, so antithetical to the imaginations of the German scientists of strategy, finds an illuminating analogue in the accounts of military action in the American Civil War offered by contemporary principals as well as by subsequent historians. One particular episode in

Grant's career offers an intriguing parallel to that of Captain Tushin and to the principle of command exhibited by Kutuzov at Borodino, when he gives no orders at all because of his conviction that "a battle is decided [...] by that elusive force known as the spirit of the troops, and he watched this force and guided it, as far as that lay in his power" (III, 2, xxxv, 805).

The so-called Miracle of Missionary Ridge took place during the battles for Chattanooga in the fall of 1863. On November 25, having repeatedly ordered an advance to no avail, Grant stood below the action, on Orchard Knob, watching "with intense interest" as Union troops at last swept along the ridge and forced the Confederates from their first line of rifle pits.[26] The order had called for Union troops to reform into columns before continuing the advance. However, finding themselves vulnerable to rifle fire from the Confederates perched above them, they appeared to swarm up the hill spontaneously. Grant writes, "Without awaiting further orders or stopping to reform, on our troops went to the second line of works."[27] No one seemed to be able to tell Grant who had ordered the advance. "When those fellows get started," one subordinate explained, "all hell can't stop them."[28]

Tempering somewhat this contemporaneous account of events directed solely by the "spirit of the troops," Brooks D. Simpson argues that while it is "improbable" that "the miracle of Missionary Ridge" was "the result of conscious design" on Grant's part, neither was Missionary Ridge "first and foremost a soldiers' battle. Grant's presence," insists Simpson, "proved indispensible to the result." Peter Cozzens suggests that when no one could tell him who had ordered the men up the ridge, Grant "resigned [himself] to letting events unfold as they might." Grant notes in his memoirs that the charge effectively carried out orders he had issued several days before, but it seems fairly certain that no commander was directly responsible for the advance.[29]

What is most important, in connection with *War and Peace,* about the events on Missionary Ridge is the myth that subsequently grew up around them. Far from being deplored, the troops' apparently spontaneous initiative—akin to that of General Burroughs's skittish horse—came to be celebrated. Herman Melville emphasized the initiative of the Union army in his poem "Chattanooga," which opens with the image of "a kindling impulse" seizing the troops, whose "hearts outran their General's plan." For Melville, the troops' independence is a product of Grant's understanding of the men he led. Commanding "without reserve," Grant could "dare" his men, "Well, go on and do your will / [...] / So master-riders fling the rein." Melville concludes, "But you must know your men." In a footnote to the poem Melville marvels at "the spontaneous enthusiasm of the troops" and dramatizes Grant as subsequently responding to "the impulse and the spectacle" on the steep slope of Missionary Ridge with the words, "I never saw any thing like it."[30]

Melville's celebration of this incident typifies a characteristic American mistrust of great men of the European model, and it offers an important counterpoint to the claim that those great men design and execute world history. During the founding period, the strain was loudest in the writing of John Adams and Thomas Jefferson; it can be traced through the work of Ralph Waldo Emerson in the nineteenth century. Suspicion of the great man's ability to seduce us from ourselves—a phenomenon represented by Tolstoy in Nikolai Rostov's "self-forgetfulness" in the presence of the tsar—stems from a political faith in the possibility of self-reliance and self-determination.

Yet these American thinkers tended to read ideology and democratic destiny where Tolstoy perceived something almost biological: the natural anarchy of "innumerable causes." Tushin may defy the order to retreat for a number of reasons—among them loyalty to the emperor, affection for his country, and hatred for its French invaders—but there is no evidence at this stage of the conflict that the "why" ultimately matters or that Tushin himself is a free agent capable of rebelling against his fate or changing the course of history. Instead, the captain is described as being "in a state similar to feverish delirium or to that of a drunken man" (I, 2, xx, 193). Tushin's actions occur not because Bagration knows him and his capabilities the way Melville claims Grant knew the character of his men: remember the first humiliating encounter between the "small, dirty" Tushin without his boots and a visiting staff officer to whom the captain jokes, "Soldiers say it's nimbler barefoot" (I, 2, xv, 173–74). Rather, like Kutuzov, Tushin accurately measures his purpose and devotes himself utterly to it.

The chaos of the battlefield—its entropy, sprawling unpredictability, manifestation of the complex interconnectedness of all things—serves for Tolstoy as an emblem of the more general workings of historical cause and effect.[31] In "the mechanism of military action," which he likens to "the mechanism of a clock," Tolstoy locates a figure for the movement of history itself: cogs, levers, wheels, and pulleys are all "obedient" to their natural movements yet ignorant of the "result and purpose" of the movement of the "whole" (I, 3, xi, 258). It is this aspect of the novel that resonates most powerfully with the contemporary historical moment, specifically with the ways in which we have begun to think about war in recent years. Several of the attributes of the wars in Iraq and Afghanistan with which the twenty-first century opened—asymmetric warfare, nonstate actors, counterinsurgency, counterterrorism, decentralized networks, ambiguous campaigns for "hearts and minds"—have intensified the so-called Clausewitzian fog, already elemental to comparatively straightforward contests between massed armies on the battlefield.

Melville's account of the events on Missionary Ridge offers a nearly contemporaneous foil to Tolstoy's depiction of battles driven by a democracy—perhaps a revolution—of innumerable causes. Examining the novel in relation to the wars in Iraq and Afghanistan opens yet another window onto Tolstoy's anarchic book as well as onto the legacies of those conflicts, the full significance of which, if we are to follow Tolstoy, we cannot yet comprehend. In its complexity and diffusiveness, early twenty-first-century conflict seems Tolstoyan in ways that previous wars have not, the product of an ultimately unknowable network of causes and effects like the one regulating the flow of events in Tolstoy's universe. Civilian policymakers, military strategists, and academics have responded to this phenomenon in a number of ways. Some regard it as an age of unpredictability, while others look to science to find hidden patterns. Few commentators, however, demonstrate much confidence in the power of individuals to control events.

In 2009, for example, a group of scientists proposed in *Nature* the use of mathematical modeling to predict the behavior of insurgent groups: "Many collective human activities, including violence," they observed, "have been shown to exhibit universal patterns."[32] One of the authors of the study, the physicist Neil Johnson, elaborated: "We found that the way in which humans do insurgent wars—that is, the number of casualties and the timing of events—is universal.... This changes the way we think insurgency works."[33] Johnson and his colleagues posit a coherent system behind violence that appears chaotic to the untutored eye.

Another pertinent model of human insurgency is the military blogger John Robb's "open-source warfare," the characteristics of which bear provocative resemblances to Tolstoy's understanding of the dynamic of war. Robb includes among the fundamental attributes of insurgencies small, autonomously functioning units, fluid networks, the splintering of one group into many, and high dimensionality (the use of network communication that overcomes geographical limitations). In this account can be discerned a technologically enhanced version of the networked theory of history and human conflict articulated by Tolstoy, whose empirical data came primarily from what we now think of as conventional warfare.[34]

United States Army doctrine's emphasis on the concept of operational adaptability in the post-9/11 era also offers what might be thought of as a Tolstoyan response to the challenge of defeating an adversary defined by its decentralization. As Martin E. Dempsey, then commanding general of U.S. Army Training and Doctrine Command, put it at a symposium in 2010, army leaders "used to sit and think that the best information came from the top down." As Dempsey explained in another speech,

> as we decentralize capability and authority *to* the edge, we also need to recognize the requirement to aggregate information and intelligence *from* the

edge—because in this complex environment of decentralized and networked adversaries operating among populations, the best information, the most important intelligence, and the context that provides the best understanding comes from the bottom up, not from the top down.[35]

Underscoring the army's need to evolve twice as fast as its adversaries, Dempsey proposed, in contrast to the old model in which information moved in one direction only—from top to bottom, from individual leaders to the broader force—a new decentralized system in which the information flow is reversed and in which knowledge from the edge is aggregated and factored into commanders' decisions.

Reversing information flow in an organization that is practically, historically, and constitutionally hierarchical requires a recalibrated understanding of military planning and preparation and a different imagining of where knowledge, perspective, and capability actually reside. It envisions a system radically different in nature from the top-down world in which Tushin commanded his battery. In its critique of this world, Tolstoy's book—which seems less grounded or rooted in, than liberated by, history—offers us an illuminating picture of the expansiveness of the longitudinal and latitudinal network in which any putatively independent action is nested. It reminds us of the need, moreover, to recognize both the contingency and the inherent, inevitable fictions of our own historical moment. As Morson argues,

> The only way anyone is effective in *War and Peace* is through alertness and adaptability to unpredictable configurations. Those who rely on planning, who treat time as a mere parameter, are always ineffective [....] The Tolstoyan world is one in which chance upsets plans, systems are always hazardous, and the narratives we construct are always at war with the lives we lead.[36]

I close by returning to one of *War and Peace*'s more subversively epic moments, one that ties together history and the imagination by looking simultaneously to past and future: Nikolenka Bolkonsky's dream at the end of the first epilogue. Nikolenka, we remember, has dreamed that he and his Uncle Pierre are at the head of "a huge army," like something out of Plutarch although not, perhaps, a vision of which Pierre himself would have approved. Yet this dream of martial glory soon becomes a nightmare, as the spectral army reveals itself to be made up of

> slanting white lines that filled the air like the spiderwebs that fly about in the fall [....] Ahead was glory, just the same as these threads, only slightly denser. They—he and Pierre—were racing lightly and joyfully nearer and nearer to their goal. Suddenly the threads that moved them began to weaken, to tangle; the going became heavy. And Uncle Nikolai Ilyich stood before them in a stern and menacing pose. (Epilogue, 1, xvi, 1177–78)

In this dream we have an image of the interconnectedness—the treacherous interconnectedness—of human beings and the deceptive ideals (glory, in this instance) they chase.[37]

Incurably afraid of the dark and of his warrior uncle, the little boy is ultimately rescued from these night terrors by the vision of his father, which fills him with love: "Nikolenka turned to look at Pierre; but there was no longer any Pierre. Pierre was his father, Prince Andrei, and his father had no image or form, but he was there, and, seeing him, Nikolenka felt weak from love: he felt strengthless, boneless, and liquid" (Epilogue, 1, xvi, 1178). Had the epilogue ended here, with the child saved by the love of a father he had never known, perhaps the question of the novel's genre might have been satisfactorily resolved. But Tolstoy persists in a scene that echoes the moment at the end of book 6 of the *Iliad*, when Hector, able to imagine in arresting detail a postwar world in which his wife and child will be consigned to a life of slavery in the hands of his enemies, nevertheless parts from his son with a prayer to Zeus that the boy might one day carry home the bloody armor of a defeated enemy in triumph.

In Tolstoy, it is not the man but the boy, the war orphan, who makes this plea:

> Mucius Scaevola burned his hand. Why shouldn't it be the same in my life? I know they want me to study. And I will study. But some day I'll stop. And then I'll do it. I ask God for only one thing: that it's the same with me as with the men in Plutarch, and I'll do the same. I'll do better. Everybody will know me, love me, admire me [....] Father! Father! Yes, I'll do something that even *he* would be pleased with..." (Epilogue, 1, xvi, 1178)

Nikolenka falls back to sleep, and the first epilogue ends with the dreams of glory that Andrei himself had repudiated long before on the field at Austerlitz, where he lay motionless and wounded under Napoleon's shadow.

A good Rousseauian child, Nikolenka reads his Plutarch with such care that he dreams heroic dreams at night. The story of Mucius Scaevola, "the left-handed," can be found in Plutarch's *Poplicola*. A defender of the early Roman republic, Scaevola earned his nickname when, after being captured during the failed assassination of Porsenna, a Tuscan ally of the tyrannical Tarquins, he defiantly thrust his hand into an open flame and stared "at Porsenna with a steadfast and undaunted countenance" while his arm burned.[38] The story of Porsenna and the ardor with which Nikolenka imagines for himself a heroic destiny suggest that Tolstoy refuses to banish altogether the heroes of antiquity from his text because he recognizes that the invisible threads that bind his characters (and readers) to them can never quite be dissolved. Dreams, by definition, refuse to obey the logical dictates of the waking day.

12

Tolstoy the International Relations Theorist

—

DAVID A. WELCH

War and Peace is much more than a novel: it is also an essay on the forces of history. Tolstoy's primary concern in *War and Peace,* understandably, was Napoleon's Russian campaign, but what he had to say about its causes and about the reasons it unfolded as it did he clearly intended to apply more generally. He said as much repeatedly. And why should it not be so? Tolstoy's understanding of the forces of history would apply as well (or as ill) to any major event in world politics as to the specific events of 1812. This makes Tolstoy an International Relations theorist.[1]

As an International Relations theorist, Tolstoy was in many respects precocious. The common wisdom is that a recognized academic field of International Relations emerged only after World War I. The world's first chair of International Relations—the Woodrow Wilson Chair at the University College of Wales, Aberystwyth—was created only in 1919.[2] Tolstoy had written *War and Peace* more than four decades earlier.[3] Of course, for many centuries historians, classicists, international legal scholars, military officers, journalists, essayists, and philosophers had written on subjects that the field of International Relations would later claim as its own. Thucydides is generally acknowledged to be the earliest, and to this day he is widely considered the father of both International Relations theory and its dominant "realist" strand.[4] So it would be wrong to describe Tolstoy as a trailblazer on the basis of timing alone. He was, however, unusual in approaching the subject at least in part through the lens of historical fiction. He was also somewhat unusual in approaching it profoundly metaphysically. Though not a trained academic, Tolstoy was both well read and thoughtful. So what he had to say on the subject repays attention.

My goal in this chapter is to sketch and situate Tolstoy's implicit International Relations theory. I argue that he successfully anticipated a number of important trends and developments in the field, though of course without access to the rather specialized vocabulary and styles of analysis that later developed within it. He identified perhaps the single most important unanswered question not only in International Relations but in the social sciences and humanities in general. In my view, his answer to this question fails. Despite this, however, I believe that *War and Peace* is a text worth taking seriously as International Relations theory.

Tolstoy's Foils: Types of History, Types of Historians

Tolstoy's basic question, which he poses periodically throughout the novel but addresses most thoroughly in part 2 of the epilogue, is the one that has preoccupied International Relations theorists since the birth of the discipline as we know it, namely, "What force moves peoples?" (Epilogue, 2, ii, 1182).[5]

Tolstoy did not have political scientists with whom to debate the question, so he debated historians instead. Historians were certainly the best foil available at the time. History and political science differ significantly both in scope and in method,[6] but they share the goal of explaining why things happen, and they make use of the same empirical record. Tolstoy was not particularly interested in taking issue with specific historians, but he was keen to take on *classes* of historians—classes that, to a first approximation, map quite neatly onto generally recognized differences between political science approaches to the study of international relations. How did he group them? For what kinds of International Relations theorists are they decent proxies? What about them did he find wanting?

Tolstoy's first and primary target was what he called "specialized biographical historians and historians of separate peoples." These writers, Tolstoy insisted, understand "the force that moves peoples" to be "the force inherent in heroes and rulers" (Epilogue, 2, ii, 1182). This great-man approach to history credits individuals with largely unfettered agency and ascribes causality to idiosyncratic personality traits. The analogue in contemporary International Relations would be scholars who privilege what Kenneth Waltz called the "first image" and what J. David Singer called "the individual level of analysis."[7] Primarily political psychologists, these scholars stress the importance in world politics of the choices and actions of specific leaders as influenced by cognition (perception, attribution, unmotivated biases and heuristics) or emotion (fear; stress; the desire to satisfy basic psychological needs for power, recognition, self-esteem, or effective control; compensation for insecurities; wishful thinking; motivated biases).[8]

A second class of historians Tolstoy calls "general historians." These are people "who deal with all peoples."

> [They] seem to recognize the incorrectness of the specialized historians' view of the force that produces events. They do not recognize this force as the power inherent in heroes and rulers, but as the result of many variously directed forces. In describing a war or the subjugation of a people, a general historian seeks the cause of an event not in the power of one person, but in the interaction of many persons connected with the event. (Epilogue, 2, ii, 1183)

General historians approach the world through either or both of Waltz's second and third images, or what Singer called the state and system levels of analysis. Here individual leaders have limited agency at most; they must respond to structural pressures or constraints. Second-image political science understands these pressures or constraints to rest primarily in domestic politics or in governmental institutions.[9] Third-image scholars locate them in the international political system.[10] Most scholars who would embrace the label "liberal" (in the empirical, not in the normative sense) would fall into the former category, and "neorealists" or "structural realists" would fall into the latter. Many classical realists[11] and English School scholars[12] would ascribe importance to structural factors at both levels of analysis, as would more recent "neoclassical realists"[13] and various other scholars who specifically study interactions between the two.[14] What unites all of these is the belief that the "rational" choices of leaders acting in a particular domestic and/or international context will generate outcomes that an unconstrained leader might not otherwise choose. Put another way, leaders don't matter much: they are more or less substitutable without loss. To the extent that they have agency of their own, they do so at the margins.

A third class of historians Tolstoy calls "historians of culture." Agreeing with general historians that individuals can have but little impact on the world and that structural pressures and constraints are vital, they nevertheless disagree that the relevant pressures and constraints are material incentives and are less inclined to assume rationality narrowly and economistically conceived. Instead, they understand the force that moves peoples "quite differently still. They see it in so-called culture, in intellectual activity" (Epilogue, 2, ii, 1184). The ultimate forces of history, in other words, are ideas. This is a view that today resonates most closely with "constructivist" International Relations scholars who stress the path-dependent evolution of norms in shaping and regulating state behavior even as they shape identities and interests.[15] The structures that pressure and constrain leaders are sociological, not economistic; "logics of appropriateness" and relative degrees of agreement or disagreement over the primary and secondary rules of international politics drive cooperation and conflict.[16]

Very little of contemporary International Relations theory cannot be related, if imperfectly, to one of Tolstoy's foils. And yet he finds them all wanting. In effect, Tolstoy rejects any and all mainstream approaches. On what basis does he do so?

Tolstoy reserves most of his disdain for the great-man approach. He demonstrates this disdain by systematically ridiculing Napoleon and his so-called genius. Napoleon hardly appears in the novel without Tolstoy's making some disparaging remark about his stature, appearance, or bearing (e.g., I, 3, xiv, 272–73; II, 2, xxi, 414–15; III, 1, vi, 620–21). Tolstoy's largely historically accurate account of the Battle of Borodino is intended to show that Napoleon was entirely ineffectual (III, 2, xxvii, 781–82).[17] "In historical events," writes Tolstoy, "the so-called great men are labels that give the event a name, which, just as with labels, has the least connection of all with the event itself" (III, 1, i, 606).

Even if biographical historians were on firm ground locating the force that moves peoples in the will and the ability of great men, Tolstoy insists that these writers provide nothing more than idiosyncratic, incommensurable accounts of events among which, on account of their selectivity and subjectivity, we cannot possibly choose.

> But once historians of different nationalities and views begin to describe the same event, the answers they give immediately lose all meaning, because each of them understands this force not only differently, but often in a totally opposite way. One historian insists that the event was produced by the power of Napoleon; another insists that it was produced by the power of Alexander; a third by the power of some third person. Besides that, historians of this sort contradict one another even in explaining that force on which the power of one and the same person is based. Thiers, a Bonapartist, says that Napoleon's power was based on his virtue and genius; Lanfrey, a republican, says it was based on his swindling and on duping the people. So that historians of this sort, by mutually demolishing each other's propositions, thereby demolish the concept of the force that produces events, and give no answer to the essential question of history. (Epilogue, 2, ii, 1182–83)

Put another way, even if there were great men in history, essentially biographical treatments could not possibly tell us much about the source, nature, or impact of their greatness.

Tolstoy has less to say by way of direct criticism of the second and third classes of historians, but his complaints are certainly pithy. He finds general history wanting, quite simply, because it understands events as the vector sum of forces—Tolstoy prefers the word "power"—but treats this vector sum as both cause and effect. This generates contradictions and lacunae that cannot be resolved within the general rubric of their operative understanding of causality. The result is that general historians must either introduce unexplained causes or selectively ignore them (Epilogue, 2, ii, 1183).

The third class of historians—cultural historians—introduce *ideas* as explanations but cannot connect them to events except through *power,* a concept they deny.

> But even allowing that all the cleverly woven arguments which fill these histories are correct, allowing that peoples are governed by some indefinable force known as an *idea*—the essential question of history either remains unanswered, or, to the former power of monarchs and to the influence of advisers and other persons introduced by the general historians, there is joined yet another new force, the *idea,* the connection of which with the masses calls for explanation. It is possible to understand that Napoleon had power, and therefore an event took place; with some flexibility it is possible to understand that Napoleon, along with other forces, was the cause of an event; but in what way the book *Le contrat social* brought it about that the French started drowning each other cannot be understood without explaining the causal connection of this new force with the event. (Epilogue, 2, ii, 1185)

This complaint shares a common thread with those that Tolstoy levels at the first and second kinds of history—namely, a presumption that to *explain* something requires a full and correct account (and *only* a full and correct account) of its prior sufficient causes.

The mechanistic Enlightenment view of causality that Tolstoy embraces is intriguing for at least two reasons, one having to do with what happens in world politics and one having to do with Tolstoy. With respect to the former, Tolstoy's presumption is entirely congenial to the so-called behavioral revolution, according to which all human action is essentially conditioned and no human action is genuinely "free." With respect to the latter, Tolstoy's implicit embrace of this view left him in the personally precarious (I would argue paradoxical) position of having to assert that free will is an illusion while at the same time embracing a religious faith and an ethical code that require free will for moral and spiritual accountability.

It is precisely here that Tolstoy's "positive" theory of history—and, by implication, his implicit International Relations theory—reveals itself. Tolstoy is not averse to the positivist, behaviorist quest for the laws of politics or history. His understanding of the term is entirely conventional, too. He refers to these laws from time to time throughout the text, never in a skeptical or dismissive vein. Here are some examples:

> Napoleon, though now, in 1812, it seemed to him more than ever that it depended on him *verser* or not *verser le sang de ses peoples* (as Alexander wrote in his last letter to him), had never been more subject than now to those inevitable

laws which forced him (acting by his own free will, as it seemed to him, with respect to himself) to do for the common cause, for history, that which had to be accomplished. (III, 1, i, 606)

Only by admitting an infinitesimal unit for observation—a differential of history, that is, the uniform strivings of people—and attaining to the art of integrating them (taking the sums of these infinitesimal quantities) can we hope to comprehend the laws of history. (III, 2, i, 822)

There are not and cannot be any causes of a historical event, except for the one cause of all causes. But there are laws that govern events, which are partly unknown, partly groped for by us. The discovery of these laws is possible only when we wholly give up looking for causes in the will of one man, just as discovering the laws of planetary movement became possible only when people gave up the notion that the earth stands still. (IV, 2, i, 987)

So Tolstoy is a believer in the laws of history. Does he also believe that he can divine them? If so, what does he divine?

The People's Will in a Deterministic World

One of the most fascinating and most revealing parts of *War and Peace* is Tolstoy's discussion of the problem of free will (Epilogue, 2, viii–x, 1200–11). It tells us much about Tolstoy's worldview, but it also flags very precisely *the* crucial unanswered question for students of world politics: namely, how can we reconcile our steadfast belief that the individual choices of at least some people (most notably, leaders of powerful countries) really do matter with our reluctance to concede that at least some of the forces of history might not themselves have fully sufficient prior causes? We are loath to say, for instance, that Napoleon had no choice but to invade Russia in 1812—what we believe about human action rebels against the idea that everything anyone does is absolutely predetermined—but our general understanding of how the world works leaves no room for uncaused causes. To his credit, Tolstoy addresses this directly and very insightfully zeroes in on it as the key issue for any philosophy of history. Contemporary International Relations theorists generally do not. I am aware of only one who has and who is actively working toward a resolution.[18]

As I have suggested, Tolstoy's solution is that free will is an illusion—though he agonizes about this and flirts with qualifications and equivocations before finally embracing it. There is no question, Tolstoy admits, that we all experience the illusion. We believe that we are the authors of our own actions at least some of the time, within at most a set of partially limiting constraints. "Whatever notion of the activity of many people or one man we examine," Tolstoy tells us, "we understand it not otherwise than as a product partly of freedom and partly of the law of necessity" (Epilogue 2, ix, 1204). But we must relinquish our belief in the free will that we feel that we experience and that we think we readily see in the actions of others. In history "what is known to us we call the laws of necessity; what is unknown to us we call the life force. The life force is only the expression of the unknown remainder of what we know about the essence of life" (Epilogue 2, x, 1211).

Relinquishing our embrace of free will is, for Tolstoy, absolutely necessary if we are to be able to claim that we can "explain" anything at all. "If there exists one free act of man," Tolstoy writes, "then not a single historical law exists or any notion of historical events" (Epilogue, 2, xi, 1212). The cost of this concession, Tolstoy recognizes, is enormous: "In the same way now it seems that we need only recognize the law of necessity and the notions of the soul, of good and evil, and all state and church institutions based on those notions will be destroyed" (Epilogue, 2, xii, 1214).

Now it is possible that Tolstoy professes a strict determinism and yet, deliberately and ironically, undermines it in the narrative itself; such, at any rate, is the argument of Gary Saul Morson.[19] Embracing this interpretation has the merit of resolving the apparent paradox of an author writing a monumental work of fiction replete with choice in which he professes that there is no such thing as choice. On this reading, Tolstoy was just kidding that everything has a fully sufficient prior cause. But resolving the paradox in this way comes at quite a cost: it requires that we infer that he was also just kidding when he offered ostensibly serious arguments against various kinds of history. It also requires that we discount just about everything he had to say that was treatiselike at any point in the novel, and in the epilogue in particular. It does seem implausible that Tolstoy fully internalized the implications of rigid determinism that he himself identified—namely, giving up on the concepts of good, evil, right, wrong, personal responsibility, and the soul—but he would not be the first to have embraced a rigid and unyielding deterministic worldview while attempting to avoid these unpleasant implications.[20] And in any case, if we are to take Tolstoy seriously as an International Relations theorist, we have no choice but to take his determinism seriously as well. The alternative is simply to say that he had nothing honest to say on the subject. So we have no choice but to leave to his biographers the question of whether he was being ironic or suffered from intense cognitive dissonance and simply ask the following question: What are the implications for his philosophy of history if he meant us to take his determinism seriously? How are we to understand the force that moves peoples in the light of it?

Tolstoy's reflections about this are both cryptic and anguished, suggesting that he desperately wanted to be able to answer his fundamental question and strained to persuade himself that he had done so. Consider, for example, the following passages.

> The period in the campaign of 1812 from the battle of Borodino to the expulsion of the French proved that a battle won is not only not the cause of a conquest, but is not even an invariable sign of conquest; it proved that the force that decides the destiny of nations lies not in conquerors, not even in armies and battles, but in *something else*. (IV, 3, i, 1032; my emphasis)

> A bee sitting on a flower stung a child. And the child is afraid of bees and says that a bee's purpose consists in stinging people. A poet admires a bee sucking from the cup of a flower and says that a bee's purpose consists in sucking up the fragrance of flowers. A beekeeper, noting how a bee gathers flower pollen and brings it to the hive, says that a bee's purpose consists in gathering honey. Another beekeeper, who has studied the life of a hive more closely, says that a bee collects pollen in order to feed the young bees and rear a queen, and that its purpose consists in reproducing its kind. A botanist notes that, as a bee lands with pollen on the pistil of a dioecious flower, it fertilizes it, and in that the botanist sees the bee's purpose. Another, observing the migration of plants, sees that the bee contributes to that migration, and this new observer may say it is in this that the bee's purpose consists. But the final purpose of the bee is exhausted neither by the one, nor the other, nor the third purpose that human reason is able to discover. The higher human reason rises in the discovery of these purposes, the more obvious for it is the inaccessibility of the final purpose.
> *All that is accessible to man* is the observation of the correspondence between the life of a bee and other phenomena of life. *It is the same for the purposes of historical figures and peoples.* (Epilogue, 1, iv, 1138; my emphasis)

> Why does a war or a revolution take place? We do not know; we only know that for the accomplishment of the one action or the other, people form themselves into certain units and all participate; and we say that this is so because it is unthinkable otherwise, because it is a law. (Epilogue, 2, vii, 1200)

These three passages are evidence of epistemic humility. The move is similar to that employed frequently by believers who are unable to reconcile faith and reason and who, in response to challenges, retreat to the shibboleth that "It's a mystery."[21] Indeed, this is Nicola Chiaromonte's interpretation in his probing essay, "Tolstoy and the Paradox of History."[22] According to this view, Tolstoy's whole point was to use epistemic humility as a vehicle for justifying a metaphysics in which pure and complete knowledge is reserved for the divine. And yet this epistemic humility rebels against confidence both in the very determinism that would generate the anguish in the first place and in Tolstoy's theological resolution.

If epistemic humility fails to solve the problem, what else might? From time to time Tolstoy flirts with tautology.

> If Napoleon had not been insulted by the demand to withdraw beyond the Vistula, and had not ordered his troops to advance, there would have been no war; but if all the sergeants had been unwilling to enlist for a second tour of duty, there also could have been no war. There also could have been no war if there had been no intrigues of the English, and if there had been no prince of Oldenburg and insulted feelings in Alexander, and if there had been no autocratic power in Russia, and if there had been no French revolution and subsequent dictatorship and empire, and all that produced the French revolution, and so on. Without any one of these causes, nothing could have happened. Therefore, all these causes—billions of causes—coincided so as to bring about what happened. And consequently none of them was the exclusive cause of the event, but *the event had to take place simply because it had to take place.* Millions of men, renouncing their human feelings and their reason, had to go from west to east and kill their own kind, just as, several centuries earlier, hordes of men had gone from east to west, killing their own kind. (III, 1, i, 604–5; my emphasis)

And yet Tolstoy is fully aware that tautology solves nothing.

> Having renounced the view of the ancients on the divine submission of the will of the people to a chosen one and on the submission of that will to a divinity, history cannot take a single step without contradiction unless it chooses one of two things: either to return to the former faith in the direct participation of the divinity in the affairs of mankind, or to explain definitely the meaning of that force productive of historical events which is known as power.
> To return to the first is impossible: belief has been destroyed, and therefore it is necessary to explain the meaning of power [....] Power is the sum total of the wills of the masses, transferred by express or tacit agreement to rulers chosen by the masses. (Epilogue, 2, iv, 1187–88)

> On what condition are the wills of the masses transferred to one person? On condition that the person express the will of the whole people. That is, power is power. That is, power is a word the meaning of which we do not understand. (Epilogue, 2, v, 1193)

At points Tolstoy seems tempted to solve the problem by relaxing determinism, admitting the possibility of degree.

> Alexander refused all negotiations because he felt himself personally offended. Barclay de Tolly tried to lead his army in the best fashion, so as to fulfill his duty and earn the glory of a great general. Rostov rode to attack against the French because he could not resist the wish to go galloping across a level field. And all the countless persons who participated in this war acted in just the same way, as a result of their personal qualities, habits, conditions, and aims. They

feared, boasted, rejoiced, resented, reasoned, supposing that they knew what they were doing and that they were doing it for themselves, and yet they were all involuntary instruments of history, and performed work hidden from them but comprehensible to us. Such is the inevitable fate of all men of action, and the higher they stand in the human hierarchy, *the less free they are*. (III, 2, i, 682; my emphasis)

In offering and accepting battle at Borodino, Kutuzov and Napoleon acted involuntarily and senselessly. And only later did historians furnish the already accomplished facts with ingenious arguments for the foresight and genius of the commanders, who, of all the involuntary instruments of world events, were the *most* enslaved and involuntary agents. (III, 2, xix, 754; my emphasis)

At the end of the day, Tolstoy provides no explicit solution. He concludes, quite simply, by asserting a strict determinism and letting the chips fall where they may.

As for astronomy the difficulty of recognizing the movement of the earth consisted in renouncing the immediate feeling of the immobility of the earth and the similar feeling of the movement of the planets, so for history the difficulty of recognizing the subjection of the person to the laws of space, time, and causes consists in renouncing the immediate feeling of the independence of one's person. But, as in astronomy the new view said: "True, we do not feel the movement of the earth, but by assuming its immobility, we arrive at an absurdity; whereas, by assuming the movement which we do not feel, we arrive at laws," so, too, in history the new view says: "True, we do not feel our dependence, but by assuming we are free, we arrive at an absurdity; whereas, by assuming our dependence on the external world, time, and causes, we arrive at laws."
   In the first case, the need was to renounce the consciousness of a nonexistent immobility in space and recognize a movement we do not feel; in the present case, it is just as necessary to renounce a nonexistent freedom and recognize a dependence we do not feel. (Epilogue, 2, xii, 1214–15)

This is, of course, ultimately unsatisfactory. And yet both Tolstoy's narrative and his treatise would appear to allow no alternative. His treatise requires it to avoid the "just kidding" objection. His narrative requires it because it is the only way to make sense of the pivotal role of Kutuzov.

Kutuzov is the linchpin of Tolstoy's answer to the question "What force moves peoples?" Like Napoleon, Kutuzov comes in for some very unflattering treatment. Tolstoy describes him, for example, as narcoleptic (I, 3, xii, 260–61) and as "grown still heavier, become flabby and swollen with fat" (III, 2, xv, 740). Kutuzov evinces nothing in the way of initiative and is both detached and easily distracted from the great task to which he has been assigned.[23] He is almost cartoonlike in his inertia.[24] Nevertheless, he is the closest thing there is to a hero in Tolstoy's political drama because *he alone gives himself up to the people's will*. Kutuzov, in short, is the only figure in the drama who does not seek to resist the force that moves peoples. Tolstoy's admiration of Kutuzov rises almost to the level of eulogy.

> In the years twelve and thirteen, Kutuzov was directly accused of blunders. The sovereign was displeased with him. And in a history written not long ago at the highest injunction, it is said that Kutuzov was a cunning court liar, fearful of the name of Napoleon, who, through his blunders at Krasnoe and the Berezina, deprived the Russian army of the glory of a complete victory over the French.
>
> Such is the destiny, not of great men, not of the *grands hommes*, whom the Russian mind does not recognize, but of those rare, always solitary men who, discerning the will of Providence, submit their personal will to it. The hatred and contempt of the crowd punish these men for their insight into the higher law.
>
> For Russian historians—strange and terrible to say—Napoleon, that most insignificant instrument of history, who never and nowhere, even in exile, displayed any human dignity—Napoleon is the object of admiration and enthusiasm; he is *grand*. While Kutuzov, a man who, from the beginning to the end of his activity in 1812, from Borodino to Vilno, while always being true to himself in all his acts and words, shows an example uncommon in history of self-denial and awareness in the present of the future significance of the event—Kutuzov seems to them something indefinite and pathetic, and when they speak of Kutuzov and the year twelve, it is as if they are always slightly embarrassed.
>
> And yet it is hard to imagine a historical figure whose activity was so invariably and constantly directed towards one and the same goal. It is hard to imagine a goal more worthy and more concurrent with the will of the whole people. It is harder still to find another example in history in which the goal that the historical figure set for himself was so perfectly attained as the goal towards which the entire activity of Kutuzov was directed in the year twelve. (IV, 4, v, 1084–85)

What is unsatisfying, of course, is the fact that by Tolstoy's own account, the Russian people *had* no will—not, at any rate, one that could be considered "free." Kutuzov was no less able to resist what fate assigned him than was Napoleon, Alexander, the Russian people, or anyone else in the novel. Automatons deserve neither praise nor admiration. Kutuzov is as unworthy of heroism as Napoleon is of villainy.

International Relations Theory's Response to Tolstoy

While I cannot pretend here to resolve the great puzzle that Tolstoy identified and yet ultimately failed to solve, I can say that contemporary International Relations theory would be skeptical of the need to solve it. I suspect that the skepticism would be less than well founded philosophically. Political scientists are not generally inclined to agonize about free will and determinism and quite confidently proceed on the assumption that structure and agency are both important in some unspecified proportion. This is not to say that a principled response is impossible—one might well ask, for example, whether greater epistemic confidence is warranted in a mechanistic account of causality than in the phenomenology of choice—but these kinds of responses are the business of philosophers, not political scientists.

With respect to the role of individuals, it is difficult to see why we should believe that leaders are substitutable without loss. Who other than Napoleon would have bothered to try conquering Russia? What is the plausible argument that World War II would have happened as it did if Otto Wels rather than Adolf Hitler had been chancellor of Germany? How likely is it that John F. Kennedy would have embroiled the United States in Vietnam?[25] And yet no one seriously imagines that leaders are utterly unconstrained. It is difficult to argue that the Iraq War of 2003 would have been possible without 9/11; the domestic and international constraints on the anti-Saddam enthusiasts in the Bush administration were simply too powerful. The common wisdom—possibly no less wise for being common—is that personality matters, at least in very specific circumstances, but always within limits. Whatever metaphysical doctrine might make sense of it, the balance between agent and structure varies but never reaches the limit at either end.[26]

Political scientists would agree with Tolstoy, however, that biographical history offers little in the way of explanatory power. Context is key. There is no agreement on whether material incentives or sociological dynamics provide a better clue to context. Put another way, the materialist/constructivist debate shows no signs of abating. Nor, for that matter, does the debate over the relative importance of domestic or international pressures and constraints (a debate best handled with nuance, since leaders of small states are generally more constrained than leaders of powerful states, and leaders of democracies more constrained than authoritarian leaders).

Where modern political scientists would perhaps most energetically engage Tolstoy is on his substantive claim that peoples have collective wills of their own. This organic notion of a popular will has a long intellectual pedigree, primarily among political theorists, but it has been a very long time indeed since empirical political scientists used it as an explanatory concept, not merely because it is difficult to define and identify (see note 5) but also because popular wills are manifestly heterogeneous. One can speak sensibly of tendencies or trends in a group's preferences or attitudes, and these may at least occasionally provide explanatory handles on events;[27] but notice what it is about "peoples" that seems most useful about them from an explanatory perspective: *ideas*. And it is precisely here at the interface between ideas and practice that we find the cutting edge of International Relations theory.[28] Despite his professed skepticism about historians of culture, Tolstoy himself was sympathetic to the power of culture and successfully if inadvertently anticipated empirical political science's eventual return to it.

Miscellaneous Precocious Insights

Although little can compete in importance with the debate between free will and determinism or with the deep question "What force moves peoples?" I conclude by noting that Tolstoy also successfully anticipated a number of other lines of inquiry that have blossomed in the field of International Relations in recent years. What he says on these subjects is little more than suggestive, but the fact that he says anything at all demonstrates a keen eye for things worth exploring.

One such insight concerns the importance of counterfactuals. Only in recent years have historians and political scientists sought to grapple with counterfactual reasoning as a technique for evaluating causal claims against the background of a fixed historical record. Counterfactual reasoning is both common and natural, and yet it is notoriously difficult to know how to use it in a disciplined, rigorous way. Tolstoy sees this very clearly and uses the insight to devastating rhetorical effect.

> Many historians say that the battle of Borodino was not won by the French because Napoleon had a cold, that if he had not had a cold, his instructions before and during the battle would have been of still greater genius, and Russia would have perished, *et la face du monde eut été changée*. For historians who accept that Russia was shaped by the will of one man—Peter the Great—and that France was turned from a republic into an empire and French troops went to Russia by the will of one man—Napoleon—such an argument, that Russia remained a power because Napoleon had a bad cold on the twenty-sixth, such an argument for such historians is inevitably consistent.
>
> If it had depended on Napoleon's will whether or not to fight the battle of Borodino, and if it had depended on his will whether to give this or that instruction, then it is obvious that a cold, having an influence on the expression of his will, could have caused the salvation of Russia, and therefore the valet who forgot to give Napoleon his waterproof boots on the twenty-fourth was the savior of Russia. (III, 2, xxviii, 783–84)

Tolstoy's determinism commits him to the view, of course, that counterfactual inferences are pointless; why attempt to articulate the implications of something that did not happen and could not possibly have happened? It seems likely that Tolstoy would not have been interested in the rather lively debate the subject has recently inspired.[29] Nevertheless, he readily saw the importance that others attach to it.

A second insight concerns the vital role of both honor and rules. Empirical political science, at least in North America, has tended to downplay or dismiss the importance of these on the assumption that material interests drive human behavior. From this perspective, honor is but window dressing, and rules are binding only on the weak.[30] Tolstoy suggests that this is an impoverished view.

> From the time of the burning of Smolensk, a war began that did not fit any of the former traditions of war. The burning of towns and villages, the retreats after battles, the blow struck at Borodino and then another retreat, the abandoning and burning of Moscow, the hunt for marauders, the cutting off of transport, the partisan war—these were all deviations from the rules.
>
> Napoleon sensed that, and from the moment when he stopped in Moscow, in the correct position of a fencer, and instead of his adversary's sword, saw a club raised over him, he never ceased complaining to Kutuzov and the emperor Alexander that the war was being conducted against all the rules. (IV, 3, i, 1033)

In this passage it is the *violation* of rules that is of consequence. Again, modern International Relations theory has been slow to recognize the importance of honor and rules, not only as crucial pillars of stability and predictability but also as fields of contestation with transformative systemic potential.[31]

Finally, Tolstoy quite brilliantly provides numerous examples of his sensitivity to the pettiness, irrationality, incoherence, confusion, and generally chaotic nature of political choice and action. It is difficult to read *War and Peace* through a unitary rational-actor lens while maintaining a straight face. The most obvious examples, of course, concern the conduct of the campaigns and battles; Tolstoy is nothing if not an eloquent critic of military "genius" and a brilliant witness to the fog of war. But he manages to lampoon high politics just as effectively (my favorite example is Bilibin's letter to Prince Andrei following the debacle at Austerlitz, II, 2, ix, 372).

If there is a final word to say about Tolstoy the International Relations theorist, it is perhaps this: that he was a keen observer of the complexity and diversity of human life and of human society—a complexity that International Relations theory is only now beginning to rediscover and explore. For too long political science has ignored what Tolstoy considered "real life with its essential concerns of health, illness, work, rest, with its concerns of thought, learning, poetry, music, love, friendship, hatred, passions," which goes on "as always, independently and outside of any political closeness or enmity with

Napoleon Bonaparte and outside all possible reforms" (II, 3, i, 418), just as it goes on independently of and apart from political science's futile attempts to pretend that it does not exist. Tolstoy may not have succeeded in answering his own question—"What force moves peoples?"—but the motion, at least, no one ever described better.

War and Peace at West Point

RICK MCPEAK

*Much of the history we teach was
made by the people we taught.*

In April 2010, the United States Military Academy at West Point hosted
a conference, *"War and Peace* at West Point," for the contributors to this
book and invited guests. The event attracted Academy faculty and students,
including ten cadets from the Department of Foreign Languages who were
studying *War and Peace* with me. Having graduated the likes of Eisenhower
and MacArthur, who made the history books not just as warriors but also
as scholars and statesmen, West Point is an ideal place to teach Tolstoy's
great war novel. During World War II, Douglas MacArthur commanded
U.S. forces in the Pacific, and Dwight D. Eisenhower led Allied forces in
Europe. After the war, Eisenhower presided over Columbia University and
MacArthur over the reconstitution of Japan. Ultimately, Eisenhower served
two terms as the thirty-fourth president of the United States. As this book is
being published, General (retired) David Petraeus, a 1974 graduate of West
Point who applied his academic, diplomatic, and military acumen to navigate
the complexities of the post-9/11 world in Iraq and Afghanistan, is leading
the Central Intelligence Agency. West Point cadets reading *War and Peace*
are preparing for critical leadership roles in Kabul, Kandahar, and other as yet
unknown places.

During the conference, academics from various disciplines—literature, philosophy, history, and international relations—presented on issues such as an
individual's potential to make history (see, e.g., chapter 6 by Love and chapter 12 by Welch). These scholars gathered at the Academy from Russia, Great
Britain, Germany, Canada, and across the United States. Donna Tussing
Orwin and I envisioned an interdisciplinary international event; much less
intentional on our part was the dynamic interaction at West Point between

theoreticians and soon-to-be practitioners of violence. From their unique disciplinary perspectives, the presenters analyzed various aspects of war and peace as depicted in the novel. Cadets listening to these presentations were preparing to become army officers who would eventually manage force across the broad spectrum from stability to combat operations. The cadets knew that Count Leo Tolstoy was a former artillery officer and decorated combat veteran, and they already respected his master work. Yet some were skeptical about the relevance to their education of a dozen talks delivered by academics with minimal connection to the military. Each speaker at the conference presented for thirty minutes and then answered questions for fifteen minutes. As analysis and debate built over fundamental questions of war, the military, and the role of history in reporting on these, the cadets plunged in.

The Academy curriculum offers cadets a top-tier liberal arts and engineering education plus sequential and progressive military training. In *War and Peace*, Tolstoy gave short shrift to the latter (see chapter 7). Tolstoy's strong views on military preparation generated the most passionate discussions among the theoreticians and the soon-to-be practitioners. The cadets knew, some of them from personal experience, that no plan survives first contact with the enemy, who always has a vote; however, they have come to value the mental discipline and unifying power of the planning process. They realize that even the most rigorous and realistic training cannot prepare them for infinite contingencies on the battlefield; nonetheless, they value preparation because it develops habits of mind that can save lives, both friendly and enemy. For the scenarios in which traditional preparation fails them, these future officers will have to rely on personal character, creativity, and critical thinking skills developed in the classrooms and in training exercises. As cadets voiced their objections to or approval of Tolstoy's theories, academic participants got a taste of the intensity of education at West Point. Discussion and debate continued day and night, during official sessions, at meals, at events, and on tours of the Academy grounds.

After reading my students' insightful reflections on "*War and Peace* at West Point," I concluded they were actually, perhaps unconsciously, most exercised about Tolstoy's views on leadership. The Academy's challenging and multifaceted curriculum constitutes a four-year leadership laboratory. Cadets focus on leadership in the classroom and practice it everywhere—in the barracks, on the parade and athletic fields, in training areas, and even overseas. Perhaps they instinctively realized something it has taken me years to grasp: the author of *War and Peace* actually knew very little about leadership in practice. Although he saw combat as a courageous junior officer, Tolstoy did not command above the squadron level. During his brief military career, he certainly observed senior leaders and, using his renowned powers of observation and description, depicted his versions of effective commanders (e.g., Bagration) and ineffective ones (e.g., Napoleon). I suspect, however, that his portrayals did not ring entirely true to the cadets. Living in an action-oriented culture with the mantra, "lead, follow, or get the hell out of the way," some struggled to relate to Tolstoy's affirmation of inaction as personified by Kutuzov; nor could many of them understand Prince Andrei's dysfunctional propensity to overthink everything. For example, most of my students sense that an ideal leader, when confronted with a spinning cannonball on the battlefield, would, in all probability, avoid reflections on his own mortality and instead hit the dirt to survive and have the chance to command his troops in combat.

My students were more sympathetic to Tolstoy's philosophy of leadership. When cadets reading *War and Peace* think about command, they cannot help but consider MacArthur and Eisenhower, whose bronze statues frame their parade field. West Point mythology promotes the great-man theory of military history so forcefully derided in *War and Peace*. Naturally, some of my students interpreted Tolstoy's debunking of the ultimate great man— Napoleon—as an indictment and dismissal of all military leaders. I urged them instead to consider Tolstoy's novel as a tribute to humility, a key aspect in the U.S. Army's current conception of servant leadership, for which Kutuzov could be a model. Tolstoy's Kutuzov, keenly aware of his own limitations and role, was a paragon of selflessness, a virtue the Academy's comprehensive leader development process strives to foster among future army leaders. During the conference, my students, who were almost all seniors, took time to reflect on their own developmental experiences and personal leadership philosophies. Most of them were high school standouts in the classroom and on the athletic fields; yet they all endured a humbling leveling process as they learned to be followers during their first—appropriately called "plebe"—year at West Point. Their comprehensive four-year, thirty-course core curriculum—composed of fifteen required courses in the humanities and social sciences and fifteen in math, science, and engineering—combined with intensive physical education and military science requirements, ultimately humbled even these highly talented scholar-athlete-leaders. Add the complexity of learning, practicing, and analyzing leadership throughout the course of study, and it becomes readily apparent why these cadets' studies and experiences promote humility and a team, rather than an individual, mentality. These future U.S. Army officers, akin to Tolstoy's Kutuzov, remain keenly aware of their commitment to something much larger and more significant than themselves.[1]

The Academy's motto—duty, honor, country—was codified by General MacArthur, who well understood that its three tenets could be in tension with one another. Ideally, all West Pointers serve their country honorably. In

reality, despite the Academy's focus on the development of leaders with impeccable character, some graduates fall short of these ideals. Several contributors to this volume (e.g., Herberg-Rothe, McPeak, and Morson) analyze
Prince Andrei Bolkonsky's ruminations on the eve of Borodino during which
he challenges the currency of "chivalry" on the battlefield. The Russian regimental commander's cynicism reaches a peak during his diatribe about the
military profession.

> The military estate is the most honored. But what is war, what is needed for
> success in military affairs, what are the morals of military society? The aim of
> war is killing, the instruments of war are espionage, treason and the encour-
> agement of it, the ruin of the inhabitants, robbing them or stealing to supply
> the army; deception and lying are called military stratagems; the morals of the
> military estate are absence of freedom, that is, discipline, idleness, ignorance,
> cruelty, depravity, and drunkenness. And in spite of that, it is the highest estate,
> respected by all. All kings except the Chinese wear military uniforms and the
> one who has killed the most people gets the greatest reward...They come to-
> gether, like tomorrow, to kill each other, they slaughter and maim tens of thou-
> sands of men, and then they say prayers of thanksgiving for having slaughtered
> so many people (inflating the numbers), and proclaim victory, supposing that
> the more people slaughtered, the greater the merit. How does God look down
> and listen to them! (III, 2, xxv, 775–76)

Needless to say, West Point cadets, who intend to join this "most honored estate" as U.S. Army officers, do not see themselves as killers, liars, thieves, monsters, or drunks in training. As part of their broad liberal arts education, they
study just-war theory and the law of armed conflict. In the classroom, they
analyze leadership failures such as those that led to abuses at the Abu Ghraib
prison in Iraq. During training exercises, they rehearse rules of engagement
specifically designed to minimize civilian casualties during military operations. In short, they study how to prosecute violence virtuously.[2]

Tolstoy's adept transformation of French and Russian histories into a compelling war narrative with authentic personages and intriguing philosophies
fascinated all the cadets. They were pleasantly surprised to learn that, even a
century after Tolstoy's death, his fiction still elicits such passionate opinions
from an array of diverse perspectives. Thanks to their own active participation
in this multifaceted approach, several of my students glimpsed the complex
simplicity of *War and Peace,* a fictive universe clearly too large for any of them
to label.

Notes

Introduction

1. The term was popularized by General John Abizaid. See Bradley Graham and Josh White, "Abizaid Credited with Popularizing the Term 'Long War,'" *Washington Post*, February 3, 2006, http://www.washingtonpost.com/wp-dyn/content/article/2006/02/02/AR2006020202242.html.

2. "Neskol'ko slov po povodu knigi 'Voina i mir,'" PSS 16:7. All translations in this introduction unless otherwise stated are my own.

3. "Cherty letopisnogo stilia v literature XIX veka," http://feb-web.ru/feb/classics/critics/eixenbaum/eih/eih-371-.htm, 375–79. Originally published in *Trudy otdela drevnerusskoi literatury Instituta russkoi literatury Akademii nauk SSSR*, vol. 14 (Moscow-Leningrad, 1958), 545–50.

4. "Cherty," 378. See entry for April 5, PSS 48:125–26.

1 Tolstoy on War, Russia, and Empire

1. M. I. Dragomirov, *Razbor romana "Voina i mir"* (Kiev, 1895), especially 42–49, 59–62, 77–85. On Tolstoy's views see, e.g., *War and Peace*, III, 2, i, 682–84, and III, 3, i and ii, 821–26. On the views of Dragomirov and other military readers of the novel, see chapter 7 ("*War and Peace* from the Military Point of View") by Donna Tussing Orwin.

2. Even Avraam Norov, who had fought at Borodino and was a strong critic of Tolstoy, conceded that his description of the battle was exceptionally powerful and authentic: A. S. Norov, *Voina i Mir 1805–1812 s istoricheskoi tochki zreniia i po vospominaniiam sovremennika* (St. Petersburg, 1868), 36.

3. Dragomirov, *Razbor*, 4–6, 17–19.

4. William C. Fuller, *Strategy and Power in Russia 1600–1914* (New York, 1992), 303–8. On Dragomirov see John W. Steinberg, *All the Tsar's Men: Russia's General Staff and the Fate of the Empire 1898–1914* (Washington, DC, 2010), 79–92. On Dragomirov's career see D. N. Shilov and Iu. A. Kuz'min, *Chleny Gosudarstvennogo Soveta Rossiiskoi Imperii 1801–1906* (St. Petersburg, 2007), 295–98.

5. On Tolstoy and Clausewitz, see chapter 10 ("Tolstoy and Clausewitz: The Dialectics of War") by Andreas Herberg-Rothe.

6. In Dominic Lieven, *Russia against Napoleon: The Battle for Europe, 1807–1814* (London, 2009), chapters 3 and 4, I attempt to show how the Russian retreat was planned and executed.

7. Dragomirov, *Razbor,* 53. Norov, *Voina i mir,* is much more generous to Barclay (see, e.g., 19, 25), but the era and regime of Nicholas I, in which he served as a minister, was much more imperial and less ethnic Russian in its ideology than was the case of late-nineteenth-century tsarism in general and Dragomirov's circle in particular.

8. Apart from sources cited in Lieven, *Russia against Napoleon,* chapters 5 and 6, see Lidiia Il'chenko, *Borodinskoe srazhenie. Istoriia russkoi versii sobytii* (Moscow, 2009). On the 1809 campaign see in particular the three-volume history by John Gill, *1809: Thunder on the Danube: Napoleon's Defeat of the Habsburgs* (London, 2007–9).

9. Kathryn B. Feuer, *Tolstoy and the Genesis of* War and Peace, ed. Robin Feuer Miller and Donna Tussing Orwin (Ithaca, 1996), 185.

10. Friedrich von Schubert, *Unter dem Doppeladler* (Stuttgart, 1962), 98–99; Lieven, *Russia against Napoleon,* chaps. 5, 6, 7, 8. On the military clergy see L. V. Mel'nikova, *Armiia i pravoslavnaia tserkov' Rossiiskoi imperii v epokhu Napoleonovskikh voin* (Moscow, 2007).

11. Dragomirov, *Razbor,* 91–95; Fuller, *Strategy and Power,* 167–74; John Keegan, *The Face of Battle* (Harmondsworth, UK, 1978), 186–88; Duke Eugen von Wurttemberg, *Memoiren des Herzogs Eugen von Wurttemberg,* 3 vols. (Frankfürt an der Oder, 1862), 2:49.

12. A late example of this is N. Troitskii, *1812. Velikii god Rossii* (Moscow, 2007), 471.

13. Lieven, *Russia against Napoleon,* chaps. 9, 11, and 12 on the Russian army's performance in the 1813 campaign.

14. A. I. Mikhailovskii-Danilevskii, *Memuary 1814–1815* (St. Petersburg, 2001), 163, 250, 267–68.

15. The best work on partisan and popular warfare is A. I. Popov, *Velikaia armiia v Rossii: Pogonia za mirazhom* (Samara, Russ., 2002).

16. Lieven, *Russia against Napoleon,* 296–99. On Chernyshev, see Frederick W. Kagan, *The Military Reforms of Nicholas I* (Houndmills, UK, 1999). On Benckendorff, Grigorii Bibikov, *A.Kh. Benkendorf i politika Nikolaia I* (Moscow, 2009).

17. This is a vast and much debated subject: see Anthony D. Smith, "War and Ethnicity: The Role of Warfare in the Formation, Self-images, and Cohesion of Ethnic Communities," *Ethnic and Racial Studies* 4, no. 4 (1981): 375–97, and Anthony D. Smith, *The Ethnic Origins of Nations* (Oxford, 1986).

18. Henry Kamen, *Imagining Spain: Historical Myth and National Identity* (New Haven, 2008), 1.

19. Kamen, *Imagining Spain,* 1–9; Charles J. Esdaile, *Fighting Napoleon: Guerrillas, Bandits and Adventurers in Spain 1808–1814* (New Haven, 2004), 1–27.

20. Esdaile, *Fighting Napoleon,* 130–59; Michael Broers, *Napoleon's Other War* (Witney, UK, 2010), passim, but especially 105–29.

21. On imperial expansion during the wars see, e.g., Michael Duffy, "World-wide War and British Expansion, 1793–1815," in *The Oxford History of the British Empire: The Eighteenth Century,* ed. Peter Marshall (Oxford, 1998), 184–207, and C. Bayly, *Imperial Meridien: The British Empire and the World 1780–1830* (London, 1989). On the forging of British identity partly through war see Linda Colley, *Britons: Forging the Nation: 1707–1837* (New Haven, 1989). Specifically on Waterloo see Peter Hofschroer's two volumes: *1815: The Waterloo Campaign* (London, 1998 and 1999).

22. Wolfgang Burgdorf, "Der Kampf um die Vergangenheit. Geschichtspolitik und Identitat in Deutschland nach 1813," in *Krieg und Umbruch in Mitteleuropa um 1800,* ed. Ute Planert (Paderborn, Ger., 2009). On the Prussian background, see Christopher Clark, *Iron Kingdom: The Rise and Downfall of Prussia, 1600–1947* (London, 2006), 345–87. On the European context see a number of useful essays in Stefan Berger, Mark Donovan, and Kevin Passmore, eds., *Writing National Histories: Western Europe since 1800* (London, 1999).

23. The term "parting of ways" is derived from Nicholas Riasanovsky, *A Parting of Ways: Government and the Educated Public in Russia 1801–1855* (Oxford, 1992). I discuss these issues in much more detail in Dominic Lieven, *Aristocracy in Europe 1815–1914* (Houndmills, UK, 1992).

24. See, e.g., an interesting piece by Alexander Martin, "Feed the Horses," *Times Literary Supplement,* November 20, 2009, 9. The most recent collection of essays on the Decembrists is O. I. Kianskaia, *Dekabristy. Aktual'nye problemy i novye podkhody* (Moscow, 2008).

25. My main work on this subject is Dominic Lieven, *Empire: The Russian Empire and Its Rivals* (London, 2001). Russian identity in the Soviet era is a complex and ambiguous issue: see Geoffrey Hosking, *Rulers and Victims: The Russians in the Soviet Union* (Cambridge, MA, 2006).

2 *The Use of Historical Sources in* War and Peace

1. Leo Tolstoy, *"The Cossacks" and Other Stories,* trans. and ed. David McDuff and Paul Foote (London, 2006), 255.

2. The early skeptics are numerous. They include military historians such as Aleksandr Vitmer, *1812 god v "Voine i mire"* (St. Petersburg, 1869), and Modest Bogdanovich, "Za i protiv. Chto takoe 'Voina i mir' grafa L. N. Tolstogo," *Golos,* May 10, 1868; veterans of 1812, most notably Avraam Norov and Prince Petr Viazemskii; and a number of reviewers, e.g., A. S. Norov, "Voina i mir (1805–1812) s istoricheskoi tochki zreniia i po vospominaniiam sovremennika," *Voennyi sbornik* 11 (1868): 189–246, and P. A. Viazemskii, "Vospominaniia o 1812 gode," *Russkii arkhiv* 1 (1869): 192–01 (there is a break of pagination in this volume with an extra insert used to print Viazemskii's essay). A negative attitude toward the historical aspect of *War and Peace* was expressed by Ivan Turgenev, who nonetheless promoted Tolstoy's novel in France, and later by Dmitrii Merezhkovskii in his influential book *Tolstoy and Dostoevsky* (1900–1901). Dmitrii Merezhkovskii, *Tolstoi i Dostoevskii,* in *Polnoe sobranie sochinenii,* 24 vols. (Moscow, 1914), vols. 9–10. Rather disparaging remarks about Tolstoy's historical preparation were made by his former consultant, Petr Bartenev: see introduction to "Zametki veterana 1812 goda," by P. S. Demenkov, *Russkii arkhiv* 49, no. 3 (1911): 385. The critical attitude toward the historical veracity of *War and Peace* peaks in Victor Shklovsky, *Material i stil' v romane Tolstogo "Voina i mir"* (Moscow, 1928; repr., The Hague, 1970). It resurfaced during the perestroika period in an article by Sergei Kormilov, a philologist at Moscow State University, "K probleme istoricheskoi dostovernosti v *Voine i mire* L. N. Tolstogo," *Vestnik MGU,* 9th ser.: Filologiia, no. 5 (1988): 3–10, and reached new—and grotesque—proportions in an article by Ekaterina Tsimbaeva, a member of the history faculty at the same university: (E. Tsimbaeva, "Historical Context in a Literary Work: Gentry Society in *War and Peace,*" *Russian Studies in Literature* 43, no. 1 (Winter 2006–7): 6–48. The Russian original was published in *Voprosy literatury* 2004, no. 5.

3. N. Gusev, *Lev Nikolaevich Tolstoi. Materialy k biografii s 1855 po 1869 g.* (Moscow, 1957), 729. Some contemporary reviewers expressed the opinion that *War and Peace* was the most truthful narrative of 1812. At the turn of the century the historical aspect of the novel received a very positive evaluation from several reputed philologists and cultural historians who also studied the specifics of Tolstoy's sources: cf. A. Kirpichnikov, *Ocherki po istorii novoi russkoi literatury* (St. Petersburg, 1896); A. Borozdin, "Istoricheskii element v romane *Voina i mir,*" *Minuvshie gody,* no. 10 (1908): 70–92; K. Pokrovskii, "Istochniki romana 'Voina i mir,'" in *"Voina i mir" Sbornik,* ed. V. P. Obninskii and T. I. Polner (Moscow, 1912), 113–28. During the Soviet period these ideas were taken to new heights in the works of such prominent Tolstoy scholars as the following: Nikolai Gusev, *Zhizn' L. N. Tolstogo. Tolstoi v rastsvete khudozhestvennogo geniia. 1862—1877* (Moscow, 1928), and *Lev Nikolaevich Tolstoi. Materialy k biografii s 1855 po 1869 g.*; Nikolai Apostolov, *Lev Tolstoi nad stranitsami istorii* (Moscow, 1928), and *Tvorcheskii put' L. N. Tolstogo* (Moscow, 1962); and Evelina Zaidenshnur, *"Voina i mir" L. N. Tolstogo. Sozdanie velikoi knigi* (Moscow, 1966). Superlatives in the assessment of Tolstoy's handling of history are present in almost every Soviet author dealing with the subject.

4. The middle-ground position can be found in Boris Eikhenbaum, *Tolstoi in the Sixties,* trans. Duffield White (Ann Arbor, 1982; Russian originally published in 1931); Liia Myshkovskaia, *Masterstvo L. N. Tolstogo* (Moscow, 1958); and, most recently, Aleksandr Gulin, *Lev Tolstoi i puti russkoi istorii* (Moscow, 2004).

5. Apostolov, *Tvorcheskii put',* 157, 170.

6. It still remains the basis for all subsequent lists and was compiled by Konstantin Pokrovskii ("Istochniki," 117–20). In 1927, it was supplemented by Nikolai Gusev and Nikolai Apostolov to include the books kept at Tolstoy's library in Iasnaia Poliana. An appendix to Shklovsky, *Material i stil'*, contains a further expanded version compiled by Vladimir Trenin. The most extensive bibliography of Tolstoy's sources, prepared by Evelina Zaidenshnur, is found in the sixteenth volume of his *Complete Works* (PSS 16:141–45).

7. Arguably some elements of presenting historical material and polemical devices used by Tolstoy can also be traced to these novels. See Dan Ungurianu, *Plotting History: The Russian Historical Novel in the Imperial Age* (Madison, 2007), 102–9.

8. Shklovsky, *Material i stil'*, 30, 43; Apostolov, *Lev Tolstoi nad stranitsami istorii*, 98.

9. V. I. Shcherbakov, "Neizvestnyi istochnik 'Voiny i mira': 'Moi zapiski' masona P. Ia. Titova," *Novoe Literaturnoe Obozrenie* 21 (1996): 130–51. For the English translation see Viktor Shcherbakov, "An Unknown Source of *War and Peace* (*My Notes* by Freemason P. Ia. Titov)," *Tolstoy Studies Journal* 9 (1997): 66–84. This is by far the most significant recent discovery pertaining to Tolstoy's sources.

10. Il'ia Radozhitskii, *Pokhodnye zapiski artillerista* (Moscow, 1835) 1:71–72.

11. Shklovsky, *Material i stil'*, 174, calls this device "transfer of the object."

12. P. A. Viazemskii, "Vospominaniia o 1812 gode," p. 192–p. 01 (see Works Cited for explanation about irregular pagination).

13. For the attribution of Riazantsev's *Memoirs* see Gulin, *Lev Tolstoi*, 202–4.

14. Kormilov, "K probleme istoricheskoi dostovernosti v *Voine i mire*," 10.

15. These calculations are taken from Zaidenshnur, *"Voina i mir,"* 328. There are also mistakes and inconsistencies pertaining to fictional characters and the relationship between the historical and novelistic chronology in *War and Peace*. For an explanation of the logic behind them see Iu. O. Birman, "O kharaktere vremeni v *Voine i mire*," *Russkaia literatura* 3 (1966): 125–31.

16. An excellent analysis of the Ostrovno episode is found in Gulin, *Lev Tolstoi*, 183–93. Among other things, Gulin draws attention to an interesting substitution concerning other participants in the battle. The drafts of the novel mention that with his improvised attack Rostov comes to the rescue of the Life-Guards Hussars, whose squadrons were indeed routed in this battle. In the final version Tolstoy replaces them with an unnamed uhlan unit. Here one might speculate that Tolstoy wanted to avoid potential "contaminations" for Rostov's instinctive decision. As a hussar officer Rostov was bound to feel a special sympathy for the plight of his fellow hussars, but at the same time there was a perennial rivalry between the army (the Pavlograd Hussars) and the Imperial Guards (the Life-Guards Hussars). The generic uhlans could not stir such emotions, but their introduction constitutes further transgression against factual accuracy, as no uhlan units took part in this battle. Moreover, the fleeing uhlans seem to wear an improbable uniform, being consistently described by Tolstoy as "orange uhlans," whereas the color of the Russian uhlan uniform was dark blue. The French dragoons are also clad improperly: they wear blue uniforms, while all regiments of the French dragoons wore green. These details have been discussed by many commentators. Gulin, *Lev Tolstoi*, 193, even suggests a consistent coloristic contrast with potentially broader implications: warm Russian colors (orange uhlans on chestnut horses) vs. cold French colors (blue dragoons on gray horses). It seems, however, that in the case of the French dragoons we are dealing with an inadvertent mistake, as Tolstoy dresses them in the blue uniform that was prevalent in the French army. If that is true, the orange uhlans might not be a mistake after all. In order to differentiate between the blue Russian uhlans and the French dragoons, who he thought also wore blue, Tolstoy mentions not the general color of the uhlans' uniform but rather the color of the officers' breastplates and facings on Russian uniforms. In *Two Hussars* he explicitly mentions the orange facings of the uhlan uniform.

17. Myshkovskaia, *Masterstvo*, 183.

18. Much has been written on the subject of veterans' criticism. For the most recent works, see Gulin, *Lev Tolstoi*, 213–30, and Ungurianu, *Plotting History*, 109–24.

19. Viazemskii, "Vospominaniia," 09–010.

20. G. P. Danilevskii, "Istoriki-ochevidtsy," in *Roman L. N. Tolstogo "Voina i mir" v russkoi kritike*, ed. I. N. Sukhikh (Leningrad, 1989), 334.

21. Such nihilism in relation to Russian history also dominated historiography, where it is associated with the academician Mikhail Pokrovskii, the chief Soviet historian of the 1920s; his "school" was condemned in the mid-1930s with the official revival of patriotism. Characteristically, Pokrovskii makes a disparaging remark about the historical veracity of *War and Peace:* "It would be very naive to mistake [...] *War and Peace* for a truthful portrayal of Russian society in the early nineteenth century. Tolstoy's heroes are by no means the contemporaries of Speransky or Pestel. [...] They are simply people from Tolstoy's own society, his neighbors, friends and relatives dressed in costumes of the epoch of the First Empire. The organizer of this masquerade ball did not take great care about the details. After all, a ball is not a museum, the only thing that matters is general resemblance! For greater verisimilitude some secondary characters are given historical names. But again, it would be extraordinarily naive to think that Tolstoy's Kutuzov and Napoleon are indeed the very same Kutuzov and Napoleon who acted on the historical arena in 1812" (N. M. Pokrovskii, foreword to *Zhenshchiny epokhi frantsuzskoi revoliutsii*, by Galina Serebriakova [Moscow, 1929], 5–6).

22. Shklovsky, *Material i stil'*, 62.

23. Iurii Pivovarov, "Dolzhnost' tsaria u nas stala vybornoi," interview by Vladimir Emel'ianenko, *Profil'*, September 1, 2008, http://www.profile.ru/items/?item=26885&page=1&comment=3.

24. L. N. Tolstoy, "Poiski nachala romana 'Voina i mir,'" in *Lev Tolstoi*, Literaturnoe nasledstvo 68 (Moscow, 1961), 387.

25. Tsimbaeva, "Historical Context," 10–11. According to Tsimbaeva, Tolstoy is well aware of his transgressions against historical veracity, his intention being to create a fairy-tale chronotope. It remains unclear how this agrees with very specific historical information in the opening lines of *War and Peace* or with the entire mass of the undoubtedly historical material in the novel.

26. *Sankt-Peterburgskie Vedomosti* (1805), 642, 653, 665, 701, 711, 721, 733, 741. (Pertinent page numbers correspond, respectively, to the issue dates cited in the text.)

3 Moscow in 1812

1. P. A. Viazemskii, "Vospominanie o 1812 gode," in *Polnoe sobranie sochinenii kniazia P. A. Viazemskogo*, 12 vols. (St. Petersburg: 1878–96), 7:195.

2. For Viazemskii's views, see his essays "Dopotopnaia ili dopozharnaia Moskva," ibid., 7:80–116, and "Kharakteristicheskie zametki i vospominaniia o grafe Rostopchine," ibid., 7:500–14.

3. These issues are discussed at greater length in my book, *Enlightened Metropolis: Constructing Imperial Moscow, 1762–1855* (Oxford, forthcoming).

4. M. N. Zagoskin, *Sochineniia*, vol. 5, *Moskva i Moskvichi* (St. Petersburg, 1889). For a different view, see Alexander Griboedov's play *Gore ot uma* (*Woe from Wit*), a satire of traditional Moscow gentry life (1823).

5. See, for example, V. Androssov, *Statisticheskaia zapiska o Moskve* (Moscow, 1832); P. Vistengof, *Ocherki Moskovskoi zhizni* (Moscow, 1842); I. T. Kokorev, *Ocherki Moskvy sorokovykh godov*, ed. N. S. Ashukin (Moscow, 1932); A. Levitov, *Moskovskie nory i trushchoby*, 2nd ed. (St. Petersburg, 1869); or the plays by Ostrovsky.

6. Laurie Manchester, *Holy Fathers, Secular Sons: Clergy, Intelligentsia, and the Modern Self in Revolutionary Russia* (DeKalb, IL, 2008), passim; Blair A. Ruble, *Second Metropolis: Pragmatic Pluralism in Gilded Age Chicago, Silver Age Moscow, and Meiji Osaka* (Washington, DC, 2001), 80–87.

7. On the portrayal of the nobility and the peasantry in *War and Peace*, see Kathryn B. Feuer, *Tolstoy and the Genesis of* War and Peace, ed. Robin Feuer Miller and Donna Tussing Orwin (Ithaca, 1996), 147–48.

8. P. I. Shchukin, ed., *Bumagi, otnosiashchiesia do Otechestvennoi voiny 1812 goda*, 10 vols. (Moscow, 1897–1908), 4:226, 228.

9. The data are drawn from an official document summarizing petitions for financial assistance filed by Muscovites in 1813: Tsentral'nyi Istoricheskii Arkhiv Moskvy, f. 20, op. 2, d. 2380.

10. In 1802, a colonel's salary was 1,040 rubles, and the governor of Tver'—whose compensation resembled that of other governors—was paid 1,800 rubles salary plus 1,200 rubles for food expenses; Heinrich Storch, *Rußland unter Alexander dem Ersten*, 9 vols. (St. Petersburg, 1804–8), 3:92, 125–31.

11. On Tolstoy's use of biological metaphors, see Olga Maiorova, *From the Shadow of Empire: Defining the Russian Nation through Cultural Mythology, 1855–1870* (Madison, 2010), 143–45.

12. Feuer, *Tolstoy and the Genesis of* War and Peace, 160–65.

13. Andrei G. Tartakovskii, "Naselenie Moskvy v period frantsuzskoi okkupatsii," *Istoricheskie Zapiski* 93 (1973): 356–79.

14. On the history of this memoir literature (including an exhaustive bibliography of published memoir texts), see Andrei G. Tartakovskii, *1812 god i russkaia memuaristika: Opyt istochnikovedcheskogo izucheniia* (Moscow, 1980).

15. Georg Reinbeck, *Flüchtige Bemerkungen auf einer Reise von St. Petersburg über Moskwa, Grodno, Warschau, Breslau nach Deutschland im Jahre 1805*, 2 vols. (Leipzig, 1806), 1:213–14; Friedrich Raupach, *Reise von St. Petersburg nach dem Gesundbrunnen zu Lipezk am Don. Nebst einem Beitrage zur Charakteristik der Russen* (Breslau, 1809), 91.

16. "Opisanie dostopamiatnykh proisshestvii v moskovskikh monastyriakh vo vremia nashestviia nepriiatelei v 1812 godu," *Chteniia v Obshchestve Istorii i Drevnostei Rossiiskikh*, v. 27, no. 4 (October–December 1858), "Materialy otechestvennye": 33–50, passim; P..... F....., "Nekotorye zamechaniia, uchinennye so vstupleniia v Moskvu frantsuzskikh voisk (i do vybegu ikh iz onoi)," in *1812 god v vospominaniiakh sovremennikov*, ed. A. G. Tartakovskii (Moscow, 1995), 29; "Otryvok iz chernovogo pis'ma neizvestnogo litsa," in Shchukin, *Bumagi*, 3:262; "Kopiia s vypiski iz pis'ma chinovnika moskovskogo pochtamta, Andreia Karfachevskogo, 6 noiabria 1812 goda," in Shchukin. *Bumagi*, 5:166.

17. Adam Glushkovskii, "Moskva v 1812 godu: Iz zapisok Adama Glushkovskogo," *Krasnyi Arkhiv*, v. 4 (1937): 154; Anton Wilhelm Nordhof, *Die Geschichte der Zerstörung Moskaus im Jahre 1812*, ed. Claus Scharf and Jürgen Kessel (Munich, 2000), 182.

18. Charles Dickens, *A Tale of Two Cities* (London, 1983), 23. I thank Julia Douthwaite for drawing my attention to this passage.

19. "Rasskaz odnogo iz byvshikh krepostnykh g. Soimonova, starichka Vasiliia Ermolaevicha," in *Rasskazy ochevidtsev o dvenadtsatom gode*, ed. T. Tolycheva [E. V. Novosil'tsova], 2nd ed. (Moscow, 1912), 68.

20. G. Ia. Kozlovskii, "Moskva v 1812 godu zaniataia frantsuzami: Vospominanie ochevidtsa," *Russkaia Starina*, v. 65 (January–March 1890): 113.

21. "Rasskaz Apollona Dmitrievicha Sysoeva, iz kupecheskogo zvaniiá," in T. N., ed., "Rasskazy ochevidtsev o dvenadtsatom gode," *Russkii Vestnik*, v. 102 (November 1872): 273.

22. L.-J. Vionnet de Maringoné, *Souvenirs d'un ex-Commandant des Grenadiers de la Vieille Garde* (Paris, 1899), 43.

23. On the Moscow plague revolt of 1771, see John T. Alexander, *Bubonic Plague in Early Modern Russia: Public Health & Urban Disaster* (Baltimore, 1980).

24. Count Philippe-Paul de Ségur, *Napoleon's Russian Campaign*, trans. J. David Townsend (Alexandria, VA, 1958), 95.

25. Ibid., 107–8.

26. This is the central thesis of Corbin's book, *The Foul and the Fragrant: Odor and the French Social Imagination*, trans. Miriam Kochan, Roy Porter, and Christopher Prendergast (Cambridge, MA, 1986).

27. Alexander M. Martin, "Sewage and the City: Filth, Smell, and Representations of Urban Life in Moscow, 1770–1880," *Russian Review* 67, no. 2 (April 2008): 243–74.

28. "Griboedovskaia Moskva v pis'makh M. A. Volkovoi k V. I. Lanskoi 1812–1818 gg.," *Vestnik Evropy* god 9, kn. 8 (August 1874): 615–16. On Tolstoy's reading of these letters, see A. V. Gulin, *Lev Tolstoi i puti russkoi istorii* (Moscow, 2004), 215.

29. "Podrobnoe donesenie Ee Imperatorskomu Velichestvu, Gosudaryne Imperatritse, Marii Feodorovne, o sostoianii moskovskogo Vospitatel'nogo Doma v bytnost' nepriiatelia v Moskve 1812 goda," *Chteniia v Obshchestve liubitelei dukhovnogo prosveshcheniia*, v. 33, no. 2 (April–June 1860): 179.

30. A. A. Smirnov, "Moskva," in *Otechestvennaia voina 1812 goda: Entsiklopediia*, ed. V. M. Bezotosnyi et al. (Moscow, 2004), 478.

31. "Griboedovskaia Moskva," 613.

32. "Rasskazy ochevidtsev o dvenadtsatom gode: Na Mokhovoi," *Moskovskie Vedomosti*, March 1, 1872.

33. A. Lebedev, "Iz rasskazov rodnykh o 1812 gode (Izvlechenie iz semeinykh zapisok)," in Shchukin, *Bumagi*, 3:259.

34. Wolfgang Schivelbusch, "The Policing of Street Lighting," in *Everyday Life*, ed. Alice Kaplan and Kristin Ross, Yale French Studies 73 (New Haven, 1987), 65–70.

35. "Dvenadtsatyi god: Sovremennye rasskazy, pis'ma, anekdoty, stikhotvoreniia," *Russkii Arkhiv*, v. 2, no. 8 (1876): 392.

36. "Pervye dni v sozhzhennoi Moskve: Sentiabr' i oktiabr' 1812-go goda (Pis'mo kn. A. A. Shakhovskogo, 1836 g., k A. I. Mikhailovskomu-Danilevskomu)," *Russkaia Starina*, v. 64 (October–December 1889): 53; F.-J. d'Ysarn-Villefort, *Relation du séjour des Français à Moscou et de l'incendie de cette ville en 1812 par un habitant de Moscou*, ed. A. Gadaruel (Brussels, 1871), 30–31.

37. "Rasskazy ochevidtsev o dvenadtsatom gode: V prikhode Petra i Pavla na Iakimanke i na Orlovom lugu," *Moskovskie Vedomosti*, March 4, 1872; N. I. T—v, "O 1812 gode (Vospominaniia iz rasskazov sovremennikov i ochevidtsev)," in Shchukin, *Bumagi*, 4:333; [Ioann Mashkov,] "1812-i god. Sozhzhenie Moskvy. Pokazaniia ochevidtsa (Protoiereia Kazanskogo na Krasnoi ploshchadi sobora)," *Russkii Arkhiv*, v. 3, no. 12 (1909): 460; "Zapiska G. N. Kol'chugina," *Russkii Arkhiv*, v. 3, no. 9 (1879): 46; N. Vishniakov, *Svedeniia o kupecheskom rode Vishniakovykh*, 3 vols. (Moscow, 1903–11), 2:39.

38. [Petr Zhdanov], *Pamiatnik Frantsuzam, ili Prikliucheniia Moskovskogo Zhitelia P....Zh....*(St. Petersburg, 1813), 4.

39. "Rasskazy ochevidtsev o dvenadtsatom gode: Na Mokhovoi."

40. "Rasskaz meshchanina Petra Kondrat'eva," in "Rasskazy ochevidtsev o dvenadtsatom gode," *Russkii Vestnik*, v. 102 (November 1872): 275–76.

41. "Rasskazy ochevidtsev o dvenadtsatom gode: V Rozhdestvenskom monastyre," *Moskovskie Vedomosti*, March 25, 1872.

42. Lebedev, "Iz rasskazov rodnykh," 257.

43. Ibid., 259.

44. "Kratkoe opisanie proizshestvii, byvshikh pri Pokhval'skoi, chto v Bashmakove, tserkvi v 1812 godu," *Chteniia v Obshchestve liubitelei dukhovnogo prosveshcheniia*, god 36 (March 1914): 71.

45. "Rasskaz Nikolaia Dmitrievicha Lavrova, sviashchennika tserkvi Spiridoniia, chto na Spiridonovke," in Tolycheva, *Rasskazy ochevidtsev*, 110.

46. [Mashkov,] "1812-i god," 457; Glushkovskii, "Moskva v 1812 godu," 153; A. Voskresenskii, "Umstvennyi vzor na protekshiia leta moei zhizni ot kolybeli i do groba (1778–1825 g.)," *Dushepoleznoe Chtenie*, no. 12 (December 1894): 593.

47. "Rasskazy ochevidtsev o dvenadtsatom gode: Rasskaz kupchikhi Anny Grigor'evny Kruglovoi, Sheremetevskoi bogadelenkoi," *Moskovskie Vedomosti*, March 13, 1872.

48. Voskresenskii, "Umstvennyi vzor," 590.

49. Nordhof, *Geschichte*, 233. See also F. Bekker, "Vospominaniia Bekkera o razzorenii i pozhare Moskvy v 1812 g.," *Russkaia Starina*, v. 38 (April–June 1883): 520.

50. Dmitrii Zavalishin, "Tysiacha vosem'sot dvenadtsatyi god (Iz vospominanii sovremennika)," *Moskovskie Vedomosti,* March 25, 1884.

51. Nordhof, *Geschichte,* 106, 276.

52. Anna Khomutova, "Vospominaniia A. G. Khomutovoi o Moskve v 1812 godu," *Russkii Arkhiv,* v. 3 (1891): 327.

53. K. B ... r, "Vospominanie o dvenadtsatom gode v Moskve," *Atenei,* no. 2 (1858): 129.

54. Bekker, "Vospominaniia," 506, 519.

55. See, for example, the works by Kokorev and Levitov cited in note 5.

56. Vladimir Dal', *Tolkovyi slovar' zhivogo velikorusskogo iazyka,* 4 vols. (1903–9; repr., Moscow, 1994), v. 4, col. 685.

4 The French at War

I thank my colleague Leighton James of the University of Swansea, who kindly provided me with the images for the two illustrations in this chapter.

1. Henry Claridge, introduction to Leo Tolstoy, *War and Peace,* trans. Louise and Aylmer Maude (London, 2001), xi.

2. Samuel Hynes, *The Soldiers' Tale: Bearing Witness to Modern War* (London, 1997), 10.

3. Martin Price, "Forms of Life and Death: Tolstoy's *War and Peace,*" in *Leo Tolstoy's War and Peace,* ed. Harold Bloom (New York, 1988), 126–27.

4. André Palluel-Guillard, "Correspondance et mentalité des soldats savoyards de l'armée napoléonienne," in *Soldats et armées en Savoie: Actes du 28e congrès des Sociétés Savantes de Savoie, Saint-Jean-de-Maurienne, 1980* (Chambéry, 1981), 198.

5. Janet S. K. Watson, *Fighting Different Wars: Experience, Memory and the First World War in Britain* (Cambridge, 2004), 6.

6. Christopher E. Forth, *Masculinity in the Modern West: Gender, Civilization and the Body* (Basingstoke, UK, 2008), 92–113.

7. Joanna Bourke, *Rape: Sex, Violence and History* (London, 2007), 359–64.

8. Bård Maeland and Paul Otto Brunstad, eds., *Enduring Military Boredom from 1750 to the Present* (Basingstoke, UK, 2009), 10–14.

9. Jacques Hantraye, *Les Cosaques aux Champs-Elysées. L'occupation de la France après la chute de Napoléon* (Paris, 2005), 56–71.

10. Linda Colley, *Britons: Forging the Nation, 1707–1837* (New Haven, 1992), 24–25.

11. Alan Forrest, Karen Hagemann, and Jane Rendall, eds., *Soldiers, Citizens and Civilians: Experiences and Perceptions of the Revolutionary and Napoleonic Wars* (Basingstoke, UK, 2009), 6–12.

12. Larry Wolff, *Inventing Eastern Europe: The Map of Civilization on the Mind of the Enlightenment* (Stanford, 1994), 1–17.

13. For an examination of German attitudes toward eastern Europe over the two centuries since 1800, see Vejas Gabriel Liulecicius, *The German Myth of the East* (Oxford, 2009).

14. René Bourgeois, *Tableau de la campagne de Moscou en 1812, par René Bourgeois, témoin oculaire* (Paris, 1814), 14.

15. Alan Forrest, *Napoleon's Men: The Soldiers of the Revolution and Empire* (London, 2002), 142–43.

16. Eric J. Leed, *The Mind of the Traveler, from Gilgamesh to Global Tourism* (New York, 1991), 189–94.

17. Désiré Fuzellier, *Journal de captivité en Russie, 1813–1814* (Paris, 2004), 156.

18. Ibid., 152.

19. Alain Fillion, *La Bérézina racontée par ceux qui l'ont vécue* (Paris, 2005), 11.

20. Léon Hennet and Emmanuel Martin, *Lettres interceptées par les Russes durant la campagne de 1812* (Paris, 1913), 61.

21. Ibid., 171.

22. Commandant Breton, "Lettres de ma captivité en Russie, 1812–14," in *Combats et captivité en Russie, mémoires et lettres de soldats français: Extraits du Carnet de la Sabretache, années 1906, 1908 et 1914–19* (Paris, 1999), 113–15.

23. Donna Tussing Orwin, "Leo Tolstoy: Pacifist, Patriot and *Molodets*," in *Anniversary Essays on Tolstoy*, ed. Donna Tussing Orwin (Cambridge, 2010), passim.

24. Alexander Kinglake, *Eothen* (London, 1845), 176, quoted in Leed, *The Mind of the Traveller*, 42–43.

25. Heinrich von Roos, *Souvenirs d'un médecin de la Grande Armée* (Paris, 2004), 92.

26. Jakob Meyer, *Jakob Meyer, soldat de Napoléon, 1808–1813: Mes aventures de guerre* (Paris, 2009), 58.

27. Shane O'Rourke, *Warriors and Peasants: The Don Cossacks in Late Imperial Russia* (Basingstoke, UK, 2000), 36–37.

28. John Ure, *The Cossacks* (London, 1999), 149.

29. Bourgeois, *Tableau de la campagne de Moscou*, 127.

30. Jean Hanoteau, ed., *Memoirs of General de Caulaincourt, Duke of Vicenza, 1812–1813* (London, 1935), 187.

31. John Bayley, "'Not a Novel ...': *War and Peace*," in Bloom, *Leo Tolstoy's War and Peace*, 9.

32. Dan Ungurianu, *Plotting History: The Russian Historical Novel in the Imperial Age* (Madison, 2007), 13.

33. Ibid., 55.

34. Liza Knapp, "The Development of Style and Theme in Tolstoy," in *The Cambridge Companion to Tolstoy*, ed. Donna Tussing Orwin (Cambridge, 2002), 162.

35. Orwin, "Leo Tolstoy," 78.

36. Kathryn B. Feuer, *Tolstoy and the Genesis of* War and Peace, ed. Robin Feuer Miller and Donna Tussing Orwin (Ithaca, 1996), 14.

37. Patricia Carden, "The Recuperative Powers of Memory: Tolstoy's *War and Peace*," in Bloom, *Leo Tolstoy's War and Peace*, 107.

38. Adam Zamoyski, *1812: Napoleon's Fatal March on Moscow* (London, 2004), xv.

39. Orlando Figes, *Crimea: The Last Crusade* (London, 2010), 409.

40. Ibid., 178.

41. Leo Tolstoy, *"The Cossacks" and Other Stories*, trans. and ed. David McDuff and Paul Foote (London, 2006), 255. Andrew Wachtel, "History and Autobiography in Tolstoy," in Orwin, *Companion to Tolstoy*, 176–77.

42. Jeff Love, *The Overcoming of History in War and Peace* (Amsterdam, 2004), 183.

43. Ungurianu, 109.

44. Joanna Bourke, *An Intimate History of Killing: Face-to-Face Killing in Twentieth-Century Warfare* (London, 1999), 13–43.

45. Donna Tussing Orwin, *Consequences of Consciousness: Turgenev, Dostoevsky and Tolstoy* (Stanford, 2007), 161.

46. Donna Tussing Orwin, *Tolstoy's Art and Thought, 1847–1880* (Princeton, 1993), 113.

47. Dominic Lieven, *Russia against Napoleon. The Battle for Europe, 1807–1814* (London, 2009), 10–11.

5 Symposium of Quotations

1. I refer to these short literary works as "aphorisms" in my forthcoming book *The Long and the Short of It: From Aphorism to Novel* (Stanford, forthcoming). I have also discussed related questions in *The Words of Others: From Quotations to Culture* (New Haven, 2011).

2. For a detailed account of Bakhtin's approach to genres, see Gary Saul Morson and Caryl Emerson, *Mikhail Bakhtin: Creation of a Prosaics* (Stanford, 1990), 271–30.

3. For Tolstoy's translation of La Rochefoucauld, see "Izbrannye aforizmy i maksimy Laroshfuko," PSS 40:283–310.

4. Leo Tolstoy, *War and Peace,* trans. Ann Dunnigan (New York, 1968), III, 1, i, 732/605. (The page number after the slash refers to the Pevear/Volokhonsky translation.) All citations from *War and Peace* are from this version, occasionally modified by comparison with the Russian version in *Polnoe sobranie sochinenii.* References are to book, part, chapter, and pages from Dunnigan and Pevear/Volokhonsky.

5. As cited in R. F. Christian, *Tolstoy's War and Peace: A Study* (Oxford, 1962), 64.

6. William Barker, ed., *The Adages of Erasmus* (Toronto, 2001), 9.

7. Clifton Fadiman and André Bernard, eds., *Bartlett's Book of Anecdotes* (Boston, 2000), 576.

8. John Dainith et al., eds., *The Macmillan Dictionary of Quotations* (Edison, NJ, 2000), 481.

9. Ibid., 481.

10. Ned Sherrin, ed., *Oxford Dictionary of Humorous Quotations* (Oxford, 1995), 350.

11. Baldesar Castiglione, *The Book of the Courtier,* trans. Charles S. Singleton (Garden City, NY, 1959), 43.

12. Dainith, *Macmillan Dictionary of Quotations,* 316.

13. Oscar Wilde, "The Critic as Artist," in *The Portable Oscar Wilde,* ed. Richard Aldington and Stanley Weintraub (New York, 1981), 134.

14. Dainith, *Macmillan Dictionary of Quotations,* 317.

15. In *The Long and the Short of It,* I call this form "apothegms."

16. Lao Tzu, *Tao Te Ching,* trans. D.C. Lau (London, 1963), 5 (opening lines of the book). For Tolstoy's translation of Lao Tzu, see PSS 40:350–63.

17. Fred R. Shapiro, *The Yale Book of Quotations* (New Haven, 2006), 584.

18. John Bartlett, *Bartlett's Familiar Quotations: A Collection of Sayings, Phrases and Proverbs Traced to Their Sources in Ancient and Modern Literature,* 15th ed., ed. Emily Morison Beck (Boston, 1980), 300 (translation adjusted).

19. Elizabeth Knowles, ed., *The Oxford Dictionary of Quotations,* 6th ed., (Oxford, 2004), 587.

20. As did Pascal's famous line about man as a "thinking reed." Donna Orwin notes the influence of Pascal on Tolstoy's sense of culture as a series of diversions from mortality: "Following Pascal, Tolstoy wrote [...] that people could either try to forget death [...] by busying themselves with 'desires and passions,' or they could look for a meaning in life that would not be destroyed by death, a meaning supplied by faith." Orwin also reminds us that "Tolstoy used the thinking reed passage as the epigram to [...] *On Life.*" See Donna Tussing Orwin, *Tolstoy's Art and Thought, 1847–1880* (Princeton, 1993), 146–47, 161–62. Tolstoy's "Thoughts of Wise People for Every Day" (1903) contains thirty-one selections from Pascal.

21. S. Marc Cohen, Patricia Curd, and C. D. C. Reeve, eds., *Readings in Ancient Greek Philosophy: From Thales to Plato* (Indianapolis, 1995), 28. I am indebted to R. Bracht Branham for his explication of the Greek original.

6 *The Great Man in* War and Peace

1. *Gorgias,* 500c 2–4: *hontina khrē tropon zdēn* (literally, how should one live?) See Plato, *Gorgias,* trans. Robin Waterfield (Oxford, 1994), 94. My initial reference uses the Stephanus page numbers, which are standard for references to Plato's text. The Greek avoids the pronoun, and the full sentence reads, "Are you somehow unaware that there's nothing that even a relatively unintelligent person would take more seriously than the issue we're discovering—the issue of how to live one's life?" That Socrates brings up this point in an encounter with the bellicose Callicles is quite relevant to the context of this chapter: combat, whether with arms or words, offers definition.

2. The first seven chapters of the second part of the epilogue give a particularly interesting treatment of the great-man theme, though it is addressed in many of the essays embedded in the text that appear from the beginning of volume III. As to the great-man view itself,

an outstanding representative of this overtly romantic mode of thought was Thomas Carlyle, whose *On Heroes, Hero-Worship and the Heroic in History* (1841) makes an impassioned argument for the importance of select individuals not only to the course of events but to advances in many fields of human endeavor. Carlyle was no friend of democracy. As to the reception of *War and Peace*, the traditional view is represented in a number of fine studies in English, among which the following deserve special mention: Isaiah Berlin, "The Hedgehog and the Fox" (Harmondsworth, UK, 1956); R. F. Christian, *Tolstoy's "War and Peace": A Study* (Oxford, 1962); Gary Saul Morson, *Hidden in Plain View: Narrative and Creative Potentials in "War and Peace"* (Stanford, 1987). For an interesting discussion of the antiheroic aspect of *War and Peace*, see Georg Lukács, *The Historical Novel* (Lincoln, NE, 1962), 85–88.

3. The terminology here is adapted from Heidegger. (See, in particular, Martin Heidegger, *Hölderlin's Hymn "The Ister,"* trans. Will McNeill [Bloomington, IN, 1996], a remarkable lecture concerning the relation of the two concepts.) But it also refers to Pascal's distinction between *l'esprit de géométrie* and *l'esprit de finesse*. In either case, the crucial difference has to do with the rise of a certain kind of mathematical physics that turns all natural processes into quantifiable transactions that may then become subject to the operations of modern mathematics such as coordinate geometry and calculus. See also Ernst Cassirer's *Determinism and Indeterminism in Modern Physics*, trans. Theodor Benfey (New Haven, 1956), for an excellent account of this epochal change.

4. The relation of legality to violence and of rest to motion is crucial for the text where reconciliation of the two is rendered impossible by contradiction. In other words, form cannot describe pure motion—what Tolstoy describes as "continuous motion"—any better than it can describe formlessness. The real issue here is to what extent form, as a kind of rest, can assimilate its opposite, motion, without transforming its opposite into itself or itself into its opposite, a much more complicated proposition, which from a narrative point of view has rich associations.

5. Here I am of course referring to the theme of role playing or playing out one's part in a greater drama—a divine one?—which emerges in the very first chapter of the novel with the description of Prince Vassily as one who speaks "lazily, the way an actor speaks in an old play."

6. The Greek refers to Plato and specifically to his distinction between the ideas, which enjoy the highest kind of being, unchanging and perfect (i.e., without defect of any kind), and their copies (*ta mē onta*), the material things that come into being and pass away.

7. Edward Gibbon, *The Decline and Fall of the Roman Empire*, vol. 1 (New York, 1993), 9.

8. While trite, the identification of Napoleon with the modern drive for mastery is nothing new: it stretches in a straight line from Hegel to Kojève. As to the modern will to mastery, this is another commonplace of German thought, particularly in the first decades of the twentieth century, when it was represented in differing ways by Cassirer, Heidegger, and their students and opponents. But even so Gallicized an observer as Tzvetan Todorov makes similar claims. See Tzvetan Todorov, *Imperfect Garden*, trans. Carol Cosman (Princeton, 2002).

9. *Posterior Analytics* 72b7–16; 83b5–9; 84a4–10, and *Physics* 239b14–29. I have used the standard Bekker page numbers for Aristotle. For a useful English edition, see Aristotle, *The Complete Works*, ed. Jonathan Barnes, 2 vols. (Princeton, 1984).

10. To speak of God in this way is to speak via analogy: God does not think. God has no need of thought. See Martin Heidegger, *The Metaphysical Foundations of Logic*, trans. Michael Heim (Bloomington, IN, 1984), 47. "This is the nature of finite knowing, which happens successively: *intellectus noster de uno in aliud discurrit*. In God, however, there is no succession; it is not as if at first he might not yet have something."

11. This is another reference to the fruits of the modern science. A particularly astute account in this connection is the one given by Hans Blumenberg in his *The Legitimacy of the Modern Age*, trans. Robert Wallace (Cambridge, MA, 1983).

12. This point is made most forcefully by an ostensibly apostate disciple of Leo Strauss, Stanley Rosen, in his *Hermeneutics as Politics*. Rosen is heir to the same tradition of thought—a largely German one—that produced Strauss, whose dissertation adviser was Cassirer and who attended a now famous lecture course by Heidegger (on Aristotle) in 1922. See Stanley Rosen, *Hermeneutics as Politics* (Oxford, 1987).

13. It is worth noting that Tolstoy seems to express a rather different view in the first chapter of the second part of the epilogue. His main complaint about the moderns is that they have retained a concept of the divinely inspired hero in practice, though they have rejected that concept in theory (Epilogue, 2, i, 1179). In other words, modern mechanistic physics does not permit the kind of expression of will that is essential to the notion of the hero, a major problem in the novel that will be resolved in favor of mechanism in the epilogue. By putting the matter thus, Tolstoy transposes the ancient distinction between theory and practice onto the modern one, except that he does not insist, at least in the epilogue, on the impossibility of bridging the gap between them, and in this regard he is distinctively modern. Yet what passes muster in the epilogue does not seem to survive the narrative, where the gap between theory and practice is much more problematic, perhaps infinitely so. Of course, this tension between essay and narrative is merely another enactment of the gap, this time showing Tolstoy's affinity with the ancients.

14. I have in mind a paradigmatic military commander like Agamemnon, who not only offends Apollo at the beginning of the *Iliad*, and must atone for that, but ends up atoning in a much more radical sense in Aeschylus's great play. It is worth noting that *hubris* and related words like the adjective *hubristēs* denote a form of violence or violence itself. In one of the most famous asides in Plato, Agathon reproaches Socrates for his aggressiveness and, by using the adjective *hubristēs* to do so, implies a kind of impiety that is obviously of considerable relevance (*Symposium* 175e8). For a useful translation, see Plato, *Symposium,* trans. Alexander Nehamas and Paul Woodruff (Indianapolis, 1989), 6.

15. See Robert Louis Jackson, *Dialogues with Dostoevsky* (Stanford, 1993), 54–74.

16. For more on this association, see Ernst Robert Curtius, *European Literature and the Latin Middle Ages,* trans. Willard R. Trask (Princeton, 1953), 353.

17. There is of course nothing new in what I say here: the connection between Tolstoy and Eastern traditions of thought is well known. The more specific connection between Tolstoy and the tradition of *wu-wei* or nonaction (literally, action without intent or exertion) has been addressed by Michael Denner. See his "Tolstoyan Nonaction: The Advantage of Doing Nothing" *Tolstoy Studies Journal* 13 (2001): 8–22. The problem here is that *wu-wei* refers less to nonaction than to action that is not connected to some intent, that is automatic and effortless. Indeed, "effortless action" is a far better translation of *wu-wei,* but it is not necessarily what Tolstoy grasped via several mediations much later in his career, as Denner helpfully points out. See also Edward Slingerland, *Effortless Action: Wu-wei as Conceptual Metaphor and Spiritual Ideal in Early China* (Oxford, 2003).

18. Zhuangzi, *Basic Writings,* trans. Burton Watson (New York, 2003), 32. Choice of translation is extraordinarily difficult in the case of Zhuangzi because he wrote in classical Chinese, whose syntactic poverty offers rich possibilities for differing interpretations of the most basic sort. Watson's translation is favored by many scholars, but, for helpful contrast, I recommend two other translations, one by the famed sinologist, Angus Graham, the other, a new translation, by Brook Ziporyn.

19. Heidegger notes that the Latin, *interesse* or *inter-esse,* suggests being *(esse) inter* or among things, being always involved with responding to things. One can take very different attitudes to this definition of interest; one might praise interest as our care for the everyday things of the world, our novelistic side, or decry our immersion in ephemera. The remarkable aspect of this praise and blame is that it hints at differing metaphysics, in the former case more positivistic and in the latter more Platonist. It is St. Augustine, after all, who railed against immersion in things as a surrender to the evil one.

20. It is a commonplace in the critical reception of *War and Peace* that Kutuzov is a rather straightforward hero or pillar of wisdom in the novel, a notion I challenge in this chapter. Indeed, this is one of the more unorthodox aspects of the interpretation I offer, for critics as different as Sir Isaiah Berlin and R. F. Christian have found themselves in general agreement as to the novel's exceedingly complimentary depiction of Kutuzov. See Berlin, "Hedgehog," 69; Christian, *Tolstoy's "War and Peace,"* 24, 90.

21. One must not forget that even Tushin is one who does violence. Tolstoy's efforts mute this aspect of Tushin and point to the general avoidance of clear depictions of Russian violence

against the enemy, a point already made incisively by Danilo Kiš in *Homo Poeticus,* ed. Susan Sontag (New York, 1995), 199–200.

22. This is nationalism as a sort of collective particularity.

23. *Oedipus at Colonus,* lines 1378–99 (in Fagles's translation). See Sophocles, *Three Theban Plays,* trans. Robert Fagles (New York, 2000), 358.

24. Derrida is apropos. He writes in *Aporias:* "Only a being-to-death can think, desire, project, indeed, 'live' immortality *as such.* Here there is an affirmation of originary finitude that Hegel thought he had reversed in Kant, not without good reason: one cannot think originary finitude without removing it as infinity, nor can one think being-to-death without starting from immortality." See Jacques Derrida, *Aporias,* trans. Thomas Dutoit (Stanford, 1993), 55. Derrida expresses a difficult paradox: that to think finitude is necessarily to surpass it—one is at once finite and not-finite, limited and unlimited. And this paradox is an affirmation of our "originary" or constitutive finitude—in simpler terms, of our being constituted by limits such as an origin.

25. Zhuangzi, *Basic Writings,* 95.

7 War and Peace *from the Military Point of View*

1. In a note from the editors on the first page of the last one that year, written by Professor Colonel A. N. Vitmer of the Imperial Nikolaevskii Military Academy. See Vitmer. "Po povodu istoricheskikh ukazanii chetvertogo toma "Voina i mir"" grafa L. N. Tolstogo," *Voennyi sbornik,* no. 12 (1868): sec. 2, 435–71; no. 1 (1869): sec. 1, 91–134. See 1868 installment, 435. Hereafter the installments of this article are cited by year and page only. Please note that the first edition of *War and Peace* contained six volumes; in the third edition in 1873, the book was reorganized into four volumes, and this remains the standard structure today.

2. N. L. [N. A. Lachinov], "Po povodu poslednego romana gr. Tolstogo," *Russkii invalid,* April 10, 1868, 3–4; N. L. [Lachinov], "Voina i mir. 4-yi tom. Sochinenie N. L. Tolstogo," *Voennyi sbornik,* no. 8 August 1868, sec. 3, 81–125; A. Vitmer, *1812 god v "Voine i mir"* (St. Petersburg, 1869). Throughout this chapter, I quote from the later, more expanded version of Lachinov's review (in *Voennyi sbornik*). In 1868 Lachinov (1834–1906?) was teaching tactics and military history at a military high school. He subsequently had a distinguished career in military journalism, serving as editor in chief of *Voennyi sbornik,* 1890–99. See E. Babaev, *Lev Tolstoi i russkaia zhurnalistika ego epokhi* (Moscow, 1993), 29–34.

3. See M. I. Dragomirov, "Razbor romana "Voiny i Mir," *Oruzheinyi sbornik,* 1868, no. 4, sec. 2, 99–138; 1869, no. 1, sec. 2, 69–122; and 1870, no. 1, sec. 2, 87–123. Major General M. I. Dragomirov (1830–1905) was teaching at the Imperial Nikolaevskii Military Academy when he wrote these essays. He became the most important theorist of military education of postreform tsarist Russia. The original installments of Dragomirov's essay are cited hereafter by year and page only.

4. M. I. Bogdanovich, "Za i protiv. Chto takoe 'Voina i mir' grafa L. N. Tolstogo," *Golos,* May 10, 1868, 1–2.

5. M. I. Bogdanovich, *Istoriia Otechestvennoi voiny 1812 goda,* 3 vols. (St. Petersburg, 1859–60).

6. See *Voennaia entsiklopediia,* vol. 4 (St. Petersburg, 1911–15).

7. Bogdanovich, "Za i protiv," 2.

8. As Vitmer wickedly remarks (1868, 438–39), if Tolstoy so despised Thiers and Mikhailovskii-Danielevskii, he ought not have used them as his most quoted sources for the period, since there were many more reliable historians whom he could have consulted.

9. *Biblioteka L'va Nikolaevicha Tolstogo v Iasnoi Poliane,* bk. 1, *Knigi na russkom iazyke,* pt. 1 (Moscow, 1958), 89, 92. The passage in Bogdanovich, *Istoriia,* is in volume 2, page 503. Unless otherwise noted, all translations in this chapter are my own.

10. Ibid., 92.

11. See, for instance, Vitmer, 1868, 444–48, and 1869, 101–2, 103.

12. Vitmer 1868, 444–46.

13. In a note on the first page, the impressed editors declare bluntly that the novel fails as history. See Vitmer, 1869, 91. For a defense of Tolstoy's accuracy as a historian, see chapter 2 by Dan Ungurianu. For an attack on it, see chapter 1 by Dominic Lieven.

14. Dragomirov, 1868, 117.

15. Ibid., 133. For other examples of posturing and vainglory provided by Dragomirov, see ibid., 130.

16. Ibid., 106–7.

17. Lachinov, *Voennyi sbornik*, 83–84. In criticizing the practical usefulness of Tolstoy's approach, Lachinov says that it puts him in the same position as Achilles trying to outrace the tortoise (metamorphosed in Lachinov's mistaken variant into a crayfish). Tolstoy, perhaps with Lachinov in mind, uses this very anecdote in the opening chapter of volume 5 in the original edition to illustrate how we can never completely break down an event into its infinitely numerous and small causes (III, 3, i). In the 1870 installment of his review, Dragomirov expands on Lachinov's critique of Tolstoy's excessively abstract and mathematical way of analyzing historical events (88–89).

18. Lachinov, *Voennyi sbornik*, 83.

19. Vitmer, 1868, 440–42.

20. Dragomirov, 1870, 108.

21. *The Overcoming of History in* War and Peace (Amsterdam, 2004), 135.

22. Ibid., 135–37.

23. Evelina Zaidenshnur, "Istoriia napisaniia i napechataniia," PSS 16:125. Recall that *War and Peace* originally came out in 6 volumes.

24. Ibid., 117, 121.

25. These connections were proposed by Boris Eikhenbaum. See Donna Tussing Orwin, *Tolstoy's Art and Thought, 1847–1880* (Princeton, 1993), 100–107, 233–34 (n15). On the role of Platon Karataev, see Orwin, "Freedom, Responsibility, and the Soul: The Platonic Contribution to Tolstoy's Psychology," *Canadian Slavonic Papers* 25, no. 4 (1983): 510–13.

26. Dragomirov, 1868, 101.

27. M. I. Dragomirov, "Vliianie rasprostraneniia nareznogo oruzhiia na vospitanie i taktiku vojsk," in *Sbornik original'nykh i perevodnykh statei*, 2 vols. (St. Petersburg, 1881), 1:23–24.

28. M. I. Dragomirov, "Po povodu sochinenii, vyzvannykh kampaniiami 1866 i 1870 godov: Stat'ia 4," in *Sbornik original'nykh i perevodnykh statei*, 1:590.

29. L. G. Besprovnyi, "M. I. Dragomirov," *M. I. Dragomirov: Izbrannye trudy*, ed. Besprovnyi (Moscow, 1956), 5.

30. Dragomirov, 1870, 114.

31. Dragomirov, 1869, 89–90.

32. Ibid., 96–97.

33. Ibid., 98.

34. Ibid., 99–100.

35. Ibid., 110.

36. Ibid., 108–9.

37. Ibid., 112–17.

38. Ibid., 117.

39. Ibid., 79–80.

40. Ibid., 83.

41. Ibid., 85; see also Dragomirov, 1870, 102.

42. See, for instance, 1869, 97, for Dragomirov's explanation of how Tolstoy could so wrongly explain Rostov's attack on the dragoons.

43. Ibid., 87–88. Note that this is a restatement of Dragomirov's characterization of Tolstoy's art as landscape painted from one point of view as opposed to the topographical map of the historian, who must take all points of view into consideration.

44. Tolstoy's mathematical theories are indebted to the ideas of S. Urusov and his circle. See B. Eikhenbaum, *Lev Tolstoy*, 2 vols. (1928–31; repr., Munich, 1968), vol. 2, pt. 4, chaps. 3 and 4 passim, and 395. For an early instance in 1862 of Dragomirov's lifelong insistence on the

cardinal importance of flexibility in the application of theory to specific battlefield conditions, see "Ob atake i oborone," in *Sbornik original'nykh i perevodnykh statei*, 1:99.

45. Dragomirov, 1870, 102–3.

46. Ibid., 104.

47. Dragomirov complains briefly about this (ibid.).

48. See, for instance, Dragomirov, 1869, 99.

49. Dragomirov, 1868, 124–34; 1869, 69–86.

50. Dragomirov, 1869, 70–71.

51. Dragomirov, 1868, 122–27, 125. General Karl von Pfühl (1757–1826) was a Prussian adviser to Alexander I whom Tolstoy mocks.

52. Dragomirov, 1869, 75–76.

53. Ibid., 86.

54. Ibid., 72.

55. E. E. Zaidenshnur, *"Voina i mir" L. N. Tolstogo: Sozdanie velikoi knigi* (Moscow, 1966), 22.

56. Iurii Lotman, "Itogi putia," in *Besedy o russkoi kul'ture. Byt i traditsii russkogo dvorianstva XVIII—nachalo XIX veka.* (St. Petersburg, 1994), 213.

57. L. N. Tolstoy, "Neskol'ko slov po povodu knigi 'Voina i mir,'" PSS 16:7–16 (published March 1868 in *Russkii arkhiv*).

8 Tolstoy and Clausewitz

The opinions expressed in this chapter are the author's own and do not necessarily reflect those of the United States Military Academy, the Department of the Army, or the Department of Defense.

1. In *Philosophers of Peace and War* (New York, 1963), W. B. Gallie compares and contrasts the philosophies of Kant, Clausewitz, Marx, Engels, and Tolstoy.

2. Kwame Anthony Appiah, in *The Honor Code: How Moral Revolutions Happen* (New York, 2010), traces the development and decline of the duel in Britain (3–51). See page 15 for links to the age of chivalry. For comprehensive information on dueling in Russia, see Irina Reyfman, *Ritualized Violence Russian Style: The Duel in Russian Culture and Literature* (Stanford, 1999). Kevin McAleer's *Dueling: The Cult of Honor in Fin-de-Siecle Germany* (Princeton, 1994) offers extensive analysis of the German tradition.

3. Iurii M. Lotman. *Besedy o russkoi kul'ture: Byt i traditsii russkogo naroda* (St. Petersburg, 1994), 164.

4. Carl von Clausewitz, *On War,* ed. and trans. Michael Howard and Peter Paret (Princeton, 1976), 75.

5. PSS 13:558, fragments 4 and 5. Pierre, who had never tested his manhood in battle, could prove his mettle by taking up arms in a duel.

6. PSS 13:560–61, fragment 12. This reversal may have been intended as a foreshadowing of Pierre's unexpected victory over the significantly more experienced duelist, Dolokhov.

7. The duel between Pierre and Dolokhov is in PSS 10:20–32. I am indebted to Bill Nickell and Donna Orwin for calling my attention to several other passages where Tolstoy depicts duels that could have happened or employs the duel as a trope.

8. My chapter thus complements chapter 10 by Andreas Herberg-Rothe. We agree on the fundamentals of Clausewitz's theory. Herberg-Rothe, however, focuses on Clausewitz's record as a practitioner of war and on the evolutionary development of the Prussian's theory of war (from existential to instrumental).

9. See, for example, Gary Saul Morson, *Hidden in Plain View: Narrative and Creative Potentials in "War and Peace"* (Stanford, 1987), especially 85–92 and 95–99. Clausewitz, *On War,* 75–89.

10. At the U.S. National War College, we referred to these enduring qualities as the DNA of war.

11. He also identifies the wrestling match as an appropriate metaphor for the struggle of wills. "Countless duels go to make up war, but a picture of it as a whole can be formed by imagining a pair of wrestlers. Each tries to compel the other to do his will; his *immediate* aim is to *throw* his opponent in order to make him incapable of further resistance." Clausewitz, *On War*, 75.

12. Ibid., 77.

13. Ibid., 89.

14. Ibid., 120.

15. Ibid., 113–21.

16. Ibid., 87.

17. See Herberg-Rothe in chapter 10 on the instrumental and existential perspectives on warfare. Clausewitz's discussions about policy are on 80–81 and 86–89 of *On War*. He defines strategy in terms of the interaction of ends and means: "The political object is the goal, war is the means of reaching it, and means can never be considered in isolation from the purpose" (87). Clausewitz concludes that "the first, the supreme, the most far-reaching act of judgment that the statesman and commander have to make is to establish [. . .] the kind of war on which they are embarking" (88).

18. Clausewitz, *On War*, 89. Also see chapter 10.

19. See chapter 10 on Tolstoy's knowledge of Clausewitz. Tolstoy's library at Iasnaia Poliana does not include any of Clausewitz's writings.

20. Leo Tolstoy, *Tolstoy's Short Fiction*, ed. and trans. Michael R. Katz (New York, 1991), 14.

21. See chapter 10 for more on Clausewitz's biography and writings about the 1812 campaign.

22. Appiah, *Honor Code*, 19. Later in the text, Appiah addresses the purpose of honor codes: "[A]n honor code says how people of certain identities can gain the right to respect, how they can lose it, and how having and losing honor changes the way they should be treated" (175).

23. See Reyfman, *Ritualized Violence*, 8–11 and 34–37, and Lotman, *Besedy*,164–66.

24. Reyfman, *Ritualized Violence*, 11.

25. Ibid., 73–85.

26. According to Reyfman, Russian duels when they were actually fought were generally more violent than their European counterparts; however, as with the near miss between Tolstoy and Turgenev in 1861, Russian nobles usually reconciled before there were any casualties (86).

27. "Honor world" is Appiah's term to describe the singular contexts in which communities exercised their unique codes of honor (*Honor Code*, 19–23).

28. I prefer to read this passage as "It's all the same to Clausewitz."

29. Morson observes that Pierre "does not challenge Dolokhov because he believes there has been an affair, he becomes convinced of the affair he has challenged Dolokhov" (*Hidden in Plain View*, 234).

30. As Reyfman notes, "[D]uelists in Russian fiction often feel regret after a duel but rarely allow Rousseau's reasoning [which would lead to reconciliation] to guide their conduct before it" (*Ritualized Violence*, 31). Also see Morson, *Hidden in Plain View*, 237–38.

31. Lotman (*Besedy*, 174) and Reyfman discuss this phenomenon, which Reyfman labels "the tyranny of the Honor Code" (*Ritualized Violence*, 178).

32. "The general unreliability of all information presents a special problem in war: all action takes place, so to speak, in a kind of twilight, which, like *fog* or moonlight, often tends to make things seem grotesque and larger than they really are" (Clausewitz, *On War*, 140; emphasis mine).

33. According to Lotman, "only strict adherence to the established order distinguished duels from murder" (*Besedy*, 169).

34. Clausewitz, *On War*, 75.

35. Interestingly, Pierre does not respond when an emotional Dolokhov begs forgiveness for the duel (III, 2, xxii, 767).

36. Seriously wounded at Austerlitz, Prince Andrei recognizes the figurative smallness of Napoleon.

9 The Awful Poetry of War

1. A. A. Saburov, *Voina i mir L. N. Tolstogo. Problematika i poetika* (Moscow, 1959), 86–87. I thank Arkadi Klioutchanski for his work as a research assistant in the preparation of this chapter. Part of this chapter appeared in *Russkaia literatura* 4 (2010): 30–38.

2. Tolstoy himself addresses the issue of the fictionalization of historical characters in the novel in his article "Neskol'ko slov po povodu knigi 'Voina i mir,'" PSS 16:9–13. I use the Pevear/Volokhonsky translation for *War and Peace*, but I alter it where necessary to clarify my meaning. All other translations are my own.

3. Compare I, 3, xiv (272–73; PSS 9:333–35) with III, 2, xxxiv (804; PSS 11:245).

4. See III, 2, xxxv, where Kutuzov follows the course of the Battle of Borodino.

5. In this chapter I take no position on the correctness of Tolstoy's philosophical ideas or his historical account of the war of 1812.

6. A. P. Skaftymov defends Kutuzov from charges of passivity in his outstanding article "Obraz Kutuzova i filosofiia istorii v romane L. Tolstogo 'Voina i mir,'" in *Skaftymov, Nravstvennye iskaniia russkikh pisatelei* (Moscow, 1972), 188–93.

7. In chapter 6 Jeff Love argues that Kutuzov is nonetheless not as perfectly wise and virtuous as Platon Karataev.

8. A. A. Saburov sees Andrei's act not as the "knightliness" (*rytsarstvo*) that he has condemned in his speech to Pierre the night before the battle but as an expression of the desperate resolve felt by the Russian troops at Borodino. See Saburov, *Voina i mir L N. Tolstogo*, 99–100.

9. M. I. Dragomirov, "*Voina i mir* gr. Tolstogo s voennoi tochki zreniia," *Oruzheinyi sbornik*, no. 4 (1868): 102.

10. Not once does Raevsky appear there, although his adjutant looking for him is the one who leads Pierre to the spot (III, 2, xxxi, 792; PSS 11:231–32). This is a sly dig by Tolstoy at the great-man theory.

11. For one example of this, see N. L. Brodskii, "'Borodino' M. Iu. Lermontova i ego patrioticheskie traditsii," in *Izbrannye trudy* (Moscow, 1964), 118–83. Brodskii discusses the influence of Lermontov's poem and Tolstoy's novel on writers during World War II. See 181–82.

12. For a very different interpretation of the function of the map as illustrative of the shortcomings of the overview it represents and also for a discussion of the painterly qualities of Tolstoy's description of Borodino, see Molly Jo Brunson, *The War (and the Peace) between the Verbal and the Visual in Russian Literary and Painterly Realism* (PhD diss., University of California, Berkeley, 2009), 157–95. Brunson has published a part of this chapter in Russian. See "Panorama P'era: Opticheskaia illiuziia i illiuziia romana 'Voina i mir,'" in *Lev Tolstoi i mirovaia literatura: Materialy v Mezhdunarodnoi nauchnoi konferentsii, prokhodivshei v Iasnoi Poliane 12–16 avgusta 2007 g.* (Tula, 2008), 81–90.

13. To tour the left side of the Russian battlefield, they would have had to recross the river and turn right, a step that Tolstoy leaves out. Thanks to Arkadi Klioutchanski for this observation.

14. An exhibit on Tolstoy at the state museum includes a map of the battle as described by Tolstoy that graphically illustrates my point. I thank the staff of the museum for their hospitality and assistance during my stay.

15. For the allegorical use that Tolstoy makes of Pierre's descent from Mozhaisk to Borodino, see Donna Tussing Orwin, *Tolstoy's Art and Thought, 1847–1880* (Princeton, 1993), 111–12.

16. See, for instance, early morning from Napoleon's and Pierre's point of view (III, 2, xxix, 788; PSS 11:226, and III, 2, xxx, 789; PSS 11:227). Tolstoy's notes on his visit include a drawing indicating the course of the sun during the battle (PSS 13: in an illustration between 40 and 41).

17. E. A. Kupreianova noted a related phenomenon in the way Tolstoy's depiction of landscape progresses from a very exact observation of nature in his diaries to the use of landscape in his prose to express an inner psychological state. For her this was a literary manifestation of the dialectic of the soul as a fundamental principle informing Tolstoy's poetics. See *Estetika L. N. Tolstogo* (Moscow, 1966), 138–56. For Richard Gustafson, what I am describing would be an example of what he called "emblematic realism," which in its narrowest manifestation indicates Tolstoy's tendency to use realistic detail emblematically and in its broadest use suggests that

Tolstoy viewed the entire world allegorically. See *Leo Tolstoy, Resident and Stranger: A Study in Fiction and Theology* (Princeton, 1986), 204 and passim.

18. See D. S. Likhachev, "Tolstoi i tysiacheletnie traditsii russkoi literatury." In G. M. Prokhorov, ed., *Russkaia i gruzinskaia srednevekovye literatury* (Leningrad, 1979), 11. Likhachev suggests that Tolstoy may have become familiar with such tales in 1853 when he read Nikolai Karamzin's famous history of Russia up to the founding of the Romanov dynasty (ibid., 7). http://www.lihachev.ru/pic/site/files/fulltext/tolstoj_i_tisjachelit_tradicii_1979.pdf.

19. "Ne med′ li v chreve Etny rzhet / I, s seroiu kipia, klokochet? / Ne ad li tiazhki uzy rvet / I cheliusti razinut′ khochet?" (M. Lomonosov, "Na vziatie Khotina"). "Vezuvii plamia izrygaet, / Stolp ognennyi vo t′me stoit, / Bagrovo zarevo ziiaet, / Dym chernyi klubom vverkh letit; / Krasneet pont, revet grom iaryi, / Udaram vsled zvuchat udary; / Drozhit zemlia, dozhd′ iskr techet; / Klokochut reki rdianoi lavy,—/ O ross! Takov tvoi obraz slavy, / Chto zrel pod Izmailom svet!" (G. Derzhavin, "Na vziatie Izmaila.")

20. For more on this metaphor see Donna Tussing Orwin, "Tolstoy and Patriotism," in *Lev Tolstoy and the Concept of Brotherhood,* ed. Andrew Donskov (Ottawa, 1996), 51–70. Another war writer in this same tradition who depends heavily on fire imagery is Denis Davydov. See V. E. Vatsuro, "Denis Davydov—Poet," in *Denis Davydov. Stikhotvoreniia. Biblioteka poeta,* ed. V. E. Vatsuro (Leningrad, 1984), 27–28. G. A. Gukovskii characterizes Davydov's war poetry as a combination of Derzhavin and V. Zhukovsky. See Gukovskii, *Pushkin i russkie romantiki* (Moscow, 1965), 160. For Tolstoy's indebtedness to Davydov in *War and Peace,* see Lauren Leighton, "Denis Davydov and *War and Peace,*" in *Studies in Honor of Xenia Gasiorowska,* ed. Lauren Leighton (Columbus, OH, 1983), 21–36.

21. This was even truer in the 1860s, when more land was under cultivation; today it is more forested. When one looks at the huge vistas of the countryside in which sky and land seem equal in size and at the rolling hills crisscrossed by streams and rivers, it is hard to believe that the area saw so much war in the seventeenth, nineteenth, and twentieth centuries.

22. In this passage and subsequent ones, the emphases on words related to grain and harvest are all mine.

23. The phrase скрытая теплота (skrytaia teplota; hidden warmth) is emphasized by Tolstoy.

24. See also III, 2, xxxix; PSS 11:263: "*Nad vsem polem,* prezhde stol′ veselo-krasivym, s ego blyostkami shtykov i dymami v utrennem solntse, stoiala teper′ mgla syrosti i dyma i pakhlo strannoi kislotoi selitry i krovi" (*Over the whole field,* once so gaily beautiful, with its gleaming bayonets and puffs of smoke in the morning sun, there now hung the murk of dampness and smoke and the strangely acidic smell of saltpeter and blood).

25. See Vladimir Dal′, *Tolkovyi slovar′ zhivogo velikorusskogo iazyka,* 4 vols. (1880–82), http://vidahl.agava.ru/.

10 Tolstoy and Clausewitz

1. Andreas Herberg-Rothe, *Clausewitz's Puzzle: The Political Theory of War* (Oxford, 2007), especially the chapter entitled "Clausewitz and Napoleon"; Carl von Clausewitz, *On War,* trans. and ed. Michael Howard and Peter Paret (Princeton, 1976, 1984); Clausewitz, *Schriften, Aufsätze, Studien, Briefe,* ed. Werner Hahlweg, 2 vols. (Göttingen, 1966 and 1990).

2. For details see Peter Paret, *Clausewitz and the State* (Princeton, 1976), still the best biography of Clausewitz.

3. Martin van Creveld, *The Transformation of War* (New York, 1991), and Harry G Summers, Jr., *On Strategy: A Critical Analysis of the Vietnam War* (Novato, CA, 1982). In van Creveld's conceptualization, the three tendencies of the trinity are incorporated into a hierarchy, whereas Clausewitz understands war as a floating balance among these tendencies. Van Creveld's concept can be meaningfully applied only to states, whereas Clausewitz's wondrous trinity can be applied to all forms of warfare. See Herberg-Rothe, *Clausewitz's Puzzle.*

4. Olav Rose, *Carl von Clausewitz. Wirkungsgeschichte seines Werkes in Rußland und der Sowjetunion 1836–1991* (Munich, 1995).

5. Raymond Aron, *Clausewitz—Philosopher of War* (New York, 1986); Rose, *Carl von Clausewitz.*

6. Rose, *Carl von Clausewitz,* 50, 55.

7. For details, see Raymond Aron, *Den Krieg denken* (Frankfurt: Propylaen, 1980), Olav Rose, *Carl von Clausewitz,* and Friedrich Doepner, "Krieg und Frieden und Vom Kriege," in *Europäische Wehrkunde,* 29 (1980): 25–30. There are also connections to Proudhon and his publication *La Guerre et la Paix,* whose title Tolstoy would borrow for his masterpiece (which was forthcoming at the time when both met in 1864).

8. One of Tolstoy's sources for the Russian campaign was probably Philippe-Paul de Ségur, *Defeat: Napoleon's Russian Campaign* (New York, 2008), first published in French in 1824 and republished in English translation in 2008. Clausewitz also knew this work, which had already been published in German in 1825 (Clausewitz, *On War,* 266 and 1209; Annotation of Werner Hahlweg in Carl von Clausewitz, *Vom Kriege,* 19th ed. [Bonn, 1980], 1209). Their common knowledge of this work might explain the similarities in Clausewitz's and Tolstoy's descriptions of the Battle of Borodino.

9. Clausewitz, "From the Campaign in Russia," in *Carl von Clausewitz: Historical and Political Writings,* ed. Peter Paret and Dan Moran (Princeton, 1992), 125 (hereafter cited as Clausewitz, "Russian Campaign").

10. Clausewitz, "Russian Campaign," 135.

11. Richard K. Riehn, *1812: Napoleon's Russian Campaign,* first published 1929 (New York, 1991), 254.

12. Herfried Münkler, "Clausewitz' Beschreibung und Analyse einer Schlacht. Borodino als Beispiel," in *Codierung von Gewalt im medialen Wandel,* ed. Steffen Martus, Marina Münkler, and Werner Röcke (Berlin, 2003), 68–91.

13. The differentiation between existential and instrumental warfare was first developed, as far as I know, by Herfried Münkler. I interpret this differentiation as an integrated part of the trinity. See Herberg-Rothe, *Clausewitz's Puzzle.*

14. Clausewitz, *Schriften,* 1:638 and 666.

15. This form of existence was not yet relevant for Clausewitz, because the French army was not waging a war of extermination against the Prussian people. In the nineteenth and twentieth centuries, however, there were wars in which nations had to fight for their very physical existence. Van Creveld focuses only on this immediate "struggle for existence" and criticizes Clausewitz for supposedly seeing war solely as instrumental. Thus van Creveld overlooks not only the views of the early Clausewitz but also the fact that there are very different forms of the struggle for existence. Most important, there are wars for political existence that cannot be limited to instrumental wars for political purposes as easily as van Creveld represents. Martin van Creveld, *Die Zukunft des Krieges* (Munich, 1998), 211–16.

16. In this respect van Creveld's criticism of Clausewitz falls far short of its mark. According to him, Clausewitz assumed that war consisted only in the purposeful killing of others. For this reason, his theory can't explain what makes men willing to risk their lives. But it takes only a superficial reading of Clausewitz's "Political Declaration of 1812" to see that it is almost exclusively concerned with justifying the risking of his own life in war; van Creveld, *Transformation,* 238; Clausewitz, "Politisches Rechnen," in *Politische Schriften und Briefe,* ed. Hans Rothfels (Munich, 1922), 221; for other similar quotations and remarks, see Herfried Münkler, *Gewalt und Ordnung* (Frankfurt, 1992), 102–7; Clausewitz, *Schriften,* 1:689; Peter Paret, *Clausewitz und der Staat* (Bonn, 1993), 268.

17. For a cohesive interpretation of the trinity see Herberg-Rothe, *Clausewitz's Puzzle.*

18. Ibid.

19. W. B. Gallie (*Philosophers of Peace and War* [Cambridge, 1978]) demonstrates this transition in his chapter about Tolstoy.

20. Clausewitz, "Russian Campaign," 201–2. He expressed this statement quite similarly in *On War,* 166–67.

21. Clausewitz, "Russian Campaign," 201.
22. Aron, *Clausewitz*, 207–208.
23. Clausewitz, *On War*, 627.
24. Clausewitz, "Russian Campaign," 202–3, 169.
25. Clausewitz, *On War*, 385.
26. Clausewitz, "Russian Campaign," 169.
27. Ibid., 167.
28. Clausewitz, *On War*, 71.
29. Carl von Clausewitz, *Der russische Feldzug von 1812* (repr., Essen, 1984), 64: "Wer die Sache gründlich durchdenkt, wird sich sagen, dass die Angriffsform die schwächere und die Verteidigungsform die stärkere im Krieg ist, dass aber die erstere die positiven, also die größern und entscheidendern, die letztere nur die negativen Zwecke hat, wodurch sich die Dinge ausgleichen und das Bestehen beider Formen nebeneinander erst möglich wird." All translations of German passages referenced in these notes are by Gerard Holden. Hereafter cited as Clausewitz, *Der russische Feldzug*. Unfortunately, this passage is missing in the Paret and Moran edition of the "Russian Campaign." Clausewitz repeats this analysis of the dialectical relationship between offense and defense in almost the same words in the first chapter of *On War*, 83–84.
30. Clausewitz, "Gedanken zur Abwehr," in *Verstreute kleine Schriften* (Osnabrück, 1980), 493–527; on this point see 497–98. Münkler, *Gewalt und Ordnung;* see the chapter "Die instrumentelle Auffassung des Krieges und die Relativierung des Vorbildcharakters der napoleonischen Strategie," 94–98; on this point see 96.
31. Clausewitz, "Russian Campaign," 204.
32. Ibid., 179.
33. Ibid., 202.
34. Aron, *Clausewitz*, 208.
35. See the conversation about Napoleon between Prince Andrei and Pierre (I, 1, v and vi, 25–30) and the commentary on Napoleon's invasion (III, 1, i, 603–6).
36. For details concerning the relation of Clausewitz and Hegel and their common changing judgment of Napoleon, see Andreas Herberg-Rothe, "Clausewitz und Hegel. Ein heuristischer Vergleich," *Forschungen zur brandenburgischen und preußischen Geschichte*, no. 1 (2000): 49–84.
37. For all references and citations in this paragraph see Clausewitz, "Russian Campaign," 202.
38. John Keegan, *A History of Warfare* (London, 1993). For Liddell Hart see René Girard, *Battling to the End* (East Lansing, MI, 2009); Beatrice Heuser, *Reading Clausewitz* (London, 2002).
39. For a good overview to this development, see Heuser, *Reading Clausewitz*.
40. This is the main thesis of his book.
41. For a detailed account of this transition, see Herberg-Rothe, *Clausewitz's Puzzle*.
42. I have slightly modified the Pevear/Volokhonsky translation to make my point about the nature of existential war clearer.
43. Clausewitz in a letter dated January 9, 1807, to his fiancée Marie, in Clausewitz, *Politische Schriften*, 10: "Verwaist irren wir Kinder eines verlorenen Vaterlandes umher und der Glanz des Staates, dem wir dienten, den wir bilden halfen, ist erloschen."
44. Carl von Clausewitz, "Historische Briefe über die großen Kriegsereignisse 1806–1807," in *Verstreute kleine Schriften* (Osnabrück, 1980), 93–125; this passage is at 124–25: "Wir haben die schönsten Hoffnungen in uns genährt; denn nie hat wohl eine Armee einen edleren Ruhm mit ihrem Blut erkauft, als der gewesen wäre, die Ehre, die Freiheit, das Bürgerglück der Deutschen Nation gerettet zu haben."
45. An inspiring overview of national mobilization since the French Revolution can be found in Daniel Moran and Arthur Waldron, eds., *The People in Arms: Military Myth and National Mobilization since the French Revolution* (Cambridge, 2003).
46. Quoted in Münkler, *Gewalt und Ordnung*, 54–6.
47. Carl von Clausewitz, "Über das Leben und den Charakter von Scharnhorst," in *Verstreute kleine Schriften*, 205–50. See also Clausewitz's reflections on the respective national characters of the French and Germans, which can be found in his essays, "Aus dem Reisejournal von 1807" and "Die Deutschen und die Franzosen," both from 1807, in Clausewitz, *Politische Schriften*,

23–34 and 35–51. These comments are not in themselves of any great significance, but they do demonstrate the way in which Clausewitz's conception of the political subject shifted from the Prussian state to the German nation.

48. Clausewitz, *Politische Schriften*, 75; Münkler, *Gewalt und Ordnung*, 103–4.

49. Clausewitz, "Politisches Rechnen," in *Carl von Clausewitz. Politik und Krieg*, ed. Hans Rothfels (Bonn, 1980), 216: "Sie wollen eine Revolution—ich habe nichts dagegen; aber wird diese Revolution in der bürgerlichen und Staatenverfassung sich nicht weit leichter machen in der Bewegung und Schwingung aller Teile, welche der Krieg hervorbringt?" In the following sentence, Clausewitz admits that no revolution is likely at present, but this does not change his basic view that such a revolution could and should be brought about via war.

50. Clausewitz, letter of January 2, 1809, in Karl Schwartz, *Leben des Generals Carl von Clausewitz und der Frau Marie von Clausewitz geb. Gräfin Brühl*, 2 vols. (Berlin, 1878), 330–31: "Einer großen und allgemeinen Revolution kann Europa nicht entgehen, es mag da Sieger bleiben, wer will [...] Von dieser großen und allgemeinen Revolution [...] würde selbst eine allgemeine Insurrektion der deutschen Völker nur ein Vorläufer sein." See also Aron, *Clausewitz*, 56.

51. Münkler, *Gewalt und Ordnung*, 104–7. The idea of violence and war as a medium for abandoning self-restraint of man, as an expression of the "mania for immortality," is described in a very graphic way by Wolfgang Sofsky, *Traktat über die Gewalt* (Frankfurt, 1996), and by Peter Berghoff, *Der Tod des politischen Kollektivs. Politische Religion und das Sterben und Töten für Volk, Nation und Rasse* (Berlin, 1997).

52. Although there are some similarities to the approaches of Frederick the Great and enlightened Russia in the eighteenth century, the new Prussian way was characterized by the education of the whole nation.

53. Ute Frevert, "Das jakobinische Modell: Allgemeine Wehrpflicht und Nationsbildung in Preußen-Deutschland," in *Militär und Gesellschaft im 19. und 20. Jahrhundert* (Stuttgart, 1987), 17–47: on this point see 25–26. One would need to look more closely at the question of whether someone like Gneisenau was simply employing "political rhetoric," as Frevert believes, when he called for a free constitution.

54. These points are taken from Aron, *Clausewitz*, 56–57, and from Schwartz, *Leben des Generals*, 330–31. The Clausewitz quotation is taken from Aron, 57, who is referring to Schwartz 330.

55. Donna Orwin, *Tolstoy's Art and Thought, 1847–1880* (Princeton, 1993), 15–16.

56. Clausewitz, *On War*, 83.

57. Clausewitz, "Die Verhältnisse Europas seit der Teilung Polens," in Schwartz, *Leben des Generals*, 401–17; Clausewitz uses the expression "ganze physische und geistige Natur."

58. Clausewitz, *On War*, 523.

59. Aron, *Clausewitz*, 623. Clausewitz seems to use the concept of polarity for the first time at a late stage in his work.

60. Clausewitz, *On War*, 83.

61. Aron, *Clausewitz*, 623.

62. Paret, *Clausewitz und der Staat*, 187.

63. See Orwin, *Tolstoy's Art and Thought*, about the influence of Goethe on Tolstoy in precisely this respect.

64. Clausewitz, *On War*, 57–77. Clausewitz developed this conception in his famous three "interactions to the extreme." For a new interpretation of this concept, see Herberg-Rothe, *Clausewitz's Puzzle*, chap. 2.

65. G. W. F. Hegel, "Vorrede zur zweiten Auflage der Wissenschaft der Logik von 1831," in Wissenschaft der Logik I, *G. W. F. Hegel: Werke*, vol. 5 (Frankfurt, 1970), 21.

66. In a letter to Gneisenau, Clausewitz mentions the books he is returning and notes that he still has the correspondence between Goethe and Schiller, published in 1828–29, which he is still working on. See Clausewitz, *Schriften*, 2:550; *Briefwechsel zwischen Schiller und Goethe in den Jahren 1794–1805*, 6 vols. (Stuttgart, 1828 and 1829). Rahel Levin is quoted by Paret, *Clausewitz und der Staat*, 14. (This quotation is missing in the English original.)

67. For both quotations see Joachim Ritter and Karlfried Gründer, eds., *Historisches Wörterbuch der Philosophie*, vol. 4 (Basel, 1976), 934.

68. Clausewitz, *Schriften,* vol. 2: on Steffens, 470 and 535; on Humboldt, 534; on the Goethe-Schiller correspondence, 550. See also Paret, *Clausewitz and the State,* for a more general discussion.

11 The Disobediences of War and Peace

The opinions expressed in this essay are the author's own and do not necessarily reflect those of the United States Military Academy, the Department of the Army, or the Department of Defense.

1. *The Four Feathers,* directed by Zoltan Korda (London Film, 1939); rereleased DVD (Criterion Collection, 2011).
2. Gary Saul Morson has argued that time has dulled readers' perceptions of the radical nature of Tolstoy's novel. See *Hidden in Plain View: Narrative and Creative Potentials in "War and Peace"* (Stanford, 1987).
3. Percy Lubbock, *The Craft of Fiction* (New York, 1947), 41.
4. Henry James, Preface to *The Tragic Muse,* in *Literary Criticism,* ed. Leon Edel, vol. 2 (New York, 1984), 1107.
5. Henry James, "Ivan Turgeneff (1818–1883)," in *Literary Criticism,* ed. Edel, vol. 2, 1029–30.
6. Arnold writes, "But the truth is we are not to take *Anna Karénine* as a work of art; we are to take it as a piece of life." See "Count Leo Tolstoi," in *The Last Word,* vol. 11 of *The Complete Prose Works of Matthew Arnold,* ed. R. H. Super (Ann Arbor, 1977), 285. Woolf suggests, "Every twig, every feather sticks to his magnet [....] Life dominates Tolstoi as the soul dominates Dostoevsky." See "The Russian Point of View," in *The Common Reader: First and Second Series Combined in One Volume,* (New York, 1948), 254–55. On lack of closure in Chekhov, see 248.
7. Pevear/Volokhosky translation. Appendix, 1217.
8. Ibid., 1217, 1219.
9. Ibid.,1217.
10. George Brimley, unsigned review, *Spectator,* September 24, 1853, reprinted in *Charles Dickens: The Critical Heritage,* ed. Philip Collins (London, 1971), 283; Henry James, "*Daniel Deronda:* A Conversation," in *Literary Criticism,* vol. 1, ed. Edel, 975–76.
11. Boris Eikhenbaum, "Lev Tolstoy" (1931), trans. George Gibian, in *War and Peace,* by Leo Tolstoy, trans. Aylmer and Louise Maude, ed. George Gibian (New York, 1966), 1127–28; George Steiner, "Tolstoy and Homer," in *Leo Tolstoy,* ed. Harold Bloom, Modern Critical Views (New York, 1986), 74. Gyorgy Lukacs proposed that Tolstoy had a "great and truly epic mentality" in "Tolstoy and the Attempts to Go beyond the Social Forms of Life," in Bloom, *Leo Tolstoy,* 9. On "[t]he tension between Tolstoy's contradictory ideas on freedom and necessity" as a source of the book's divided identity as epic and novel, see Paul Debreczeny, "Freedom and Necessity: A Reconsideration of *War and Peace,*" *Papers in Language and Literature* 7, no. 2 (1971): 198.
12. M. M. Bakhtin, *The Dialogic Imagination: Four Essays,* ed. Michael Holquist, trans. Caryl Emerson and Michael Holquist, University of Texas Press Slavic Series 1 (Austin, 1981), 16. On Bakhtin's use of Tolstoy as straw man, see Caryl Emerson, "The Tolstoy Connection in Bakhtin," *PMLA* 100, no. 1 (January 1985): 68–80.
13. David Quint, *Epic and Empire: Politics and Generic Form from Virgil to Milton* (Princeton, 1993), 9.
14. Georg Wilhelm Friedrich Hegel, *The Philosophy of History,* trans. J. Sibree (New York, 1902), 77.
15. Morson argues that the novel does not "really begin *in medias res* [...] [b]ecause no real beginning or ending can be isolated" (*Hidden,* 162).
16. Tolstoy's critique resembles that of Plutarch, who disparages interpreters who take delight in making "fortuitous occurrences [...] look like works of a rational power and design."

See "Sertorius," in *Plutarch's Lives,* Dryden translation, rev. Arthur Hugh Clough, 2 vols. (New York, 2001), 2:1.

17. Morson, "*War and Peace,*" in *The Cambridge Companion to Tolstoy,* ed. Donna Tussing Orwin (Cambridge, 2002), 72.

18. "A Few Words," 1222.

19. "[T]he real shortcoming in the whole creation [...] is the lack of any *development in the plot.* The novel does not move." "Annenkov on *War and Peace,*" in *Tolstoy: The Critical Heritage,* ed. A. V. Knowles (London, 1978), 105.

20. Leopold von Ranke, preface to *Histories of the Latin and Germanic Nations from 1494–1514,* reprinted in *The Varieties of History: From Voltaire to the Present,* ed. Fritz Stern, 2nd ed. (New York, 1973), 57. Brackets in the reprinted edition, not author's interpolation.

21. Edward Hallett Carr, *What Is History?* (New York, 1962), 55. For a summary of this evolution, see Alan Munslow, "Biography and Life Writing," in *The Routledge Companion to Historical Studies,* 2nd ed. (London, 2006), 45–48.

22. "A Few Words," 1224.

23. The Russian military historian M. I. Dragomirov suggested that fictional soldiers such as Tushin "illumine that internal side of the battle better than the majority of multi-tomed descriptions of wars in which faceless characters pass fleetingly by.... These fictional characters live and act before you in such a way that invaluable practical lessons may be learnt from their activity by anyone who has decided to devote himself to military affairs." See "Dragomirov on Prince Andrey and the Art of War," in Knowles, *Tolstoy: The Critical Heritage,* 154–55. See also chapter 7 of this book, by Donna Tussing Orwin.

24. On new-model obedience in late-eighteenth- and nineteenth-century America, see Elizabeth D. Samet, *Willing Obedience: Citizens, Soldiers, and the Progress of Consent in America, 1776–1898* (Stanford, 2004).

25. Ulysses S. Grant, *Personal Memoirs of U. S. Grant,* in *Memoirs and Selected Letters,* ed. Mary Drake McFeely and William S. McFeely (New York, 1990), 638.

26. Ibid., 446.

27. Ibid., 445.

28. Brooks D. Simpson, *Ulysses S. Grant: Triumph over Adversity, 1822–1865* (Boston, 2000), 242.

29. Ibid., 244; Peter Cozzens, *The Shipwreck of Their Hopes: The Battles for Chattanooga* (Urbana, IL, 1996), 282. Grant, *Personal Memoirs,* 446.

30. Herman Melville, *Battle-Pieces and Aspects of the War* (1866; repr., New York,1995), 90, 249.

31. Morson reads battle "as a microcosm of the historical process" in the novel. *Hidden,* 88.

32. Juan Camilo Bohorquez, et al., "Common Ecology Quantifies Human Insurgency," letter in *Nature,* December, 2009, 911.

33. Johnson quoted in Natasha Gilbert, "Modellers Claim Wars Are Predictable," *Nature,* December 16, 2009, http://www.nature.com/news/2009/091215/full/462836a.html.

34. See Global Guerrillas Blog, "Characteristics of Open Source Warfare," http://globalguerrillas.typepad.com/globalguerrillas/2010/02/characteristics-of-open-source-warfare.html. See also John Robb, *Brave New War: The Next Stage of Terrorism and the End of Globalization* (Hoboken, NJ, 2007).

35. Martin E. Dempsey, "TRADOC Perspective," speech at Association of the United States Army (AUSA) Institute of Land Warfare Winter Symposium and Exposition, Ft. Lauderdale, FL, February 25, 2010; Dempsey, keynote address, AUSA chapter presidents' dinner, Washington, DC, October 4, 2009.

36. Morson, *Hidden,* 94, 129.

37. There is a provocative analogue to this model of human interconnectedness in *Moby-Dick,* when Ishmael, the habitual loner, suddenly finds his own fate literally tied to that of Queequeg through the safety line that holds the latter while he is engaged in the precarious business of stripping blubber from a captured whale. "I saw that this situation of mine was the

precise situation of every mortal that breathes; only, in most cases, he [...] has this Siamese connection with a plurality of other mortals. If your banker breaks, you snap; if your apothecary by mistake sends you poison in your pills, you die." See Herman Melville, *Moby-Dick,* ed. Harold Beaver (New York, 1987), 426.

38. Plutarch, "Poplicola," in *Lives,* 1:139. This episode also had a significant impact on the young Rousseau, who reports seizing a hot chafing dish at the dinner table one day in imitation of his republican hero. See Jean-Jacques Rousseau, *The Confessions,* trans. J. M. Cohen (New York, 1953), 20–21. On the enduring seductiveness of the martial dream for Tolstoy, see Donna Tussing Orwin, "Leo Tolstoy: Pacifist, Patriot, and Molodets," in *Anniversary Essays on Tolstoy,* ed. Donna Tussing Orwin (Cambridge, 2010).

12 Tolstoy the International Relations Theorist

I thank Rick McPeak, Donna Orwin, the participants in the April 2010 conference "*War and Peace* at West Point," and two anonymous reviewers for their helpful comments and suggestions; and Tim Ormond both for expert research assistance and for perceptive insights on various translation issues.

1. Throughout I will employ Hollis and Smith's helpful practice of capitalizing International Relations when referring to the discipline and using lowercase when referring to its subject matter. Martin Hollis and Steve Smith, *Explaining and Understanding International Relations* (Oxford, 1991), 2.

2. The first holder was Sir Alfred Zimmern, a classicist by training. See Polly Low, *Interstate Relations in Classical Greece: Morality and Power* (Cambridge, 2007), 7.

3. Torbjørn Knutsen argues that a recognized academic field actually developed during the 1890s, in the United States—still two decades after *War and Peace.* Torbjørn L. Knutsen, "A Lost Generation? IR Scholarship before World War I." *International Politics* 45 (November 2008): 650–74.

4. Robert B. Strassler and Richard Crawley, eds., *The Landmark Thucydides: A Comprehensive Guide to the Peloponnesian War* (New York, 1996); but cf. David A. Welch, "Why International Relations Theorists Should Stop Reading Thucydides," *Review of International Studies* 29 (July 2003): 301–19.

5. Tolstoy's word here—*narody*—is commonly translated by others as "nations": e.g., Constance Garnett (New York, 1976); Louise and Aylmer Maude (Oxford, 1998); and Rosemary Edmonds (London, 1978). States—sovereign, territorial political units—were of course the principal actors in the international system in the nineteenth century, as they are today. States, not peoples or nations, field armies. There are no universally accepted definitions of "peoples" or "nations." Benedict Anderson leaves the notion inherently vague by calling a nation an "imagined community": *Imagined Communities: Reflections on the Origin and Spread of Nationalism* (London, 1991). My own preference is to conceive of a people as "[a] group united by common culture, tradition, or sense of kinship (though not necessarily by blood, race, or political ties), typically sharing a language and system of beliefs," and a nation as a people with "strong ties to a particular territory, and, usually, aspirations for political autonomy." Joseph S. Nye, Jr., and David A. Welch, *Understanding Global Conflict and Cooperation: An Introduction to Theory and History,* 8th ed. (New York, 2010), 330. The ambiguity here is a function of the fact that the adjectives *French* and *Russian* equally well modify all three nouns: state, people, and nation.

6. Robert Jervis, "International Politics and Diplomatic History: Fruitful Differences," http://www.h-net.org/~diplo/ISSF/PDF/ISSF-Jervis-InaguralAddress.pdf.

7. Kenneth N. Waltz, *Man, the State and War* (New York, 1959); J. David Singer, "The Levels of Analysis Problem in International Relations," in *International Politics and Foreign Policy,* ed. James N. Rosenau (New York, 1969), 20–29.

8. The literature is vast, but particularly important works include Irving L. Janis and Leon Mann, *Decision Making: A Psychological Analysis of Conflict, Choice, and Commitment*

(New York, 1977); Robert Jervis, *Perception and Misperception in International Politics* (Princeton, 1976); Robert Jervis, Richard Ned Lebow, and Janice Gross Stein, *Psychology & Deterrence* (Baltimore, 1985); Richard Ned Lebow, *Between Peace and War: The Nature of International Crisis* (Baltimore, 1981); Rose McDermott, *Political Psychology in International Relations* (Ann Arbor, MI, 2004); and Jerrold M. Post and Alexander George, *Leaders and Their Followers in a Dangerous World: The Psychology of Political Behavior* (Ithaca, 2004).

9. James Rosenau, ed., *Domestic Sources of Foreign Policy* (New York, 1967); Graham T. Allison, *Essence of Decision: Explaining the Cuban Missile Crisis* (Boston, 1971); Morton H. Halperin, *Bureaucratic Politics and Foreign Policy* (Washington, DC, 1974); Jack Snyder, *Myths of Empire: Domestic Politics and International Ambition* (Ithaca, 1991).

10. Kenneth N. Waltz, *Theory of International Politics* (New York, 1979); Robert O. Keohane, ed., *Neorealism and Its Critics* (New York, 1986); Barry Buzan, Charles Jones, and Richard Little, *The Logic of Anarchy: Neorealism to Structural Realism* (New York, 1993).

11. E.g., E. H. Carr, *The Twenty Years Crisis, 1919–1939: An Introduction to the Study of International Relations* (London, 1940); and Hans J. Morgenthau, *Politics among Nations: The Struggle for Power and Peace* (New York, 1948).

12. E.g., Hedley Bull, *The Anarchical Society: A Study of Order in World Politics* (London, 1977).

13. Steven E. Lobell, Norrin M. Ripsman, and Jeffrey W. Taliaferro, eds., *Neoclassical Realism, the State, and Foreign Policy* (New York, 2009).

14. Peter Gourevitch, "The Second Image Reversed: The International Sources of Domestic Politics," *International Organization* 32 (Autumn 1978): 881–912; Robert Putnam, "Diplomacy and Domestic Politics: The Logic of Two-Level Games," *International Organization* 42 (Summer 1988): 428–60.

15. Nicholas Greenwood Onuf, *World of Our Making: Rules and Rule in Social Theory and International Relations* (Columbia, SC, 1989); Alexander Wendt, *Social Theory of International Politics* (Cambridge, 1999); Audie Klotz and Cecelia Lynch, *Strategies for Research in Constructivist International Relations* (Armonk, NY, 2007); Richard Ned Lebow, "Identity and International Relations," *International Relations* 22 (December 2008): 473–92.

16. Mark Raymond, "Social Change in World Politics: Secondary Rules and Institutional Politics" (PhD diss., University of Toronto, 2011).

17. Cf. Alexander Mikaberidze, *The Battle of Borodino: Napoleon against Kutuzov* (Barnsley, Yorkshire, UK, 2007).

18. Namely, Alexander Wendt, who is in the early stages of a research program on "quantum social science"—an attempt to determine whether the apparently non-Aristotelian and non-Cartesian characteristics of quantum physical phenomena might scale up to the behavior of individual humans and their social and political interactions.

19. Gary Saul Morson, *Hidden in Plain View: Narrative and Creative Potentials in* War and Peace (Stanford, 1987).

20. Perhaps the clearest and strongest example is Spinoza, who in his *Ethics* reconceived "freedom" as the knowledge that one is not at all "free"—a move that would seem to reduce "ethics" to a descriptive category. Benedictus de Spinoza, *Ethics,* trans. G. H. R. Parkinson (Oxford, 2000). Tolstoy's "A Few Words apropos of the Book *War and Peace,*" published in the *Russian Archive* in 1868 (and reprinted in the Pevear/Volkhonsky translation of *War and Peace* on pp. 1217–24) suggests that he meant his determinism very seriously, but it includes a number of remarks that suggest a sliding scale of the kind I discuss below.

21. See, e.g., C. S. Lewis, *Mere Christianity* (London, 1955).

22. In Nicola Chiaromonte, "Tolstoy and the Paradox of History," in *The Paradox of History: Stendhal, Tolstoy, Pasternak, and Others* (Philadelphia, 1986), 17–50.

23. See, e.g., Kutuzov's tender interaction with Prince Andrei, at a time of acute national emergency, following Andrei's father's death (III, 2, xvi, 743–45).

24. A particularly telling illustration is Kutuzov's almost impertinent interaction with the tsar immediately prior to Austerlitz (I, 3, xv, 276–77).

25. Fredrik Logevall, *Choosing War: The Lost Chance for Peace and the Escalation of War in Vietnam* (Berkeley, 1999); James G. Blight, janet M. Lang, and David A. Welch, *Virtual JFK: Vietnam If Kennedy Had Lived* (Lanham, MD, 2010).

26. Alexander Wendt, "The Agent-Structure Problem in International Relations Theory," *International Organization* 41 (Summer 1987): 335–70; David Dessler, "What's at Stake in the Agent-Structure Debate?" *International Organization* 43 (Summer 1989): 441–74.

27. See generally http://www.worldvaluessurvey.org/.

28. Vincent Pouliot, "'Sobjectivism': Toward a Constructivist Methodology," *International Studies Quarterly* 51 (June 2007): 359–84.

29. Neal J. Roese, and James N. Olson, *What Might Have Been: The Social Psychology of Counterfactual Thinking* (Mahwah, NJ, 1995); Philip E. Tetlock and Aaron Belkin, eds., *Counterfactual Thought Experiments in World Politics: Logical, Methodological, and Psychological Perspectives* (Princeton, 1996); David Sylvan and Stephen Majeski, "A Methodology for the Study of Historical Counterfactuals," *International Studies Quarterly* 42 (1998): 79–108; Niall Ferguson, *Virtual History: Alternatives and Counterfactuals* (New York, 1999); Richard Ned Lebow, "What's So Different about a Counterfactual?," *World Politics* 52 (July 2000): 550–85.

30. An intriguing exception is Barry O'Neill, *Honor, Symbols, and War* (Ann Arbor, MI, 1999), which takes honor and rules seriously but gives them a rational-choice interpretation.

31. Richard Ned Lebow, *A Cultural Theory of International Relations* (Cambridge, 2008); Raymond, "Social Change in World Politics."

War and Peace *at West Point*

The opinions expressed in this essay are the author's own and do not necessarily reflect those of the United States Military Academy, the Department of the Army, or the Department of Defense.

1. Because we engaged in a collaborative learning experience, I am sincerely indebted to all ten of the cadets in my *War and Peace* course. Specific appreciation goes to Cadet Aleksandr Klevenskiy, who reminded me that, while West Point mythology promotes the great-man theory of military history, the Academy's leader development process actually fosters humility.

2. I also thank Cadet Rudy Weisz, who informed my analysis of Prince Andrei's ruminations on the eve of Borodino.

Works Cited

Alexander, John T. *Bubonic Plague in Early Modern Russia: Public Health & Urban Disaster.* Baltimore: Johns Hopkins University Press, 1980.

Allison, Graham T. *Essence of Decision: Explaining the Cuban Missile Crisis.* Boston: Little, Brown, 1971.

Anderson, Benedict. *Imagined Communities: Reflections on the Origin and Spread of Nationalism.* London: Verso, 1991.

Androssov, V. *Statisticheskaia zapiska o Moskve.* Moscow: V tipografii Semena Selivanovskogo, 1832.

Annenkov, P. "Historical and Aesthetic Questions in Count L. N. Tolstoy's Novel 'War and Peace.'" *Vestnik Evropy* 2 (1868). Reprinted in *Tolstoy: The Critical Heritage,* ed. A. V. Knowles, 100–114. London: Routledge & Kegan Paul, 1978.

Apostolov, Nikolai. *Lev Tolstoi nad stranitsami istorii.* Moscow: Komissiia po oznamenovaniiu stoletiia so dnia rozhdeniia L.N. Tolstogo, 1928.

———. *Tvorcheskii put' L. N. Tolstogo.* Moscow: AN SSSR, 1962.

Appiah, Kwame Anthony. *The Honor Code: How Moral Revolutions Happen.* New York: Norton, 2010.

Aristotle. *The Complete Works.* Ed. Jonathan Barnes, 2 vols. Princeton: Princeton University Press, 1984.

Arnold, Matthew. "Count Leo Tolstoi." In *Essays in Criticism: Second Series,* 186–219. Vol. 4 of *The Works of Matthew Arnold.* London: Macmillan, 1903.

Aron, Raymond. *Clausewitz—Philosopher of War.* New York: Simon & Schuster, 1986.

———. *Den Krieg denken.* Frankfurt: Propylaen, 1980.

Auerbach, Erich. *Mimesis: The Representation of Reality in Western Literature.* Trans. Willard R. Trask. Princeton: Princeton University Press, 1953.

B . . . r, K. "Vospominanie o dvenadtsatom gode v Moskve." *Atenei,* no. 2 (1858): 119–134.

Babaev, E. *Lev Tolstoi i russkaia zhurnalistika ego epokhi.* Moscow: MGU, 1993.

Bakhtin, M. M. *The Dialogic Imagination: Four Essays.* Ed. Michael Holquist. Trans. Caryl Emerson and Michael Holquist. Austin: University of Texas Press, 1981.

Barker, William, ed. *The Adages of Erasmus.* Toronto: University of Toronto Press, 2001.

Bartenev, Petr. Introduction to "Zametki veterana 1812 goda," by P. S. Demenkov. *Russkii arkhiv* 49, no. 3 (1911): 385.

Bartlett, John. *Bartlett's Familiar Quotations: A Collection of Sayings, Phrases and Proverbs Traced to Their Sources in Ancient and Modern Literature*. Ed. Emily Morison Beck. Boston: Little, Brown, 1980.

Bayley, John. "Not a Novel . . . : *War and Peace*." In *Leo Tolstoy's* War and Peace, ed. Harold Bloom, 7–39. Modern Critical Views. New York: Chelsea House, 1988.

Bayly, C. *Imperial Meridien: The British Empire and the World 1780–1830*. London: Longman, 1989.

Bekker, F. "Vospominaniia Bekkera o razzorenii i pozhare Moskvy v 1812 g." *Russkaia Starina* 38 (April–June 1883): 507–524.

Berger, Stefan, Mark Donovan, and Kevin Passmore, eds. *Writing National Histories: Western Europe since 1800*. London: Routledge, 1999.

Berghoff, Peter. *Der Tod des politischen Kollektivs: Politische Religion und das Sterben und Töten für Volk, Nation und Rasse*. Berlin: Akademie, 1997.

Berlin, Isaiah. *The Hedgehog and the Fox*. Harmondsworth, UK: Penguin, 1956.

Besprovnyi, L. G. "M. I. Dragomirov." Introduction to *M. I. Dragomirov: Izbrannye trudy*, ed. L. G. Besprovnyi, 3–39. Moscow: Voennoe izdatel'stvo Ministerstva Oborony Soiuza SSR, 1956.

Bibikov, Grigorii. *A.Kh. Benkendorf i politika Nikolaia I*. Moscow: Tri Kvadrata, 2009.

Birman, Iu. O. "O kharaktere vremeni v *Voine i mire.*" *Russkaia literatura* 3 (1966): 125–31.

Blight, James G., janet M. Lang, and David A. Welch. *Virtual JFK: Vietnam If Kennedy Had Lived*. Lanham, MD: Rowman & Littlefield, 2010.

Bloom, Harold, ed. *Leo Tolstoy*. Modern Critical Views. New York: Chelsea House, 1986.

——, ed. *Leo Tolstoy's* War and Peace. Modern Critical Views. New York: Chelsea House, 1988.

Blumenberg, Hans. *The Legitimacy of the Modern Age*. Trans. Robert Wallace. Cambridge, MA: MIT Press, 1983.

Bogdanovich, Modest. *Istoriia Otechestvennoi voiny 1812 goda*. 3 vols. St. Petersburg: Tipografiia Torgovogo doma S. Strugovshchikova, G. Pokhitonova, N. Vodova, i Co., 1859–60.

——. "Za i protiv. Chto takoe 'Voina i mir' grafa L. N. Tolstogo." *Golos*, May 10, 1868, 1–2.

Bohorquez, Juan Camilo et al. "Common ecology quantifies human insurgency." Letter in *Nature*, December 17, 2009, 911–14.

Borozdin, A. "Istoricheskii element v romane *Voina i mir.*" *Minuvshie gody*, no 10 (1908): 70–92.

Bourgeois, René. *Tableau de la campagne de Moscou en 1812, par René Bourgeois, témoin oculaire*. Paris: J.-G. Dentu, 1814.

Bourke, Joanna. *An Intimate History of Killing: Face-to-Face Killing in Twentieth-Century Warfare*. London: Granta, 1999.

——. *Rape: Sex, Violence and History*. London: Virago, 2007.

Briefwechsel zwischen Schiller und Goethe in den Jahren 1794–1805. 6 vols. Stuttgart: Cotta'sche Buchhandlung, 1828 and 1829.

Brimley, George. Unsigned review. *Spectator*, September 24, 1853. Reprinted in *Charles Dickens: The Critical Heritage*, ed. Philip Collins, 283–86. London: Routledge & Kegan Paul, 1971.

Brodskii, N. L. "'Borodino' M. Iu. Lermontova i ego patrioticheskie traditsii." In *Izbrannye trudy*, 118–83. Moscow: Prosveshchenie, 1964.

Broers, Michael. *Napoleon's Other War*. Witney, UK: Peter Lang, 2010.

Brunson, Molly Jo. "Panorama P'era: Opticheskaia illiuziia i illiuziia romana 'Voina i mir.'" In *Lev Tolstoi i mirovaia literatura: Materialy v Mezhdunarodnoi nauchnoi konferentsii, prokhodivshei v Iasnoi Poliane 12–16 avgusta 2007 g.* 81–90. Tula: Izdatel'skii dom Iasnaia Poliana, 2008.

———. "The War (and the Peace) between the Verbal and the Visual in Russian Literary and Painterly Realism." PhD diss. University of California, Berkeley, 2009.

Bull, Hedley. *The Anarchical Society: A Study of Order in World Politics.* London: Macmillan, 1977.

Burgdorf, Wolfgang. "Der Kampf um die Vergangenheit. Geschichtspolitik und Identität in Deutschland nach 1813." In *Krieg und Umbruch in Mitteleuropa um 1800,* ed. Ute Planert, 333–57. Paderborn: Ferdinand Schoningh, 2009.

Buzan, Barry, Charles Jones, and Richard Little. *The Logic of Anarchy: Neorealism to Structural Realism.* New York: Columbia University Press, 1993.

Carden, Patricia. "The Recuperative Powers of Memory: Tolstoy's *War and Peace.*" In *Leo Tolstoy's* War and Peace, ed. Harold Bloom, 103–21. Modern Critical Views. New York: Chelsea House, 1988.

Carlyle, Thomas. *On Heroes, Hero-Worship and the Heroic in History.* London: Chapman and Hall, Ltd., 1841.

Carr, E. H. *The Twenty Years Crisis, 1919–1939: An Introduction to the Study of International Relations.* London: Macmillan, 1940.

———. *What Is History?* London: Vintage, 1961.

Cassirer, Ernst. *Determinism and Indeterminism in Modern Physics.* Trans.Theodor Benfey. New Haven: Yale University Press, 1956.

Castiglione, Baldesar. *The Book of the Courtier.* Trans. Charles S. Singleton. Garden City, NY: Doubleday, 1959.

Chiaromonte, Nicola. "Tolstoy and the Paradox of History." In *The Paradox of History: Stendhal, Tolstoy, Pasternak, and Others,* 17–50. Philadelphia: University of Pennsylvania Press, 1986.

Christian, R. F. *Tolstoy's "War and Peace": A Study.* Oxford: Oxford University Press, 1962.

Chuang Tzu. *Basic Writings.* Trans. Burton Watson. New York: Columbia University Press, 1964.

Claridge, Henry. Introduction to *War and Peace* by Leo Tolstoy, v–xiii. Trans. Louise and Aylmer Maude. Ware in Hertfordshire, UK: Wordsworth Editions, 2001.

Clark, Christopher. *Iron Kingdom: The Rise and Downfall of Prussia, 1600–1947.* London: Allen Lane, 2006.

Clausewitz, Carl von. "Aus dem Reisejournal von 1807." In *Politische Schriften und Briefe,* ed. Hans Rothfels, 23–34. Munich: Drei Masken Verlag, 1922.

———. *Der russische Feldzug von 1812.* Essen: Magnus, 1984.

———. "Die Deutschen und die Franzosen." In *Politische Schriften und Briefe,* ed. Hans Rothfels, 35–51. Munich: Drei Masken Verlag, 1922.

———. "Die Verhältnisse Europas seit der Teilung Polens." In *Leben des Generals Carl von Clausewitz und der Frau Marie von Clausewitz geb. Gräfin Brühl,* by Karl Schwartz, 401–17. 2 vols. Berlin: Ferd. Dümmlers Verlags-Buchhandlung, 1878.

———. "From the Campaign in Russia." In *Carl von Clausewitz: Historical and Political Writings,* ed. Peter Paret and Dan Moran, 110–204. Princeton: Princeton University Press, 1992.

———. "Gedanken zur Abwehr." In *Verstreute kleine Schriften,* 493–527. Osnabrück: Biblio-Publishers, 1980.

———. "Historische Briefe über die großen Kriegsereignisse 1806–1807." In *Verstreute kleine Schriften,* 93–125. Osnabrück: Biblio-Publishers,1980.

———. Letter of January 2, 1809. In *Leben des Generals Carl von Clausewitz und der Frau Marie von Clausewitz geb. Gräfin Brühl,* by Karl Schwartz, 330–31. 2 vols. Berlin: Ferd. Dümmlers Verlags-Buchhandlung, 1878.

———. *On War.* Ed. and trans. Michael Howard and Peter Paret. Princeton, Princeton University Press, 1976.

——. "Politisches Rechnen." In *Carl von Clausewitz. Politik und Krieg,* by Hans Rothfels, 212. Bonn: Duemmler, 1980.

——. *Politische Schriften und Briefe.* Ed. Hans Rothfels. Munich: Drei Masken Verlag, 1922.

——. *Schriften, Aufsätze, Studien, Briefe.* Ed. Werner Hahlweg. 2 vols. Göttingen: Vandenhoeck & Ruprecht, 1966 and 1990.

——. "Über das Leben und den Charakter von Scharnhorst." In *Verstreute kleine Schriften,* 205–50. Osnabrück: Biblio-Publishers, 1980.

——. *Verstreute kleine Schriften.* Osnabrück: Biblio-Publishers, 1980. 205–50; 493–527.

——. *Vom Kriege.* 19th Edition. Bonn: Duemmler, 1980.

Cohen, S. Mark, Patricia Reed, and C. D. C. Reeve, eds. *Readings in Ancient Greek Philosophy: From Thales to Plato.* Indianapolis: Hackett, 1995.

Colley, Linda. *Britons: Forging the Nation, 1707–1837.* New Haven: Yale University Press, 1992.

Collins, Philip, ed. *Charles Dickens: The Critical Heritage.* London: Routledge & Kegan Paul, 1971.

Combats et captivité en Russie: Mémoires et lettres de soldats français. Paris: F. Teissèdre, 1999.

Corbin, Alain. *The Foul and the Fragrant: Odor and the French Social Imagination.* Trans. Miriam Kochan, Roy Porter, and Christopher Prendergast. Cambridge, MA: Harvard University Press, 1986.

Cozzens, Peter. *The Shipwreck of Their Hopes: The Battles for Chattanooga.* Champaign: University of Illinois Press, 1996.

Curtius, Ernst Robert. *European Literature and the Latin Middle Ages.* Trans. Willard R. Trask. Princeton: Princeton University Press, 1953.

Dainith, John et al., eds. *The Macmillan Dictionary of Quotations.* Edison, NJ: Chartwell, 2000.

Dal', Vladimir. Tolkovyi slovar' zhivogo velikorusskogo iazyka, 4 vols. 1880–82. http://vidahl.agava.ru/.

Danilevskii, G. P. "Istoriki-ochevidtsy." In *Roman L. N. Tolstogo "Voina i mir" v russkoi kritike,* ed. I. N. Sukhikh, 33–35. Leningrad: Izdatel'stvo Leningradskogo universiteta, 1989.

Davydov, Denis. *Stikhotvoreniia. Biblioteka poeta,* ed. V. E. Vatsuro. Leningrad: Sovetskii pisatel', 1984.

Debreczeny, Paul. "Freedom and Necessity: A Reconsideration of *War and Peace." Papers in Language and Literature* 7, no. 2 (1971): 185–98.

Dempsey, Martin E. Keynote address. AUSA chapter presidents dinner. Washington, DC, October 4, 2009.

——. "TRADOC Perspective." Speech at the Association of the United States Army (AUSA) Institute of Land Warfare Winter Symposium and Exposition. Ft. Lauderdale, Florida, February 25, 2010.

Denner, Michael. "Tolstoyan Nonaction: The Advantage of Doing Nothing." *Tolstoy Studies Journal* 13 (2001): 8–22.

Derrida, Jacques. *Aporias.* Trans. Thomas Dutoit. Stanford: Stanford University Press, 1993.

Dessler, David. "What's at Stake in the Agent-Structure Debate?" *International Organization* 43 (Summer 1989): 441–74.

Dickens, Charles. *A Tale of Two Cities.* London: Cathay Books, 1983.

Doepner, Friedrich. "Krieg und Frieden und Vom Kriege." *Europaeische Wehrkunde* 29 (1980): 25–30.

Donskov, Andrew, ed. *Lev Tolstoy and the Concept of Brotherhood.* Ottawa: Legas, 1996.

Dragomirov, M. I. "Ob atake i oborone." In *Sbornik original'nykh i perevodnykh statei*, 1:97–110.

———. "Po povodu sochinenii, vyzvannykh kampaniiami 1866 i 1870 godov: Stat'ia 4." In *Sbornik original'nykh i perevodnykh statei*, 1:583–608.

———. "Razbor romana "Voina i Mir." [Also called "'Voina i mir' gr. Tolstogo s voennoi tochki zreniia.] *Oruzheinyi sbornik*, 1868, no. 4, sec. 2, 99–138; 1869, no. 1, sec. 2, 69–122; and 1870, no. 1, sec. 2, 87–123.

———. *Razbor romana "Voina i mir."* Kiev: Izdatel'stvo N. Ia Oglobina, 1895.

———. *Sbornik original'nykh i perevodnykh statei M. I. Dragomirova, 1858–1880.* 2 vols. St. Petersburg: Tipografiia V. S. Balasheva, 1881.

———. "Vliianie rasprostraneniia nareznogo oruzhiia na vospitanie i taktiku vojsk." In *Sbornik original'nykh i perevodnykh statei*, 1:23–62.

———. "'War and Peace' from a Military Point of View." In *Weapons Miscellany* [Oruzheinyi sbornik], 1868 (no. 4) and 1869 (no. 1). Reprinted as "Dragomirov on Prince Andrey and the Art of War," in *Tolstoy: The Critical Heritage*, ed. A. V. Knowles, 153–58. London: Routledge & Kegan Paul, 1978.

Duffy, Michael. "World-wide War and British expansion, 1793–1815." In *The Oxford History of the British Empire: The Eighteenth Century*, ed. Peter Marshall, 184–207. Oxford: Oxford University Press, 1998.

"Dvenadtsatyi god: Sovremennye rasskazy, pis'ma, anekdoty, stikhotvoreniia." *Russkii Arkhiv* 2, no. 8 (1876): 386–409.

Eikhenbaum, Boris, "Cherty letopisnogo stilia v literature XIX veka," http://feb-web.ru/feb/classics/critics/eixenbaum/eih/eih-371-.htm, 371–79. Originally published in *Trudy otdela drevnerusskoi literatury Instituta russkoi literatury Akademii nauk SSSR.* Moscow: Izdatel'stvo AN SSSR, 1958, 14: 545–50.

———. *Lev Tolstoy.* 2 vols. (1928–31). Munich: Wilhelm Fink Verlag, 1968.

———. "Lev Tolstoy" (1931). In *War and Peace*, by Leo Tolstoy. Trans. and ed. George Gibian, 1126–28. New York: Norton, 1966.

———. *Tolstoi in the Sixties.* Trans. Duffield White. Ann Arbor, MI: Ardis, 1982 (Russian originally published in 1931).

Emerson, Caryl. "The Tolstoy Connection in Bakhtin." *PMLA* 100, no. 1 (January 1985): 68–80.

Esdaile, Charles J. *Fighting Napoleon: Guerrillas, Bandits and Adventurers in Spain 1808–1814.* New Haven: Yale University Press, 2004.

Fadiman, Clifton, and André Bernard, eds. *Bartlett's Book of Anecdotes.* Boston: Little Brown, 2000.

Ferguson, Niall. *Virtual History: Alternatives and Counterfactuals.* New York: Basic Books, 1999.

Feuer, Kathryn B. *Tolstoy and the Genesis of* War and Peace. Ed. Robin Feuer Miller and Donna Tussing Orwin. Ithaca: Cornell University Press, 1996.

Figes, Orlando. *Crimea: The Last Crusade.* London, 2010.

Fillion, Alain. *La Bérézina racontée par ceux qui l'ont vécue.* Paris: Editions France-Empire, 2005.

Forrest, Alan. *Napoleon's Men: The Soldiers of the Revolution and Empire.* London: Hambledon and London, 2002.

Forrest, Alan, Karen Hagemann, and Jane Rendall, eds. *Soldiers, Citizens and Civilians: Experiences and Perceptions of the Revolutionary and Napoleonic Wars.* Basingstoke, UK: Palgrave, 2009.

Forth, Christopher E. *Masculinity in the Modern West: Gender, Civilization and the Body.* Basingstoke, UK: Palgrave, 2008.

Four Feathers, The. DVD. MGM Video, 2005.

Frevert, Ute. "Das jakobinische Modell: Allgemeine Wehrpflicht und Nationsbildung in Preußen-Deutschland." In *Militär und Gesellschaft im 19. und 20. Jahrhundert,* 17–47. Stuttgart: Klett-Cotta, 1987.

Fuller, William. C. *Strategy and Power in Russia 1600–1914.* New York: Free Press, 1992.

Fuzellier, Désiré. *Journal de captivité en Russie, 1813–1814.* Paris: Ginkgo, 2004.

Gallie, W.B. *Philosophers of Peace and War.* Cambridge: Cambridge University Press, 1978.

Gibbon, Edward. *The Decline and Fall of the Roman Empire.* Vol. 1. New York: Knopf, 1993.

Gilbert, Natasha. "Modellers Claim Wars Are Predictable." *Nature* 462, December 16, 2009, 836. http://www.nature.com/news/2009/091215/full/462836a.html.

Gill, John. *1809. Thunder on the Danube: Napoleon's Defeat of the Habsburgs.* 3 vols. London: Frontline Books, 2007–9.

Girard, Rene. *Battling to the End.* East Lansing, MI: Michigan State University Press, 2009.

Global Guerrillas Blog. "Characteristics of Open Source Warfare." http://globalguerrillas. typepad.com/globalguerrillas/2010/02/characteristics-of-open-source-warfare.html.

Glushkovskii, Adam. "Moskva v 1812 godu: Iz zapisok Adama Glushkovskogo," *Krasnyi Arkhiv* 4 (1937): 121–59.

Gourevitch, Peter. "The Second Image Reversed: The International Sources of Domestic Politics." *International Organization* 32 (Autumn 1978): 881–912.

Grant, Ulysses S. *Personal Memoirs.* In *Ulysses S. Grant: Memoirs and Selected Letters,* ed. Mary Drake McFeely and William S. McFeely. New York: Library of America, 1990.

"Griboedovskaia Moskva v pis'makh M. A. Volkovoi k V. I. Lanskoi 1812–1818 gg." *Vestnik Evropy,* 9 god, kn. 8 (August 1874): 572–666.

Gukovskii, G. A. *Pushkin i russkie romantiki.* Moscow: Izdatel'stvo khudozhestvennoe, 1965.

Gulin, A. V. *Lev Tolstoi i puti russkoi istorii.* Moscow: IMLI RAN, 2004.

Gusev, Nikolai. *Lev Nikolaevich Tolstoi. Materialy k biografii s 1855 po 1869 g.* Moscow: AN SSSR, 1957.

——. *Zhizn' L. N. Tolstogo: Tolstoi v rastsvete khudozhestvennogo geniia, 1862–1877.* Moscow: Tolstovskii muzei, 1928.

Gustafson, Richard. *Leo Tolstoy, Resident and Stranger: A Study in Fiction and Theology.* Princeton: Princeton University Press, 1986.

Hahlweg, Werner, ed. *Schriften, Aufsätze, Studien, Briefe.* 2 vols. Göttingen:Vandenhoeck & Ruprecht, 1966 and 1990.

Halperin, Morton H. *Bureaucratic Politics and Foreign Policy.* Washington, DC: Brookings, 1974.

Hanoteau, Jean, ed. *Memoirs of General de Caulaincourt, Duke of Vicenza, 1812–1813.* London: Cassell, 1935.

Hantraye, Jacques. *Les Cosaques aux Champs-Elysées: L'occupation de la France après la chute de Napoléon.* Paris: Belin, 2005.

Hegel, Georg Wilhelm Friedrich. *The Philosophy of History.* Trans. J. Sibree. New York: American Home Library, 1902.

——. "Vorrede zur zweiten Auflage der Wissenschaft der Logik von 1831." In *Wissenschaft der Logik I,* 5:19–34. Frankfurt: Suhrkamp, 1970.

Heidegger, Martin. *Hölderlin's Hymn "The Ister."* Trans. Will McNeill. Bloomington: Indiana University Press, 1996.

——. *The Metaphysical Foundations of Logic.* Trans. Michael Heim. Bloomington: Indiana University Press, 1984.

Hennet, Léon, and Emmanuel Martin. *Lettres interceptées par les Russes durant la campagne de 1812.* Paris: La Sabretache, 1913.

Herberg-Rothe, Andreas. "Clausewitz und Hegel: Ein heuristischer Vergleich." *Vorschungen zur brandenburgischen und preußischen Geschichte,* no. 1 (2000): 49–84.

——. *Clausewitz's Puzzle: The Political Theory of War.* Oxford: Oxford University Press, 2007.

Heuser, Beatrice. *Reading Clausewitz.* London: Pimlico, 2002.

Hofschroer, Peter. *1815: The Waterloo Campaign.* 2 vols. London: Greenhill Books, 1998 and 1999.

Hollis, Martin, and Steve Smith. *Explaining and Understanding International Relations.* Oxford: Clarendon Press, 1991.

Hosking, Geoffrey. *Rulers and Victims: The Russians in the Soviet Union.* Cambridge, MA: Harvard University Press, 2006.

Hynes, Samuel. *The Soldiers' Tale: Bearing Witness to Modern War.* London: Pimlico, 1997.

Il'chenko, Lidiia. *Borodinskoe srazhenie: Istoriia russkoi versii sobytii.* Moscow: Kvadriga, 2009.

Jackson, Robert Louis. *Dialogues with Dostoevsky.* Stanford: Stanford University Press, 1993.

James, Henry. "*Daniel Deronda:* A Conversation." In *Partial Portraits,* 65–93. London: Macmillan, 1888.

——. "Ivan Turgeneff (1818–1883)." In *Literary Criticism.* New York: Library of America, 1984, 2:1027–34.

——. *The Novels and Tales of Henry James.* New York: Scribner's, 1908.

Janis, Irving L., and Leon Mann. *Decision Making: A Psychological Analysis of Conflict, Choice, and Commitment.* New York: Free Press, 1977.

Jervis, Robert. "International Politics and Diplomatic History: Fruitful Differences." http://www.h-net.org/~diplo/ISSF/PDF/ISSF-Jervis-InaguralAddress.pdf.

——. *Perception and Misperception in International Politics.* Princeton: Princeton University Press, 1976.

Jervis, Robert, Richard Ned Lebow, and Janice Gross Stein. *Psychology & Deterrence.* Baltimore: Johns Hopkins University Press, 1985.

Kagan, Frederick W. *The Military Reforms of Nicholas I.* Houndmills, UK: Macmillan, 1999.

Kamen, Henry. *Imagining Spain: Historical Myth and National Identity.* New Haven: Yale University Press, 2008.

Kaplan, Alice, and Kristin Ross, eds. *Everyday Life.* Yale French Studies 73. New Haven: Yale University Press, 1987.

Keegan, John. *The Face of Battle.* Harmondsworth, UK: Penguin, 1978.

——. *A History of Warfare.* London: Hutchinson, 1993.

Keohane, Robert O., ed. *Neorealism and Its Critics.* New York: Columbia University Press, 1986.

Khomutova, Anna. "Vospominaniia A. G. Khomutovoi o Moskve v 1812 godu." *Russkii Arkhiv* 3 (1891): 309–28.

Kianskaia, O. I. *Dekabristy: Aktual'nye problemy i novye podkhody.* Moscow: RGGU, 2008.

Kinglake, Alexander. *Eothen.* London, 1845, 176. Quoted in *The Mind of the Traveller, from Gilgamesh to Global Tourism,* by Eric J. Leed, 42–43. New York: Basic Books, 1991.

Kirpichnikov, A. *Ocherki po istorii novoi russkoi literatury.* St. Petersburg: Izd. L. F. Panteleeva, 1896.

Kiš, Danilo. *Homo Poeticus.* Ed. Susan Sontag. New York: Farrar, Strauss and Giroux, 1995.

Klotz, Audie, and Cecelia Lynch. *Strategies for Research in Constructivist International Relations.* Armonk, NY: M.E. Sharpe, 2007.

Knapp, Liza. "The Development of Style and Theme in Tolstoy." In *The Cambridge Companion to Tolstoy,* ed. Donna Tussing Orwin, 156–75. Cambridge: Cambridge University Press, 2002.

Knowles, A. V., ed. *Tolstoy: The Critical Heritage*. London: Routledge & Kegan Paul, 1978.

Knowles, Elizabeth, ed. *The Oxford Dictionary of Quotations*. 6th ed. Oxford: Oxford University Press, 2004.

Knutsen, Torbjørn L. "A Lost Generation? IR Scholarship before World War I." *International Politics* 45 (November 2008): 650–74.

Kokorev, I. T. *Ocherki Moskvy sorokovykh godov*. Ed. N. S. Ashukin. Moscow: Academia, 1932.

Kormilov, S. I. "K probleme istoricheskoi dostovernosti v *Voine i mire* L. N. Tolstogo." *Vestnik MGU,* 9th ser.: Filologiia, no. 5 (1988): 3–10.

Kozlovskii, G. Ia. "Moskva v 1812 godu zaniataia frantsuzami: Vospominanie ochevidtsa." *Russkaia Starina* 65 (January–March 1890): 105–14.

"Kratkoe opisanie proizshestvii, byvshikh pri Pokhval'skoi, chto v Bashmakove, tserkvi v 1812 godu." *Chteniia v Obshchestve liubitelei dukhovnogo prosveshcheniia,* March 1914, 54–76.

Kupreianova, E. A. *Estetika L. N. Tolstogo*. Moscow: Izdatel'stvo Nauka, 1966.

[Lachinov, N. A.] N. L. "Po povodu poslednego romana gr. Tolstogo." *Russkii invalid,* April 10, 1868, 3–4.

——. "Voina i mir. 4-yi tom. Sochinenie L. N. Tolstogo." *Voennyi sbornik,* no. 8 (August 1868), sec. 3, 81–125.

Lao Tzu. *Tao Te Ching*. Trans. D.C. Lau. London: Penguin, 1963.

Lebedev, A. "Iz rasskazov rodnykh o 1812 gode (Izvlechenie iz semeinykh zapisok)." In *Bumagi, otnosiashchiesia do Otechestvennoi voiny 1812 goda*. Ed. P. I. Shchukin. 10 vols. Moscow: Tov-vo tip. A. I. Mamontova, 1897–1908, 3:255–261.

Lebow, Richard Ned. *Between Peace and War: The Nature of International Crisis*. Baltimore: Johns Hopkins University Press, 1981.

——. *A Cultural Theory of International Relations*. Cambridge: Cambridge University Press, 2008.

——. "Identity and International Relations." *International Relations* 22 (December 2008): 473–92.

——. "What's So Different about a Counterfactual?" *World Politics* 52 (July 2000): 550–85.

Leed, Eric J. *The Mind of the Traveller, from Gilgamesh to Global Tourism*. New York: Basic Books, 1991.

Leighton, Lauren. "Denis Davydov and *War and Peace.*" In *Studies in Honor of Xenia Gasiorowska,* ed. Lauren Leighton, 21–36. Columbus, OH: Slavica, 1983.

Lev Tolstoi i mirovaia literatura: Materialy v Mezhdunarodnoi nauchnoi konferentsii, prokhodivshei v Iasnoi Poliane 12–16 avgusta 2007 g. Tula: Izdatel'skii dom Iasnaia Poliana, 2008.

Levitov, A. *Moskovskie nory i trushchoby*. 2nd ed. St. Petersburg: Izdanie V. E. Genkelia, 1869.

Lewis, C. S. *Mere Christianity*. London: Collins, 1955.

Lieven, Dominic. *Aristocracy in Europe 1815–1914*. Houndmills, UK: Macmillan, 1992.

——. *Empire: The Russian Empire and Its Rivals*. London: John Murray, 2001.

——. *Russia against Napoleon: The Battle for Europe, 1807–1814*. London: Allen Lane, 2009.

Likhachev, D. S. "Tolstoi i tysiacheletnie traditsii russkoi literatury." In *Russkaia i gruzinskaia srednevekovye literatury,* 5–19. Leningrad: Nauka, 1979. Originally published in *Russkaia i gruzinskaia srednevekovye literatury,* ed. G. M. Prokhorov, 5–19. Leningrad: Nauka, 1979. http://www.lihachev.ru/pic/site/files/fulltext/tolstoj_i_tisjachelit_tradicii_1979.pdf.

Liulecicius, Vejas Gabriel. *The German Myth of the East*. Oxford: Oxford University Press, 2009.

Lobell, Steven E., Norrin M. Ripsman, and Jeffrey W. Taliaferro, eds. *Neoclassical Realism, The State, and Foreign Policy.* New York: Cambridge University Press, 2009.

Logevall, Fredrik. *Choosing War: The Lost Chance for Peace and the Escalation of War in Vietnam.* Berkeley: University of California Press, 1999.

Lotman, Iurii M. *Besedy o russkoi kul'ture: Byt i traditsii russkogo naroda.* Saint Petersburg: Iskusstvo-SPB, 1994.

Love, Jeff. *The Overcoming of History in War and Peace.* Amsterdam: Rodopi, 2004.

Low, Polly. *Interstate Relations in Classical Greece: Morality and Power.* Cambridge: Cambridge University Press, 2007.

Lubbock, Percy. *The Craft of Fiction.* New York: Scribner's, 1921.

Lukács, Georg [Lukacs, Gyorgy]. *The Historical Novel.* Lincoln: University of Nebraska Press, 1962.

——. "Tolstoy and the Attempts to Go Beyond the Social Forms of Life." In *Leo Tolstoy's War and Peace,* ed. Harold Bloom, 9–14. Modern Critical Views. New York: Chelsea House, 1988.

Maeland, Bård, and Paul Otto Brunstad, eds. *Enduring Military Boredom from 1750 to the Present.* Basingstoke, UK: Palgrave, 2009.

Maiorova, Olga. *From the Shadow of Empire: Defining the Russian Nation through Cultural Mythology, 1855–1870.* Madison: University of Wisconsin Press, 2010.

Manchester, Laurie. *Holy Fathers, Secular Sons: Clergy, Intelligentsia, and the Modern Self in Revolutionary Russia.* DeKalb: Northern Illinois University Press, 2008.

Maringoné, L.-J. Vionnet de. *Souvenirs d'un ex-Commandant des Grenadiers de la Vieille Garde.* Paris: Imprimerie & librairie militaires Edmond Dubois, 1899.

Marshall, Peter, ed. *The Oxford History of the British Empire: The Eighteenth Century.* Oxford: Oxford University Press, 1998.

Martin, Alexander M. *Enlightened Metropolis: Constructing Imperial Moscow, 1762–1855* (forthcoming).

——. "Feed the Horses." *Times Literary Supplement,* November 20, 2009, 9.

——. "Sewage and the City: Filth, Smell, and Representations of Urban Life in Moscow, 1770–1880." *Russian Review* 67, no. 2 (April 2008): 243–74.

[Mashkov, Ioann]. "1812-i god. Sozhzhenie Moskvy. Pokazaniia ochevidtsa (Protoiereia Kazanskogo na Krasnoi ploshchadi sobora)." *Russkii Arkhiv* 3, no. 12 (1909): 455–63.

McAleer, Kevin. *Dueling: The Cult of Honor in Fin-de-Siecle Germany.* Princeton: Princeton University Press, 1994.

McDermott, Rose. *Political Psychology in International Relations.* Ann Arbor: University of Michigan Press, 2004.

McFeely, Mary Drake, and William S. McFeely, eds. *Ulysses S. Grant: Memoirs and Selected Letters.* New York: Library of America, 1990.

McNeillie, Andrew, ed. *The Common Reader: First Series.* New York: Harcourt-Harvest, 1984.

Melville, Herman. *Battle-Pieces and Aspects of the War.* 1866; repr., New York: Da Capo, 1995.

——. *Moby-Dick.* Ed. Harold Beaver. New York: Penguin, 1987.

Mel'nikova, L. V. *Armiia i pravoslavnaia tserkov' Rossiiskoi imperii v epokhu Napoleonovskikh voin.* Moscow: Kuchkovo pole, 2007.

Merezhkovskii, Dmitrii. *Tolstoi i Dostoevskii.* In *Polnoe sobranie sochinenii.* 24 vols. Moscow: Tip. I. D. Sytina, 1914, vols. 9–10.

Meyer, Jakob. *Jakob Meyer, soldat de Napoléon, 1808–1813: Mes aventures de guerre.* Paris: Autrement, 2009.

Mikaberidze, Alexander. *The Battle of Borodino: Napoleon against Kutuzov.* Barnsley, Yorkshire, UK: Pen & Sword, 2007.

Mikhailovskii-Danilevskii, A. I. *Memuary 1814–1815*. St. Petersburg: Russkaia natsional'naia Biblioteka, 2001.

Militär und Gesellschaft im 19. und 20. Jahrhundert. Stuttgart: Klett-Cotta, 1987.

Moran, Daniel, and Arthur Waldron, eds. *The People in Arms: Military Myth and National Mobilization since the French Revolution*. Cambridge: Cambridge University Press, 2003.

Morgenthau, Hans J. *Politics among Nations: The Struggle for Power and Peace*. New York: Knopf, 1948.

Morson, Gary Saul. *Hidden in Plain View: Narrative and Creative Potentials in "War and Peace."* Stanford: Stanford University Press, 1987.

——. *The Long and the Short of It: From Aphorism to Novel*. Stanford, forthcoming.

——. *"War and Peace."* In *The Cambridge Companion to Tolstoy*, ed. Donna Tussing Orwin, 65–79. Cambridge: Cambridge University Press, 2002.

——. *The Words of Others: From Quotations to Culture*. New Haven: Yale University Press, 2011.

Morson, Gary Saul, and Caryl Emerson. *Mikhail Bakhtin: Creation of a Prosaics*. Stanford: Stanford University Press, 1990.

Münkler, Herfried. "Clausewitz' Beschreibung und Analyse einer Schlacht. Borodino als Beispiel." In *Codierung von Gewalt im medialen Wandel*, ed. Steffen Martus et al., 68–91. Berlin: Akademie, 2003.

——. *Gewalt und Ordnung*. Frankfurt: Fischer, 1992.

Munslow, Alan. *The Routledge Companion to Historical Studies*. 2nd ed. London: Routledge, 2006.

Myshkovskaia, L. M. *Masterstvo L. N. Tolstogo*. Moscow: Sovetskii pisatel', 1958.

Nordhof, Anton Wilhelm. *Die Geschichte der Zerstörung Moskaus im Jahre 1812*. Ed. Claus Scharf and Jürgen Kessel. Munich: Haraldt Boldt Verlag im R. Oldenbourg Verlag, 2000.

Norov, A. S. *Voina i Mir 1805–1812 s istoricheskoi tochki zreniia i po vospominaniiam sovremennika*. St. Petersburg: Tipografiia Departamenta Udelov, 1868.

——. "Voina i mir (1805—1812) s istoricheskoi tochki zreniia i po vospominaniiam sovremennika." *Voennyi sbornik* no. 11 (1868): 189–246.

Nye, Joseph S., Jr., and David A. Welch. *Understanding Global Conflict and Cooperation: An Introduction to Theory and History*. 8th ed. New York: Pearson/Longman, 2010.

Obninskii, V. P., and T. I. Polner, eds. *Voina i mir. Sbornik*. Moscow: Zadruga, 1912.

O'Neill, Barry. *Honor, Symbols, and War*. Ann Arbor: University of Michigan Press, 1999.

Onuf, Nicholas Greenwood. *World of Our Making: Rules and Rule in Social Theory and International Relations*. Columbia: University of South Carolina Press, 1989.

"Opisanie dostopamiatnykh proisshestvii v moskovskikh monastyriakh vo vremia nashestviia nepriiatelei v 1812 godu." *Chteniia v Obshchestve Istorii i Drevnostei Rossiiskikh* 27, no. 4 (October–December 1858), sec. "Materialy otechestvennye": 33–50.

O'Rourke, Shane. *Warriors and Peasants: The Don Cossacks in Late Imperial Russia*. Basingstoke, UK: Macmillan, 2000.

Orwin, Donna Tussing, ed. *The Cambridge Companion to Tolstoy*. Cambridge: Cambridge University Press, 2002.

——. *Consequences of Consciousness: Turgenev, Dostoevsky and Tolstoy*. Palo Alto: Stanford University Press, 2007.

——. "Freedom, Responsibility, and the Soul: The Platonic Contribution to Tolstoy's Psychology." *Canadian Slavonic Papers* 25, no. 4 (1983): 510–13.

——. "Leo Tolstoy: Pacifist, Patriot and *Molodets*." In *Anniversary Essays on Tolstoy*, ed. Donna Tussing Orwin, 76–95. Cambridge: Cambridge University Press, 2010.

——. "Tolstoy and Patriotism." In *Lev Tolstoy and the Concept of Brotherhood*, ed. Andrew Donskov, 51–70. Ottawa: Legas, 1996.

——. *Tolstoy's Art and Thought, 1847–1880*. Princeton: Princeton University Press, 1993.

Palluel-Guillard, André. "Correspondance et mentalité des soldats savoyards de l'armée napoléonienne." In *Soldats et armées en Savoie: Actes du 28e congrès des Sociétés Savantes de Savoie, Saint-Jean-de-Maurienne, 1980*, 197–208. Chambéry: Union des Sociétés Savantes de Savoie, 1981.

Paret, Peter. *Clausewitz and the State*. Princeton: Princeton University Press, 1976.

——. *Clausewitz und der Staat*. Bonn: Duemmler, 1993.

Paret, Peter, and Dan Moran. *Carl von Clausewitz: Historical and Political Writings*. Princeton: Princeton University Press, 1992.

"Pervye dni v sozhzhennoi Moskve: Sentiabr' i oktiabr' 1812-go goda (Pis'mo kn. A. A. Shakhovskogo, 1836 g., k A. I. Mikhailovskomu-Danilevskomu)." *Russkaia Starina* 64 (October–December 1889): 31–55.

Pivovarov, Iurii, "Dolzhnost' tsaria u nas stala vybornoi." Interview by Vladimir Emel'ianenko. *Profil'*, September 1, 2008. http://www.profile.ru/items/?item=26885&page=1&comment=3.

Planert, Ute, ed. *Krieg und Umbruch in Mitteleuropa um1800*. Paderborn: Ferdinand Schoeningh, 2009.

Plato. *Gorgias*. Trans. Robin Waterfield. Oxford: Oxford University Press, 1994.

——. *Symposium*. Trans. Alexander Nehamas and Paul Woodruff. Indianapolis: Hackett, 1989.

Plutarch. "Poplicola," In *Plutarch's Lives*. Dryden translation, rev. Arthur Hugh Clough. 2 vols. New York: Modern Library, 2001, 1:129–43.

——. "Sertorius." In *Plutarch's Lives*, 2:1–22.

"Podrobnoe donesenie Ee Imperatorskomu Velichestvu, Gosudaryne Imperatritse, Marii Feodorovne, o sostoianii moskovskogo Vospitatel'nogo Doma v bytnost' nepriiatelia v Moskve 1812 goda." *Chteniia v Obshchestve liubitelei dukhovnogo prosveshcheniia* 33, no. 2 (April–June 1860): 161–84.

Pokrovskii, K. "Istochniki romana *Voina i mir.*" In *"Voina i mir." Sbornik*, ed. V. P. Obninskii and T. I. Polner, 113–28. Moscow: Zadruga, 1912.

Pokrovskii, N.M. Foreword to *Zhenshchiny epokhi frantsuzskoi revoliutsii*, by Galina Serebriakova, 5–11. Moscow: Academia, 1929.

Popov, A. I. *Velikaia armiia v Rossii: Pogonia za mirazhom*. Samara: NTTs, 2002.

Post, Jerrold M., and Alexander George. *Leaders and Their Followers in a Dangerous World: The Psychology of Political Behavior*. Ithaca: Cornell University Press, 2004.

Pouliot, Vincent. "'Sobjectivism': Toward a Constructivist Methodology." *International Studies Quarterly* 51 (June 2007): 359–84.

Price, Martin. "Forms of Life and Death: Tolstoy's *War and Peace*." In *Leo Tolstoy's War and Peace*, ed. Harold Bloom, 123–30. Modern Critical Views. New York: Chelsea House, 1988.

Putnam, Robert. "Diplomacy and Domestic Politics: The Logic of Two-Level Games." *International Organization* 42 (Summer 1988): 428–60.

Quint, David. *Epic and Empire: Politics and Generic Form from Virgil to Milton*. Princeton: Princeton University Press, 1993.

Radozhitskii, Il'ia. *Pokhodnye zapiski artilleristas 1812 po 1816 god*. Moscow: V tip. Lazarevykh, 1835.

Ranke, Leopold von. "Preface: Histories of the Latin and Germanic Nations from 1494–1514." In *The Varieties of History: From Voltaire to the Present*, ed. Fritz Stern, 55–58. New York: Vintage, 1973.

"Rasskaz Apollona Dmitrievicha Sysoeva, iz kupecheskogo zvaniia." In T. N., ed., "Rasskazy ochevidtsev o dvenadtsatom gode." *Russkii Vestnik* 102 (November 1872): 269–74.

"Rasskaz meshchanina Petra Kondrat'eva." In "Rasskazy ochevidtsev o dvenadtsatom gode." *Russkii Vestnik* 102 (November 1872): 275–80.

"Rasskazy ochevidtsev o dvenadtsatom gode: Na Mokhovoi." *Moskovskie Vedomosti,* March 1, 1872.

"Rasskazy ochevidtsev o dvenadtsatom gode: Rasskaz kupchikhi Anny Grigor'evny Kruglovoi, Sheremetevskoi bogadelenkoi." *Moskovskie Vedomosti,* March 13, 1872.

"Rasskazy ochevidtsev o dvenadtsatom gode: V prikhode Petra i Pavla na Iakimanke i na Orlovom lugu." *Moskovskie Vedomosti,* March 4, 1872.

"Rasskazy ochevidtsev o dvenadtsatom gode: V Rozhdestvenskom monastyre." *Moskovskie Vedomosti,* March 25, 1872.

Raupach, Friedrich. *Reise von St. Petersburg nach dem Gesundbrunnen zu Lipezk am Don. Nebst einem Beitrage zur Charakteristik der Russen.* Breslau: Wilhelm Gottlieb Korn, 1809.

Raymond, Mark. "Social Change in World Politics: Secondary Rules and Institutional Politics." PhD diss., University of Toronto, 2011.

Reinbeck, Georg. *Flüchtige Bemerkungen auf einer Reise von St. Petersburg über Moskau, Grodno, Warschau, Breslau nach Deutschland im Jahre 1805.* 2 vols. Leipzig: Wilhelm Rein und Comp., 1806.

Reyfman, Irina. *Ritualized Violence Russian Style: The Duel in Russian Culture and Literature.* Stanford: Stanford University Press, 1999.

Riasanovsky, Nicholas. *A Parting of Ways: Government and the Educated Public in Russia 1801–1855.* Oxford: Oxford University Press, 1992.

Riehn, Richard K. *1812. Napoleon's Russian Campaign.* New York: Wiley, 1991.

Ritter, Joachim and Karlfried Gründer, eds. *Historisches Wörterbuch der Philosophie.* Vol. 4. Basel: I–K, 1976.

Roese, Neal J., and James N. Olson. *What Might Have Been: The Social Psychology of Counterfactual Thinking.* Mahwah, NJ: Lawrence Erlbaum, 1995.

Roos, Heinrich von. *Souvenirs d'un médecin de la Grande Armée.* Paris: Perrin, 2004.

Rose, Olav. *Carl von Clausewitz: Wirkungsgeschichte seines Werkes in Rußland und der Sowjetunion 1836–1991.* Munich: Oldenbourg, 1995.

Rosen, Stanley. *Hermeneutics as Politics.* Oxford: Oxford University Press, 1987.

Rosenau, James, ed. *Domestic Sources of Foreign Policy.* New York: Free Press, 1967.

Rothfels, Hans. *Carl von Clausewitz. Politik und Krieg.* Bonn: Duemmler 1980.

——, ed. *Politische Schriften und Briefe.* Munich: Drei Masken Verlag, 1922.

Rousseau, J.J. *The Confessions.* Trans. J. M. Cohen. New York: Penguin Classics, 1953.

Ruble, Blair A. *Second Metropolis: Pragmatic Pluralism in Gilded Age Chicago, Silver Age Moscow, and Meiji Osaka.* Washington, DC: Woodrow Wilson Center Press, 2001.

Saburov, A. A. *Voina i mir L. N. Tolstogo. Problematika i poetika.* Moscow: Izdatel'stvo Moskovskogo un-ta, 1959.

Samet, Elizabeth D. *Willing Obedience: Citizens, Soldiers, and the Progress of Consent in America, 1776–1898.* Stanford: Stanford University Press, 2004.

Sankt-Peterburgskie Vedomosti. 1805: 642, 653, 665, 701, 711, 721, 733, and 741.

Shcherbakov, Viktor. "Neizvestnyi istochnik 'Voiny i mira': 'Moi zapiski' masona P. Ia. Titova." *Novoe Literaturnoe Obozrenie* 21 (1996): 130–51.

——. "An Unknown Source of *War and Peace* (*My Notes* by Freemason P. Ia. Titov)." Trans. Ilia Pomerantsev and Donna Orwin. *Tolstoy Studies Journal* 9 (1997): 66–84.

Schivelbusch, Wolfgang. "The Policing of Street Lighting." In *Everyday Life,* ed. Alice Kaplan and Kristin Ross, 61–74. Yale French Studies 73. New Haven: Yale University Press, 1987.

Schubert, Friedrich von. *Unter dem Doppeladler.* Stuttgart: Koehler Verlag, 1962.

Schwartz, Karl. *Leben des Generals Carl von Clausewitz und der Frau Marie von Clausewitz geb. Gräfin Brühl.* 2 vols. Berlin: Ferd. Dümmlers Verlags-Buchhandlung, 1878.

Ségur, Count Philippe-Paul de. *Defeat: Napoleon's Russian Campaign.* New York: New York Review Books Classics, 2008.

——. *Napoleon's Russian Campaign.* Trans. J. David Townsend. Alexandria, VA: Time-Life Books, 1958.

Shapiro, Fred R., ed. *The Yale Book of Quotations.* New Haven: Yale University Press, 2006.

Shchukin, P. I. ed. *Bumagi, otnosiashchiesia do Otechestvennoi voiny 1812 goda.* 10 vols. Moscow: Tov-vo tip. A. I. Mamontova, 1897–1908.

Sherrin, Ned, ed. *Oxford Dictionary of Humorous Quotations.* Oxford: Oxford University Press, 1995.

Shilov, D. N., and Iu. A. Kuz'min. *Chleny Gosudarstvennogo Soveta Rossiiskoi Imperii 1801–1906.* St. Petersburg: Dmitrii Bulanin, 2007.

Shklovsky,Victor. *Material i stil' v romane Tolstogo "Voina i mir."* Moscow: Federatsiia, 1928; repr., The Hague: Mouton, 1970.

Simpson, Brooks D. *Ulysses S. Grant: Triumph over Adversity, 1822–1865.* Boston: Houghton Mifflin, 2000.

Singer, J. David. "The Levels of Analysis Problem in International Relations." In *International Politics and Foreign Policy,* ed. James N. Rosenau, 20–29. New York: Free Press, 1969.

Skaftymov, A. P. "Obraz Kutuzova i filosofiia istorii v romane L. Tolstogo 'Voina i mir.'" In Skaftymov, *Nravstvennye iskaniia russkikh pisatelei,* 188–93. Moscow: Izdatel'stvo Khudozhestvennaia literatura, 1972.

Slingerland, Edward. *Effortless Action: Wu-wei as Conceptual Metaphor and Spiritual Ideal in Early China.* Oxford: Oxford University Press, 2003.

Smirnov, A. A. "Moskva." In *Otechestvennaia voina 1812 goda: Entsiklopediia,* ed. V. M. Bezotosnyi et al., 476–79. Moscow: ROSSPEN, 2004.

Smith, Anthony D. *The Ethnic Origins of Nations.* Oxford: Blackwell, 1986.

——. "War and Ethnicity: The Role of Warfare in the Formation, Self-images, and Cohesion of Ethnic Communities." *Ethnic and Racial Studies* 4, no. 4 (1981): 375–97.

Snyder, Jack. *Myths of Empire: Domestic Politics and International Ambition.* Ithaca: Cornell University Press, 1991.

Sofsky, Wolfgang. *Traktat über die Gewalt.* Frankfurt: Fischer, 1996.

Soldats et armées en Savoie: Actes du 28e congrès des Sociétés Savantes de Savoie, Saint-Jean-de-Maurienne, 1980. Chambéry: Union des Sociétés Savantes de Savoie, 1981.

Sophocles. *Three Theban Plays.* Trans. Robert Fagles. New York: Penguin, 2000.

Spinoza, Benedictus de. *Ethics.* Trans. G. H. R. Parkinson. Oxford: Oxford University Press, 2000.

Steinberg, John W. *All the Tsar's Men: Russia's General Staff and the Fate of the Empire 1898–1914.* Washington DC: Woodrow Wilson Center Press, 2010.

Steiner, George. "Tolstoy and Homer." In *Leo Tolstoy,* ed. Harold Bloom, 67–74. Modern Critical Views. New York: Chelsea House, 1986.

Stern, Fritz, ed. *The Varieties of History: From Voltaire to the Present.* New York: Vintage, 1973.

Storch, Heinrich. *Rußland unter Alexander dem Ersten.* 9 vols. St. Petersburg: Johann Friedrich Hartknoch, 1804–8.

Strassler, Robert B., and Richard Crawley, eds. *The Landmark Thucydides: A Comprehensive Guide to the Peloponnesian War.* New York: Free Press, 1996.

Summers, Harry G., Jr. *On Strategy: A Critical Analysis of the Vietnam War.* Novato, CA: Presidio Press, 1982.

Sylvan, David, and Stephen Majeski. "A Methodology for the Study of Historical Counterfactuals." *International Studies Quarterly* 42 (1998): 79–108.

T—v, N. I. "O 1812 gode (Vospominaniia iz rasskazov sovremennikov i ochevidtsev)." In *Bumagi, otnosiashchiesia do Otechestvennoi voiny 1812 goda,* ed. P. I. Shchukin. 10 vols. Moscow: Tov-vo tip. A. I. Mamontova, 1897–1908, 4:331–46.

Tartakovskii, Andrei G, ed. *1812 god i russkaia memuaristika: Opyt istochnikovedcheskogo izucheniia.* Moscow: Izdatel'stvo Nauka, 1980.

——. *1812 god v vospominaniiakh sovremennikov.* Moscow: Izdatel'stvo Nauka, 1995.

——. "Naselenie Moskvy v period frantsuzskoi okkupatsii." *Istoricheskie Zapiski* 93 (1973): 356–79.

Tetlock, Philip E., and Aaron Belkin, eds. *Counterfactual Thought Experiments in World Politics: Logical, Methodological, and Psychological Perspectives.* Princeton: Princeton University Press, 1996.

Todorov, Tzvetan. *Imperfect Garden.* Trans. Carol Cosman. Princeton: Princeton University Press, 2002.

Tolstoy, L.N. *Biblioteka L'va Nikolaevicha Tolstogo v Iasnoi Poliane,* bk. 1, *Knigi na russkom iazyke,* pt. 1. Moscow: Izdatel'stvo Sovetskaia Rossiia, 1958.

——. *"The Cossacks" and Other Stories.* Trans. and ed. David McDuff and Paul Foote. London: Penguin, 2006.

——. "Izbrannye aforizmy i maksimy Laroshfuko." In *Polnoe sobranie sochinenii,* 40:283–310.

——. "Neskol'ko slov po povodu knigi 'Voina i mir.'" In *Polnoe sobranie sochinenii,* 16:9–13.

——. *Polnoe sobranie sochinenii* (PSS). 90 vols. Moscow: Gosudarstvennoe izdatel'stvo Khudozhestvennaia literatura, 1928–58.

——. *Tolstoy's Short Fiction.* Ed. and trans., Michael R. Katz. New York: Norton, 1991.

——. *War and Peace.* Trans. Ann Dunnigan. New York: Signet, 1968.

——. *War and Peace.* Trans. Rosemary Edmonds. London: Folio Society, 1978.

——. *War and Peace.* Trans. Constance Garnett. New York: Thomas Y. Crowell, 1976.

——. *War and Peace.* Ed. George Gibian. New York: Norton, 1966.

——. *War and Peace.* Trans. Louise and Aylmer Maude. Oxford: Oxford University Press, 1998.

——. *War and Peace.* Trans. Richard Pevear and Larisa Volokhonsky. New York: Vintage Books, 2007.

Tolycheva, T. [E. V. Novosil'tsova], ed.,"Rasskaz Nikolaia Dmitrievicha Lavrova, sviashchennika tserkvi Spiridoniia, chto na Spiridonovke." In *Rasskazy ochevidtsev o dvenadtsatom gode,* 106–12. Moscow: Tipografiia G. Lissnera i D. Sobko, 1912.

——, ed. "Rasskaz odnogo iz byvshikh krepostnykh g. Soimonova, starichka Vasiliia Ermolaevicha." In *Rasskazy ochevidtsev o dvenadtsatom gode,* 67–76. Moscow: Tipografiia G. Lissnera i D. Sobko, 1912.

Troitskii, N. *1812. Velikii god Rossii.* Moscow: Omega, 2007.

Tsentral'nyi Istoricheskii Arkhiv Moskvy, f. 20, op. 2, d. 2380.

Tsimbaeva, E. "Historical Context in a Literary Work: Gentry Society in *War and Peace.*" *Russian Studies in Literature* 43, no. 1 (Winter 2006–7): 6–48 (Russian original in *Voprosy literatury,* no. 5 [2004]).

Ungurianu, Dan. *Plotting History: The Russian Historical Novel in the Imperial Age.* Madison: University of Wisconsin Press, 2007.

Ure, John. *The Cossacks.* London: Constable, 1999.

van Creveld, Martin. *Die Zukunft des Krieges.* Munich: Gerling Akademie Verlag, 1998.

——. *The Transformation of War.* New York: Free Press, 1991.

Vatsuro, V. E. "Denis Davydov—Poet." In *Denis Davydov: Stikhotvoreniia. Biblioteka poeta,* ed. V. E. Vatsuro, 5-48. Leningrad: Sovetskii pisatel', 1984.

Viazemskii, P. A. "Vospominanie o 1812 gode," in *Polnoe sobranie sochinenii kniazia P. A. Viazemskogo*, vol. 7. 12 vols. St. Petersburg: Izd. Grafa S. D. Sheremeteva, 1878–96.

——. "Vospominaniia o 1812 gode." *Russkii arkhiv* 1 (1869): 181–192, 01–016 (please note irregular pagination: the two segments in this article are contiguous with no explanation for why the pagination changes).

Vishniakov, N. *Svedeniia o kupecheskom rode Vishniakovykh*. 3 vols. Moscow: Tipografiia G. Lissnera i A Geshelia [v. 2–3: G. Lissnera i D. Sobko], 1903–11.

Vistengof, P. *Ocherki Moskovskoi zhizni*. Moscow: V tipografii S. Selivanovskogo, 1842.

Vitmer, Aleksandr. *1812 god v "Voine i mire."* St. Petersburg, 1869.

——. "Po povodu istoricheskikh ukazanii chetvertogo toma 'Voina I Mir'" grafa L. N. Tolstogo." *Voennyi sbornik*, no. 12 (1868): sec. 2, 435–71; no. 1 (1869): sec. 1, 91–134.

Voennaia entsiklopediia. Vol. 4. St. Petersburg: Sytin Publishing, 1911–15.

Voskresenskii, A. "Umstvennyi vzor na protekshiia leta moei zhizni ot kolybeli i do groba (1778–1825 g.)." *Dushepoleznoe Chtenie*, no. 12 (December 1894): 596–600.

Wachtel, Andrew. "History and Autobiography in Tolstoy." In *The Cambridge Companion to Tolstoy*, ed. Donna Tussing Orwin, 176–90. Cambridge: Cambridge University Press, 2002.

Waltz, Kenneth N. *Man, the State and War*. New York: Columbia University Press, 1959.

——. *Theory of International Politics*. New York: Random House, 1979.

Watson, Janet S. K. *Fighting Different Wars: Experience, Memory and the First World War in Britain*. Cambridge: Cambridge University Press, 2004.

Welch, David A. "Why International Relations Theorists Should Stop Reading Thucydides." *Review of International Studies* 29 (July 2003): 301–19.

Wendt, Alexander. "The Agent-Structure Problem in International Relations Theory." *International Organization* 41 (Summer 1987): 335–70.

——. *Social Theory of International Politics*. Cambridge: Cambridge University Press, 1999.

Wilde, Oscar. *The Portable Oscar Wilde*. Ed. Richard Aldington and Stanley Weintraub. New York: Penguin, 1981.

Wolff, Larry. *Inventing Eastern Europe: The Map of Civilization on the Mind of the Enlightenment*. Stanford: Stanford University Press, 1994.

Woolf, Virginia. "The Russian Point of View." In *The Common Reader*, ed. Andrew McNeillie, 173–82. New York: Harcourt-Harvest, 1984. http://www.worldvaluessurvey.org/.

Wurttemberg, Duke Eugen von. *Memoiren des Herzogs Eugen von Wurttemberg*, 3 vols. Frankfurt an der Oder: Gustav Harnecher, 1862.

Ysarn-Villefort, F.-J. d'. *Relation du séjour des Français à Moscou et de l'incendie de cette ville en 1812 par un habitant de Moscou*. Ed. A. Gadaruel. Brussels: Fr.-J. Olivier, 1871.

Zagoskin, M. N. *Sochinenii*, vol. 5. 7 vols. St. Petersburg: V. I. Shtein, 1889.

Zaidenshnur, Evelina. "Istoriia napisaniia i napechataniia." In *Polnoe sobranie sochinenii* (PSS), 16:125.

——. "Poiski nachala romana 'Voina i mir': Piatnadtsadt' nabroskov." In *Lev Tolstoi*, 1: 291–324. 2 vols. Literaturnoe nasledstvo, vols. 68–69. Moscow: AN SSSR, 1961.

——. *"Voina i mir" L. N. Tolstogo: Sozdanie velikoi knigi*. Moscow: Kniga, 1966.

Zamoyski, Adam. *1812: Napoleon's Fatal March on Moscow*. London: Harper Collins, 2004.

"Zapiska G. N. Kol'chugina." *Russkii Arkhiv* 3, no. 9 (1879): 45–62.

Zavalishin, Dmitrii. "Tysiacha vosem'sot dvenadtsatyi god (Iz vospominanii sovremennika)." *Moskovskie Vedomosti*, March 25, 1884.

[Zhdanov, Petr]. *Pamiatnik Frantsuzam, ili Prikliucheniia Moskovskogo Zhitelia P.... Zh ...* St. Petersburg: Tipografiia I. Baikova, 1813.

Contributors

Alan Forrest is professor of modern history at the University of York in the United Kingdom.

Andreas Herberg-Rothe is senior lecturer of political sciences on the faculty of social and cultural studies at the University of Applied Sciences in Fulda, Germany.

Dominic Lieven is a senior research fellow at Trinity College, Cambridge University.

Jeff Love is professor of Russian and German at Clemson University.

Alexander M. Martin is associate professor of history at the University of Notre Dame.

Rick McPeak is a colonel in the United States Army and head of the Department of Foreign Languages at the United States Military Academy at West Point.

Gary Saul Morson is Frances Hooper Professor of the Arts and Humanities at Northwestern University.

Donna Tussing Orwin is professor of Russian literature and chair of the Department of Slavic Languages and Literatures at the University of Toronto.

Elizabeth D. Samet is professor of English at the United States Military Academy at West Point.

Dan Ungurianu is professor of Russian studies and chair of the Department of Russian Studies at Vassar College.

David A. Welch is CIGI Chair of Global Security at the Balsillie School of International Affairs and professor of political science at the University of Waterloo.

Index